Articles on CALVIN *and* CALVINISM

A FOURTEEN-VOLUME ANTHOLOGY OF SCHOLARLY ARTICLES

edited by

RICHARD C. GAMBLE
CALVIN THEOLOGICAL SEMINARY

A GARLAND SERIES

Contents of Series

VOLUME 2

CALVIN'S
Early Writings and Ministry

edited by

RICHARD C. GAMBLE

GARLAND PUBLISHING, INC.
NEW YORK & LONDON
1992

Library of Congress Cataloging-in-Publication Data

Calvin's early writings and ministry / edited by Richard C. Gamble.
p. cm. — (Articles on Calvin and Calvinism ; v. 2)
Includes bibliographical references.
ISBN 0-8153-1043-9 (alk. paper)
1. Calvin, Jean, 1509-1564. 2. Reformed Church—Doctrines—History—16th century. I. Gamble, Richard C. II. Series.
BX9418.A74 1992 vol. 2
284'.2—dc20
[284'.2'092] 92-30028
CIP

Printed on acid-free, 250-year-life paper
Manufactured in the United States of America

Contents

Introduction

There is a marked contrast between the life and work of Calvin in his last half-decade and in the beginning of his scholarly career and ministry. Calvin's early life was marked by a number of failures, including the failure to receive notoriety for his first published work, a scholarly piece which did not sell well at all. His early ministry was capstoned by the dubious honor of expulsion from the city of Geneva together with his faithful friend and fellow minister, William Farrel.

Moving to the bustling city of Strasbourg, his tumultuous life in Geneva was left behind, and Calvin had a few years of peace and literary production. He met his bride, composed his first biblical commentary, and restructured the *Institutes*, so that its shape in 1539 was more like that of the final version produced twenty years later.

Volume 2 investigates the influences on Calvin prior to and immediately after his conversion to Evangelical or Protestant Christianity. This volume also provides historical and literary analysis of the early writings of Calvin including his commentary on Seneca's *De Clementia,* the *Psychopannychia*, the Cop address, the 1536 *Institutes*, and the *Reply to Sadoleto*. In addition is a study of Calvin's conception of church music, reminding us that Calvin was concerned with very practical church concerns, including the possibility of translating some Psalms for singing.

10. JACQUES LEFÈVRE D'ETAPLES (c. 1455-1536). CALVIN'S FORERUNNER IN FRANCE

PROF. P.E. HUGHES*

Early in the year 1534 a young man, twenty-five years of age, made the journey to Nérac in the south-west of France in order to meet and confer with an old man, more than three times his age. That young man was John Calvin, and the aged fellow countryman he had sought out was Jacques Lefèvre d'Etaples. We know nothing of what transpired between the two, except that Theodore Beza, Calvin's colleague and successor in Geneva, records that Lefèvre gave Calvin a cordial welcome and, delighted with his visit, "predicted that he would be a distinguished instrument in the restoration of the kingdom of heaven in France" *(Johannis Calvini Vita)*.

This encounter took place at a time when Calvin was very definitely in a state of transition. He was in transition *physically*, uncertain as to what the future might hold for him and as to what might prove to be the right place for him to settle and work in. Not many weeks previously he had fled in disguise from Paris in order to avoid arrest and imprisonment, and perhaps execution. The occasion of this undignified exodus had been the delivery of a public oration in the capital by his friend Nicolas Cop, son of the king's physician, in his capacity as the newly appointed Rector of the University of Paris. The oration was a remarkably bold and clear declaration of evangelical beliefs, affirming the blessedness of those who suffer persecution for the sake of the Gospel and the uniqueness of the grace of God, who through his Word engenders faith and opens our hearts to receive the Gospel. It has been widely held that the real author of this oration was Calvin, not Cop: but this is questionable for a number of reasons. For one thing, the opening section is closely indebted to the exhortation which Erasmus prefixed to the third edition of his New Testament; for another, there seems to be demonstrable dependence on Bucer's Latin translation of a sermon of Luther's on the Beatitudes; and, further, as Wendel has remarked, there is much in the oration that accords

* His address is: 1565 Cherry Lane, Rydal, PA 19046, USA.

with the evangelical position of Lefèvre — though Wendel is inexcusably misleading when he goes on to make the astonishing assertion that, "after an impartial examination of Lefèvre's writings, whatever has been advanced to show that Levèvre ever really adhered to the Reform or to its theological principles can be cast into the limbo of tendentious legend" *(Calvin: The Origins and Development of his Religious Thought,* 1963, pp. 41, 42). I believe I shall be able to demonstrate that the opposite is the truth. However, whatever the origin of Nicolas Cop's oration, there can be no doubt that Calvin was associated with him in its preparation. Its delivery evoked an immediate response of extreme hostility. Pressed by the Franciscans and the Sorbonne scholastics, the Parliament issued an order for the arrest of Cop and Calvin. Both, going separate ways, managed to make good their escape, the latter, it is said, from an upper window of the collège Fortet by means of a hastily knotted rope of bed-curtains and his identity concealed beneath the garb of a common vineyard labourer (see E. Doumergue, *Jean Calvin: Les hommes et les choses de son temps,* Vol. I, 1899, p. 354).

Calvin was also in transition *spiritually and intellectually.* The Cop incident indicated that his sympathies had been transferred from the unreformed traditions of his upbringing to the doctrines of the evangelical faith, though probably not yet openly so. The meeting with Lefèvre at Nérac may well have decided him to take his stand publicly with the evangelical cause. After the visit to Lefèvre he made the long journey to the town of his birth, Noyon, in the north, and surrendered the benefices which had been procured for him in childhood through his father's influence. He now knew what he had to do. From Noyon he made his way, with stops at Poitiers and Orléans, down to the city of Basel, and there, in the company of congenial spirits, including Nicolas Cop who had found refuge there, he worked diligently at the composition of his famous *Institutes of the Christian Religion (Christianae Religionis Institutio).* It was published in March 1536, a slender handbook of six chapters, which over the next two dozen years would grow into the much more massive work of twenty-eight chapters in four volumes now so familiar to us. The *Institutes* was essentially a contribution to the evangelical cause: addressed by a dedicatory letter to the King of France, the work was an *apologia* designed to win understanding and espousal of the reforming movement by clearly setting forth the biblical principles by which it was animated. The time of the publication of this first edition of the *Institutes* was also the time of the death of Lefèvre (who departed this life in the first months of 1536). The torch that he had lit and carried was now in the hands of John Calvin.

Something else of momentous significance to Calvin took place in the year 1536. He had decided to settle in Strassbourg, where the reformed faith had for some time been firmly established under the leadership of Martin Bucer, feeling that there he would find the peace and detachment which would enable him to give himself to study and authorship. The conflict between Francis I and Charles V made it advisable for Calvin to make a détour by way of Geneva, and in the month of July he arrived in that city with the intention of spending no more than one night there. These were perilous times and he was travelling under the assumed name of d'Espeville (in Basel he had used the pseudonym Lucanius); but his identity was made known to William Farel, who, in a manner typical of his fiery zeal, persuaded Calvin to remain in Geneva by pronouncing a curse on the seclusion he was seeking in Strassbourg and demanding that he should devote himself to the promotion of the reformation to which the city was already dedicated. It may be said that Lefèvre, though now dead, had a hand in this crisis of Calvin's career, for Farel had been brought to the evangelical faith in Paris a quarter of a century earlier through the witness of Lefèvre with whom he was then studying.

Who was this man Jacques Lefèvre d'Etaples? And why has the name of this personage, who courageously blazed the trail of evangelical renewal in France and whose reputation was on a level with that of his friend Erasmus (who died in the same year as Lefèvre) at the head of European scholarship in his day, fallen into such neglect? Perhaps the answer to the latter question is to be found in the fact that the reform of the French Church for which he lived and toiled indefatigably was never realized. Today, however, Lefèvre and his worth are being rediscovered and there are encouraging signs that he is at last beginning to gain once more the recognition that is his due.

Lefèvre, a native of Picardy like Calvin, was born in Etaples, a town on the channel coast at the north-east corner of France. The date of his birth is uncertain, but it was probably about the year 1455. As a youth he came to Paris and remained there for many years, first as a student and then as a teacher of philosophy and mathematics at the collège du Cardinal Lemoine, an institution founded for the education of scholars from his home region of Picardy. He was also ordained to the priesthood of the church. If there is one characteristic that gave direction and purpose to the whole of his life, it was his insistence on authenticity; and this authenticity was to be found only at the source, in the genuine and unsullied original or fountainhead of whatever subject one might be studying. In this respect he was a representative of the very best spirit of Renaissance humanism. Together with this went his intense and unremitting dedication as a scholar and a teacher to the work that he had in hand. His prolific output was the harvest of this application. For centuries a polluted stream of Aristotelian philosophy that had wandered far from the source had flowed through the schools and universities of Europe. Lefèvre set himself to remedy this situation by fulfilling the great labour of preparing for the press accurate Latin translations, together with commentaries and annotations, of the many works of the Aristotelian corpus. It is not surprising that his contemporaries praised him as the outstanding Aristotelian scholar of his day.

But the scope of his interest extended far beyond Aristotle. Interspersed with the Aristotelian publications were carefully edited works on mathematics and philosophy, often with his own running commentary, by a variety of authors which issued from Lefèvre's study; editions also of the Hermetic writings, of the works of Dionysius the Areopagite, of the mystical compositions of Ramon Lull, Jan van Ruysbroeck, Nicholas of Cusa, and others; *The Orthodox Faith* by John of Damascus and other works of a theological nature; and then, in the last decades of his life, his immense industry as he concentrated his energies on the task of translating and commenting on the text of Holy Scripture. But this was not all, for his hand was very much in the flow of publications that came from the able younger scholars who were his students and colleagues and who enjoyed the stimulation of his keen intellectual direction and supervision.

Lefèvre was ever a churchman of deep piety and seriousness. But he was none the less searching during the earlier part of his life searching for the pure fountain of truth, first in the philosophers of antiquity, whom he then regarded as theologians close, by reason of their antiquity, to the source of wisdom, and then feeling the attraction of mystical theology with the prospect it held out of the immediate experience of God, and then, finally, his discovery of the Gospel of the grace of God through the mediation of Jesus Christ. His publication, in 1499, of the works of Dionysius is instructive in this respect because it illustrates the transition that was then in process. We now know that these are pseudonymous writings, the composition of an unidentified author probably of the sixth century; indeed, as Lefèvre was aware, Nicholas of Cusa earlier in the fifteenth century had dismissed the author as a Platonist and Nicholas's contemporary Lorenzo Valla had incisively demonstrated the impossibility of the genuineness of these works. Lefèvre, however, was unwilling to abandon the conviction, which had for centuries prevailed in the Church and was still regarded as sacrosanct by the great majority of his contemporaries, that these writings had in fact been composed by St. Paul's Athenian convert, Dionysius the Areopagite (Acts 17:34). Consequently, he saw them as taking us back all but to St Paul himself and held them to be virtually a fount of apostolic and canonical truth.

We should take the publication of the works of the Pseudo-Dionysius, then, as an indication that Lefèvre was moving closer, in intention, even if not in actuality, to the authentic source of Holy Scripture; but it would be another decade before he succeeded in finding the reality for which he was feeling. Moreover, his enthusiasm at this juncture for the compositions of Dionysius was animated by another significant element in the make-up of his personality, namely, his intense spirit of patriotism: he constantly longed and laboured to wean his fellow countrymen away from unworthy preoccupations and to raise them to the highest level of spirituality. Hence his fearless assaults upon the soulless scholasticism and arid sophistries by which the academic world had for so long been dominated, and not least the University of Paris, and his denunciation of the currupt texts retained and used with such complacency and the futile formalities of medieval disputations over piffling points that had not the slightest relevance for serious scholarship or spiritual integrity or, for that matter, for the affairs of everyday life. It was little wonder that Lefèvre had bitter enemies among the self-inflated theologasters of the Sorbonne. The publication of the works of Dionysius fits within the pattern of his compaign for authenticity, and for the improvement not only of his university but of his country; for, according to a tradition which Lefèvre at that time gladly accepted, Dionysius the Areopagite had been the original apostle to France and the first bishop of Paris. Accordingly, he exhorted his fellow citizens: "Applaud your apostle, your first bishop, your parent who first brought you life and light, receive with honour his sacred teachings, and study them to your profit day and night". As always, Lefèvre is completely sincere; there is no suspicion of self-seeking on his part.

A significant milestone in lefèvre's spiritual pilgrimage was reached with the publication, in 1509, of his *Fivefold Psalter (Quincuplex Psalterium).* Even though he had not yet bidden a final farewell to the ancient philosophers and the medieval mystics, the appearance of this work gave notice that the focus of his attention was now beginning to concentrate on the text of Holy Scripture, in which he had at last discovered the uniquely true source of all knowledge and wisdom.

Lefèvre was now definitely on the way to becoming the man of one book. His heart was now involved as well as his mind. This is made clear in dramatic fashion in the letter of dedication addressed to Cardinal Briçonnet.

While virtually all studies may be expected to bring some degree of pleasure and usefulness [Lefèvre writes], the study of divine truth alone promises not just pleasure and usefulness but the highest happiness: 'Blessed are they who search thy testimonies', the psalmist declares (Psalm 119:2). What study, then, should we pursue more eagerly or embrace more willingly?

Then follows Lefèvre's witness to the crisis of his own personal experience:

> For a long time [he confesses] I pursued human studies and paid little more than lip service to the study of divine things ...; but once I had tased them as it were from a distance, so much light shone forth that human learning seemed to me to be darkness in comparison, and so wonderful was the fragrance they breathed that nothing can be found on earth to compare with its sweetness ... I am accustomed to the cloistered life [he continues], but those who do not know this sweetness in my judgment have never tasted the true food of the soul.

In 1508, the year prior to the publication of the *Fivefold Psalter,* Lefèvre had moved to the Abbey of Saint-Germain-des-Prés at the invitation of his influential friend Guillaume Briçonnet, bishop of Lodève (son of the cardinal of the same name), who was then the abbot and wished with his aid to effect some salutary monastic reforms. Many of the monks, resentful of any change in the *status quo,* took themselves elsewhere, and thus left the way open for serious students to move into the cells they had vacated and to take advantage both of Lefèvre's devout learning and also of the abbey's splended library. Lefèvre told Cardinal Briçonnet that on many occasions he had asked monks who sought nourishment from the Scriptures what sweetness they had derived from their reading, and that for the most part they had replied that they had found nothing but some kind of "literal" sense, especially when they were trying to understand the Psalms (recited in their daily offices), and that this had left them dissatisfied and dejected.

The *Fivefold Psalter* of 1509 was Lefèvre's response to this situation. With its five different Latin versions, the fifth of which was Lefèvre's own revision of the Vulgate, corrected by comparison with the Hebrew original, this work was, in part, a pioneering essay in textual criticism, and as such it called forth the displeasure of the theological establishment. But more important than this, it was a pioneering work in practical hermeneutics. In the preface Lefèvre propounded his principle of biblical exegesis which was destined to change the course of interpretation in the Church. Though he formulated this principle quite independently, it was a rediscovery rather than an innovation; and the time was undoubtedly ripe for its reappearance. For centuries a fourfold scheme of exposition (comprising four different senses: literal, allegorical, tropological, and anagogical) had been dominant, but in such a way that the literal sense was despised as superficial and of little worth, while the other three senses, which could all be subsumed under the one heading of the allegorical or mystical sense, purported to give the deep "spiritual" significance hidden beneath the rough surface of the scriptural text.

The effect on the Church of the allegorical method was pernicious, because it inevitably fostered an attitude of disdain and disregard for the plain, natural sense of the text and reduced the Bible to a book of intellectual word-puzzles; it led, further, to the spinning out of interpretations of the most elaborate and fantastic character which were as unedifying as they were fanciful; and, worst of all, it had the effect of taking the Bible out of the hands of the common people, who were regarded as ignorant and incapable of delving below the surface, and making it the preserve of inventive academics.

What Lefèvre did was to rescue the *literal* sense of the Scriptures. And by literal he did not mean literalistic; nor did he mean that there could be only one sense for the whole of Scripture. Depending on the context and the *genre* of a passage, the literal sense might be historical, allegorical, ethical, or eschatological, or even two or more of these together. The literal sense, moreover, was the *intended* sense. The psalmist, for example, was not merely writing about his own affairs, but was writing as a prophet through whom the Holy Spirit was speaking. Lefèvre insisted, then, that the proper literal sense was the sense intended by the Holy Spirit. But this sense was missed if the Holy Spirit was not present with regenerative power in the heart and mind of the reader or student of the Bible; and this consideration caused Lefèvre to postulate a *twofold literal sense:* (1) "the improper sense of those who are blind and fail to see, and who therefore understand divine things only in a carnal manner"; and (2) "the proper sense of those who see and are enlightened". "The former sense", he adds, "is fabricated by human reason; the latter is imparted by the divine Spirit". This explains the dejection of the monks with whom he had spoken: they had advanced no further than the improper literal sense of the Psalms. Accordingly, it was with the purpose of displaying the proper literal sense that Lefèvre "attempted to write a short exposition of the Psalms, with Christ as helper, who is the key of David" (of. Rev. 3:7). He showed how, under the inspiration of God's Spirit, the apostolic authors of the New Testament took passages from the Psalms and proclaimed their literal fulfilment in the person and work of Christ, and he arrived at the important conclusion that *"the literal sense and the spiritual sense coincide",* the true sense being "not what is called allegorical or tropological, but the sense which the Holy Spirit speaking through the prophet intends". This sense was accessible to all persons, whether learned or uneducated, provided they were not strangers to the vital working of the Holy Spirit in their lives.

Lefèvre's hermeneutical principle was adopted and applied by the Continental and British reformers who followed him. Thus it was he who prepared the ground for the restoration of the interpretation of Scripture in accordance with its sane, natural, and christological sense. And one of the first to come under his influence in this respect was an as yet unknown monk named Martin Luther. A little under a hundred years ago (in 1885) a copy of the first (1509) edition of the *Fivefold Psalter* was found in the library of Dresden: its margins were profusely annotated in the handwriting of Luther — an eloquent witness to the great care with which the volume had been studied by the young German scholar. Like Lefèvre, Luther's first endeavours in biblical exegesis were devoted to the Book of Psalms (on which he started lecturing in 1513). It was from Lefèvre that he learnt the primary importance of the literal sense and the twofold distinction within that sense; and in expounding the Psalter he, too, sought to bring out the native sense, that, namely, intended by both divine and human authors, which he described as the "prophetic" literal sense, and which, distinct from the "historic" literal sense, pointed to and was fulfilled in the person and work of Christ. 1509, it may be worth noticing, was not only the year of the publication of Lefèvre's *Fivefold Psalter* but also the year of the birth of John Calvin.

Some three years later, in December 1512, Lefèvre's massive and masterly *Commentary on the Epistles of St Paul,* was published in Paris. This work marks a very considerable advance on the road to reform, for we now find Lefèvre crossing over the boundary into the territory of biblically reformed theology in advance of the Reformers themselves and scaling the heights of theological comprehension which would subsequently be occupied by those whose names were to become famous as leaders of evangelical revival in Europe. In 1512, Luther's nailing of his Ninety-Five Theses to the door of the cathedral in Wittenburg was still five years off, as also was Zwingli's campaign for reform in Zürich, and Calvin was an infant but three years of age. The doctrines which such men would proclaim as belonging to the very heart of the Gospel Lefèvre had already proclaimed with assurance in his commentary on St Paul's Epistles. The work was Lefèvre's own; it was not a rehash of the notions of earlier writers, not a chain of quotations from others, but the result of his own penetration into the mind and spirit of the great apostle. The ground on which he was now taking his stand was that of *sola scriptura.*

It must suffice for me to draw attention to Lefèvre's firm grasp of that doctrine which is central to the Gospel, namely, that the sinner is justified by the grace of God alone *(sola gratia)* through faith in Christ alone *(sola fide),* with the consequence that all the glory must be ascribed to God alone *(soli Deo gloria).* Indeed, these very Latin expressions, which were to become the banner-headlines of Reformation theology, occur and recur in his commentary. Thus he insists that saving righteousness "flows solely from the mercy of God" and that therefore "men ought to give the glory to God alone *(soli Deo gloria),* since it is impossible for them to be saved of themselves and by their own works". He actually calls it "the righteousness of faith and grace".

> Our sins [he writes] are not forgiven except through that propitiation set before God and interceding on our behalf by the blood of redemption, which was shed in the great sacrifice on the wooden altar. All these things are given to us freely; but he alone trod the winepress.

And he applies christologically, and in truly apostolic fashion, the affirmation of Isaiah 53:4f.: "He bore our griefs and he carried our sorrows; the Lord laid on him the iniquity of us all; the chastisement of our peace was upon him; and by his bruising we have been healed"

And who is the sinner [he asks] that, turning to the contemplation and heartfelt invocation of such great goodness of God, does not, with so great a Mediator, find pardon? And when the Apostle speaks of God as justifying him who has faith in Jesus he shows that this righteousness and justification are from God and not from men. Therefore no one should glory in himself and in his own works as though he could be saved by them; for there is no cause for glory save in God alone, in the wounds of Christ, and in his blood (on Rom. 3:21ff.).

All the blessings of the Gospel are effected by God's grace and mercy; and they are most of all necessary for us who have come from the death of sin to life in the Spirit as persons who are in extreme need and poverty. By grace alone *(per solam gratiam)* can we be saved ... For we are saved by his grace through faith - saved not because of ourselves, but by God's grace. For grace is a gift, not a work. And lest we should think that the faith by means of which we are justified is ours, even this is God's gift. Therefore we should attribute everything to God and nothing to ourselves, and so we should glory neither in ourselves nor in works, but in God's grace and mercy alone *(in sola Dei gratia et misericordia)* (on Eph. 2:8ff.).

This is the authentic note of that evangelical faith which is commonly associated with the theologians of the Reformation, but which, as the Commentary on the Pauline Epistles shows, Lefèvre sounded ahead of them. Through diligent study of the Scriptures he had found his own way to the great liberating truths of the Gospel. There were still advances in understanding for him to make and misguided notions for him to discard, but he would never deviate from the straight path along which he was now walking with assurance.

The sincerity of Lefèvre's commitment to the Gospel of grace is strikingly demonstrated in the conversion of William Farel (1489-1565). It was some two or three years before the appearance of the Commentary on Paul's Epistles that Farel, a young aristocrat from Gap (Dauphiné) in south-east France, arrived in Paris to join the company of scholars who were pursuing their studies under the direction of Lefèvre at Saint Germain-des-Prés. In a letter written years later (on 7 September 1527; for the text see A.L. Herminjard, *Correspondance des réformateurs dans les pays de langue française,* 9 vols., 1866-1897, Vol. II, pp. 42ff).

Farel described how he had come as a young man to Paris "burdened with the grossest superstition". "The more I endeavoured to advance and improve myself", he wrote, "the more I slipped backwards". The reading of many religious works left him unsatisfied. "I wished to be a Christian like Aristotle", he explained, "whom virtually all treated as Christian, hoping to eat good fruit from a bad tree". He turned away from the light of the plain teaching of Scripture. But then he went on to describe how the "saintly" Lefèvre was the instrument whose "gentle guidance" God used to bring him to trust in Christ as his sole Saviour and Mediator: "to him, after being driven hither and thither, my soul, once it had reached the haven, clung, and to him alone", he testified. Moreover, "things now took on a new appearance; Scripture began to be full of meaning, the Prophets plain, the Apostles clear, the voice of the Shepherd, Master, and Teacher Christ recognized".

Later, in his autobiographical *Letter to all Lords and Peoples and Pastors* of 1530, Farel narrated how Lefèvre had encouraged him to become a preacher of the Gospel and had "often said to me that God would renew the world and that I would see it"; and he acknowledged that it was Lefèvre who had persuaded him that there was no merit in anyone except Christ alone:

> By his instruction he drew me away from false opinions of merit, teaching me that we have no merits at all, but that all comes from the grace and mercy of God alone, without anyone else possessing any merit. And I believed this as soon as it was said to me.

In 1521 Lefèvre left Paris for Meaux, a city some twenty miles east of the capital, in response to an invitation from William Briçonnet who had been appointed bishop of Meaux at the end of 1515, and who previously had called Lefèvre to his side at Saint-Germain-des-Prés. He now wished Lefèvre to lead the work of reform in his diocese which he had taken over in a deplorable condition of spiritual apathy and disrepair. Lefèvre probably found it a welcome move. His bitter enemies at the Sorbonne had long been demanding his blood. Opponents of his reforming zeal were venomously denouncing him, together with Luther, Erasmus, and Reuchlin, as an antichrist. Lefèvre's impatience with the futile sophistries of academic scholasticism, his insistence on the natural interpretation of Scripture, his defence of Reuchlin in the Pfefferkorn affair, and his challenging, on biblical grounds, of a number of long entrenched traditions and practices were resented by those who could not bear the bubble of their authoritarian self-importance to be pricked.

Convinced as he now was that scriptural ground was the only secure ground, Lefèvre was able to view this hostility with serenity. "Do not take it amiss that many are opposed to my writings", he wrote in 1519 (to Cornelius Agrippa of Nettesheim). "... I believe the day is coming when the truth of these things will be more clearly seen ... Falsehood withers away by itself and at length collapses without an attacker".

Once Lefèvre was at Meaux the prospects for the advance of the Gospel in that diocese and from there to other parts of France looked bright. Briçonnet, the bishop of Meaux, who was himself a member of an influential family and a distinguished ecclesiastical statesman, gave him the full weight of his support and collaborated with him in bringing together a team of outstanding young men to put into effect the programme for the evangelization and spiritual revitalization of the diocese. Briçonnet, moreover, was the close friend and confidant of the king's sister, Marguerite d'Angoulême, who had aligned herself with the evangelicals and was a constant advocate of their cause at the court. The king's attitude seemed to be more vacillating, largely because of vacillating fortunes in the game of international politcs in which he was involved, but he repeatedly came forward as the protector of Lefèvre against the designs of those who wished to do him ill. There was much justification, therefore, for his bright vision of the conquest of France by the Gospel and for his confidence that God would renew the world, even though he might not live to see it. Meanwhile this is the grand objective to which he devoted all of his considerable energy with undeviating singleness of purpose.

In June 1522 his Latin *Commentary on the Four Gospels (Commentarii initiatorii in Quatuor Evangelia)* was published. It confirms the conclusion that the Word of God was now his sole and passionate obsession.

Thus in the preface, addressed to "Christian readers", he affirmed:

> The Word of God is sufficient; this alone is enough for the discovery of the life which knows no end; this rule alone is the guide to eternal life; all else on which the Word of God does not shine is as unnecessary as it is superfluous.

It is, indeed, an appeal to the Church to return to the pure source of the living waters of the Gospel:

> Would that standard of belief might be sought from the

> primitive Church which consecrated so many martyrs to Christ, which knew no rule apart from the Gospel, which had no goal but Christ, and which offered worship to none except the Triune God. Truly, if we lived according to this custom, the eternal Gospel of Christ would flourish now as it flourished then.

But Latin was for scholars, and Lefèvre was well aware that if the populace as a whole were to be reached it would have to be in their own language (this was another basic principle of reform). Accordingly, he set himself to the translation of the Bible into the language of the French people, and in June 1523, just a year after his Latin commentary on the Gospels, his French translation of the Gospels issued from the press. Five months later this French version of the New Testament was completed with the appearance of a volume containing the Pauline Epistles, the Catholic Epistles, the Acts of the Apostles, and the Apocalypse in that order. This work of translation meant, as Lefèvre explained in the preface to the earlier volume, that "the simple members of the body of Christ, having this in their own language, can be as certain of the evangelical truth as those who have it in Latin".

Next to appear, again at an interval of just a few months (in February 1524), was Lefèvre's French translation of the Psalms, and the labour of translating to Old Testament into French was completed in four volumes which were published successively between April and September in 1528; and then, in 1530, Lefèvre's translation of the whole Bible was brought out in a single volume. Thus by tireless application to the task he had set before himself he gave practical expression to his conviction that "the time has now come when our Lord Jesus Christ, our sole salvation, truth, and life, wishes that his Gospel should be purely proclaimed throughout the whole world" (in the preface to the translation of the Gospels). Another work belonging to this period, his *Commentary on the Catholic Epistles,* which was the last of his Latin commentaries, was completed, it seems, late in 1524, though not published until the middle of 1527.

The year 1525 proved to be a year of crisis. During the course of that year — probably in the summer, though the date is uncertain — the publication took place of an anonymous volume in the French language containing the *Epistles and Gospels for the Fifty-Two Weeks of the Year,* each of which was followed by a brief homily or exhortation which was simple, practical, and evangelical in tone. The anonymity may possibly be attributable to an edict of the Sorbonne of

1523 forbidding the publication of any French translations of the Scriptures; but as it was a volume intended in the first place not for the academic world but for use in the parishes of the diocese of Meaux, the mention of authorship probably seemed irrelevant. In any case, Lefèvre's enemies in Paris seized on it and unhesitatingly described it as the work of "Jacques Lefèvre and his disciples". The evidence, in fact, is conclusive that the volume's exhortations were fundamentally the work of Lefèvre, though actually prepared under his close supervision by four of his younger colleagues. The work was essentially an instrument of reform, designed to make an explanation of the teaching of the Bible available to all in simple terms and in the language of the people.

On 6 November 1525 the theologians of the Sorbonne censured 48 propositions extracted from the exhortations, denouncing them variously as heretical, scandalous, odious, false, rash, impious, erroneous, schismatic, Lutheran, etc. A scrutiny of the doctrines condemned by the Sorbonne as "diabolical inventions and heretical fantasies" shows very plainly that they bore what was becoming the hallmark of the teaching of the Reformation, though Lefèvre had learned them from his own independent and prior study of Scripture: such doctrines, for example, as those which affirm that the salvation of the sinner is owed entirely to the grace of God and not at all to any supposed human merit, that justification is not in any degree by works but solely by faith in the perfect atoning work of Jesus Christ, and that therefore it is not to any saint or angel or other creature that we must look for grace and help but only to God, to whom alone belongs all the glory for our redemption.

All the circumstances seemed to be in favour of Lefèvre's adversaries. The king of France (Francis I), who had previously given instructions that Lefèvre was not to be molested, had suffered defeat in battle at Pavia in February of 1525 and been carried off captive to Spain. A few weeks before the Sorbonne's censure of the 48 propositions the Parliament had been persuaded to issue an edict requiring Lefèvre and others to be brought to judgment in Paris. The captive king actually tried to intervene from afar by sending an injunction to stop the persecution of these persons. He reminded the Parliament that the Sorbonnists had previously (in 1523) assailed Lefèvre with accusations and calumnies of which he had been completely cleared, and he demanded that Lefèvre should be free from slander and violence. But the enemies of Levèvre, feeling that the king's message from his Spanish prison could safely be disregarded, were determined to go their own way. Meanwhile however, Lefèvre and some of his friends who had avoided arrest had succeeded in fleeing the country. Lefèvre found refuge and hospitality in the home of Capito in Strassbourg. There he enjoyed the stimulating fellowship of Martin Bucer and other reforming leaders. But the exile did not last long, for the release of the king and his return to France in the spring of 1526 opened the way for Lefèvre and his friends to resume their ministry in the homeland. At the invitation of the king Lefèvre went to Blois, near Orléans, where he was given the double responsibility of organizing the royal library and serving as tutor to Charles, the youngest of the royal princes, then only four years old (his two elder brothers were being held hostage in Spain). Otherwise his energies were concentrated on the task of completing the translation of the Bible into French. The closing years of his life, from 1530 onwards, were spent in the peaceful security of Marguerite's chateau at Nérac, and it was there that Calvin paid him the visit mentioned at the beginning of this paper.

Calvin first came to Paris as a young student in 1523, that is, at a time when Lefèvre was no longer himself in the capital, though not far away in Meaux. It was a time, moreover, when Lefèvre's reputation as a scholar was at its height and his person the centre of controversy, with distinguished friends on the one hand and bitter enemies on the other. It is impossible that Calvin should have been unaware of his fame and unlikely that he would have been unfamiliar with his work and his writings. Was it then that he first felt the influence of this remarkable man? It would be gratifying to have a definite answer to this question, but as things are we must be content to remain in uncertainty.

However much the ways of Lefèvre and Calvin may have differed ecclesiastically, it is not unjust to say that theologically Calvin followed closely the path that had been pioneered by Lefèvre. The provision of the best possible version of the Bible in the language of the people became a matter of the greatest importance for him. His cousin, Pierre Robert Olivétan, was then working on a revision, by careful comparison with the Hebrew and Greek originals, of Lefèvre's translation of the Scriptures which had been published in Antwerp in 1530, and Calvin now joined him in this work. The resulting volume was brought out the following year (1535) in Neuchâtel. Calvin continued to labour at the improvement of the French version of the Scriptures for many years after this. Affinities to the thought of

Lefèvre are evident in the two prefaces (one in Latin and one in French) that Calvin wrote for Olivétan's Bible, not least in the expression of the intense desire to increase in christlikeness, or *christiformitas* as Lefèvre called it, and in the emphasis on the redemptive knowledge of Christ as the supreme purpose of the doctrine of Scripture. The sum of all biblical study and searching, Calvin asserted, is "to know Jesus Christ and the infinite riches comprised in him".

> What more could we demand for the spiritual doctrine of our souls than to know God, to be transformed in him, and to have his glorious image stamped upon us? ... Let all our understanding be concentrated on this point, to learn in Scripture to know Jesus Christ and him only, in order that we may be led by him straight to the Father, who contains in himself all perfection.

In such aspirations the hearts and minds of Lefèvre and Calvin were entirely at one.

MARTIN BUCER AND THE CONVERSION OF JOHN CALVIN

High above the names of all the other leaders of the Reformed Churches history has written in large, clear letters: "John Calvin;" yet, how he became a Protestant, and what influences caused his conversion, the most painstaking historical research has failed to reveal. In April, 1532, he was still a Roman Catholic absorbed in humanistic studies, and manifesting no more than a literary interest in the Bible. In 1535 he cast upon the troubled waters of the Reformation a theological treatise that did more to direct the current of subsequent Protestant thought than any other book of the age. Beyond all question it was the fruit of a revolutionary religious experience, but who sowed the seed and when, no one has been able to tell. Surely the *Institutes* were not the product of completely spontaneous and independent thought; for that would require a superhuman originality. From what quarry, then, did he take the marble which he carved into the Calvinistic System, and who were the masters, if any, who taught him to use the hammer and chisel?

The latest theory is that he was greatly influenced in his religious development by Martin Bucer, the reformer of Strasbourg. Their first recorded meeting was at the Synod of Bern in 1537. On the nature of their intercourse before this event, historians have differed widely, some describing it in vague and indefinite terms, others limiting it to an epistolary acquaintance, while one biographer has audaciously declared that in 1528 Calvin was actually a student in Bucer's classes at Strasbourg.[1] Even such conservative critics as the editors of Calvin's correspondence in the *Corpus Reformatorum* have advanced the query, "what if at that time [1528] Bucer

---

[1] Kampschulte makes this claim (F. W. Kampschulte, *Johann Calvin*, 1869, I, 231 and n. 2). *Cf.*, W. Walker, *Jean Calvin*, 1909, p. 73 ff.; A. Lang, "Die Bekehrung Johannes Calvins," in *Studien zur Geschichte der Theologie und der Kirche*, II, Heft I, 16-17; A. Lefranc, *La Jeunesse de Calvin*, 1888, p. 56; E. Doumergue, *Jean Calvin*, 1899, ff., I, 298, 556-557.

entertained the young Frenchman in his own home?"[2] To answer "Yes" would be no less than to assert that it was Martin Bucer who prepared the soil in which the *Institutes* were rooted and from which they grew. History demands, however, that this question be answered in the negative, for reasons which it is the purpose of this article to set forth. There is no sound basis in fact for the legend that Calvin was converted by Bucer. Those who have advanced it have been misled because their interest was primarily in Calvin, not Bucer. While every known source for a knowledge of the French reformer's life has been scrutinized with painstaking care, his biographers have shown themselves unfamiliar with the movements of the German theologian. A little further investigation of the latter's activities will show that Bucer exercised no personal influence upon Calvin before the Synod of Bern.

General considerations would favor the hypothesis that Calvin took his first steps in the Reformed faith under the guiding hand of Martin Bucer, for no other of the evangelical leaders of Germany was in closer personal touch with France than he. It was Bucer who had translated into Latin Luther's commentary on the Epistles of Peter and Jude, in order that the French might read it; and for the same purpose he published in 1525 a Latin edition of Luther's sermons, dedicating it to the "Brethren in France."[3] For their sakes he assumed the pseudonym of "Aretius Felinus" when he published a commentary on Psalms, thus planning to avoid the restrictions of ecclesiastical censorship.[4] By him many exiles from France, who found in Strasbourg a city of refuge, were heartily welcomed. Roussel and Lefèvre sought

---

[2] *Corpus Reformatorum, Calvini Opera*, Xb, 22, n. 1.

[3] A. L. Herminjard, *Correspondance des Réformateurs dans les Pays de Langue française*, I, 318-320. *Cf.* F. Mentz, "Bibliographische Zusammenstellung der gedruckten Schriften Bucers" (*Zur 400 jährigen Geburtsfeier Martin Butzers*, nos. 5, 9).

[4] T. Schiess, *Briefwechsel der Brüder Ambrosius und Thomas Blaurer*, I, 204.

safety in the Silver-City[5] in 1525,[6] and during the years that followed, hundreds of Frenchmen fled to her walls for protection. Though Bucer was never wealthy, he gladly received many of them beneath the shelter of his own roof.[7] William Farel spent many months at Strasbourg,[8] and Bucer was intimate not with him alone, but also with John Sturm,[9] Olivétan,[10] John Sleidan,[11] Nicholas and Henry Cop,[12] Marguerite of Navarre,[13] and many others.[14] So famous a protector of French exiles and so energetic a leader in the spreading of Protestant propaganda in France, might very naturally have established a personal relationship with Calvin.

But this general probability is not supported by the evidence. Our knowledge of their relations before the Synod of Bern, 1537, rests almost entirely upon three letters, the first, from Bucer to Farel, dated merely May 1; the second, from Calvin to Bucer, dated September 4; and the third, from Bucer to Calvin, dated November 1, 1536. While some writers have contended that these letters furnish evidence of a direct influence by Bucer upon the younger reformer, a more careful investigation, correlated with the events of Bucer's life, will demonstrate that there was no such influence.

In the first letter, undoubtedly written on May 1, 1528,[15] Bucer informs Farel, "I have here a youth of Noyon, who, cast out of Orleans by persecution, where he undertook the

---

[5] The Latin name for Strasbourg was *Argentoratum*.

[6] Herminjard, *op. cit.*, I, 404-405.

[7] *Cf.* Schiess, *op. cit.*, I, 502, II, 813.

[8] Herminjard, *op. cit.*, I, 431, 451.

[9] Herminjard, *op. cit.*, III, 271-274, 308, n. 6.

[10] Herminjard, *op. cit.*, III, 44.

[11] M. Lenz, *Kleine Historische Schriften*, p. 104.

[12] M. Lenz, *Briefwechsel Landgraf Philipps des Grossmüthigen von Hessen mit Bucer*, I, 216; *Corpus Reformatorum*, II, 498-499; Herminjard, *op. cit.*, III, 158-159.

[13] Herminjard, *op. cit.*, V, 38.

[14] Bucer to Antonius, "Thesaurus Baumianus," IV, 209-210.

[15] The text is published by Herminjard, *op cit.*, II, 131-133, and in *Calvini Opera*, Xb, 1-2. The original manuscript is in the *Bibliothèque des Pasteurs* at Neuchâtel. On the date *cf.* Herminjard, *op. cit.*, II, 131, n. 1, and H. Eells, "The Correct Date for a Letter to Zwingli" (*Revue belge de Philologie et d'Histoire*, July 1922, p. 516, ff).

study of letters, has wandered here. He relates that there is one at Orleans who is suitable [to assist Farel]. We will write concerning him to Peregrinus . . . The [youth of] Noyon resolves to study languages, in which, as yet, he is entirely ignorant of Greek and Hebrew." The bearing of this passage upon the present investigation is best exemplified by the theory which Kampschulte has advanced in these words, "A letter of the Strasbourg reformer Bucer at this time, can even make room for the conjecture, that already from Orleans Calvin had turned his gaze toward Germany, and crossing over as early as the year 1528, had established himself in the city of Bucer and Capito;"[16] and in a foot-note he continues, "It is plain that the passage applies exactly to Calvin in every detail."[17] In spite of Kampschulte's calm assurance, it may well be questioned if he is right in this "conjecture" that Calvin was a pupil of Bucer and Capito in the spring of 1528. Undoubtedly, several characteristics of this "youth of Noyon" might accurately be applied to Calvin, but a closer examination of the passage shows that he could not have been the student of whom Bucer writes.

First, except for this letter there is not the slightest evidence of a sojourn by Calvin in Strasbourg in the spring of 1528. Kampschulte, vainly seeking such support for his claim, conjectures still further that Calvin wrote to Bucer as an old acquaintance in his "Letter of September 4," and that in 1534 he sent to Capito his work on the sleep of the soul. Even assuming that this was the case, and there is good reason to believe that it is only legend, Kampschulte can only establish a vague probability that this hypothetical acquaintance originated at Strasbourg in 1528.

Against this vague probability there exists conclusive internal and external evidence, proving that Calvin was not the student to whom Bucer refers. Calvin himself testifies that he was not "cast out of Orleans by persecution," for in the preface to his commentary on the Psalms, he wrote, "And,

[16] Kampschulte, *op. cit.*, I, 231.
[17] Kampschulte, *op. cit.*, I, 231, n. 1.

in fact, leaving the country of France, I came into Germany for the express purpose that I might live there in some unknown corner, as I had always desired. But observe, while I resided at Basel, being hidden there and known to a few people, they persecuted many faithful and holy people in France."[18] From this statement it is clear that the persecution commenced, or became severe, after his departure; and that he went to Basel, not Strasbourg. Calvin did not study under the faculty of letters at Orleans but under the faculty of law.[19] It was at Paris that he began the study of Greek,[20] and in 1534 at Basel he first became acquainted with the intricacies of Hebrew.[21] Even Kampschulte finds "room" for only a short stay at Strasbourg.[22]

In addition there are three incontestable proofs that Calvin could not have taken refuge in Strasbourg from persecution as early as 1528. His *Commentary on Seneca's Treatise on Clemency* is not the work of one who had accepted evangelical beliefs, had suffered for his decision, and listened, even for a short time to the fervent evangelical teaching of Bucer and Capito.[23] If Calvin found refuge in Strasbourg in 1528, why did he go to Basel to live in 1535? Most conclusive of all is the fact that Bucer wrote to the French reformer on November 1, 1536, "For it is impossible for me to tell you how sorry I am that I was not permitted to know you and speak to you when you were here."[24] Surely Bucer would not have said this to a former pupil, for above all else Bucer took an interest in men. Whoever he was, the "youth of Noyon" was not John Calvin. Herminjard has suggested that it was Olivétan, and this probably is as good a guess as can be made.[25]

---

[18] *Calvini Opera*, XXXI, 24.
[19] Walker, *op. cit.*, p. 53.
[20] Walker, *op. cit.*, p. 63.
[21] "Vie de Calvin," *Calvini Opera*, XXI, 58.
[22] Kampschulte, *op. cit.*, I, 231, n. 1.
[23] Walker, *op. cit.*, p. 69, ff.
[24] *Calvini Opera*, Xb, 68.
[25] Herminjard, *op. cit.*, III, 44 and n. 20.

The second letter which furnishes evidence as to the relations between Bucer and Calvin before the Synod of Bern, 1537, was written by Calvin to the Strasbourg reformer on September 4 from Noyon.[26] The letter itself is peculiar and puzzling in many ways, but the greatest enigma is the year of its origin, which Calvin has not mentioned and no historian has been able to ascertain. Devoted entirely to a recommendation of an unknown French Protestant refugee, the letter is characterized by two significant features: it is the epistle of a firm convert to evangelical beliefs, and it is marked by an apparently "familiar tone" which sounds as if this was not Calvin's first letter to the reformer of Strasbourg. The whole significance of the letter hinges upon the nature of this "familiar tone" and since this is confined to the first and last paragraphs, it will suffice to quote them alone.

The grace and peace of the Lord be with thee through the mercy of God and the victory of Christ.

I would have had neither leisure to write, nor warrant, nor even good reason, had it not seemed proper in a few words to bring to thy notice with my deep sympathy the pitiful condition of this excellent brother, which certain friends of unquestionable trustworthiness and probity have made known to me by letter. Yet whether I [merely] indulge my sorrow and sympathy, or advance his interests, I could not restrain myself from writing.

. . . .

I beseech of thee, Dr. Bucer, if my prayers, if my tears have any avail, to relieve his misery. To thee is committed the poor; thou wilt be the helper of the fatherless. Do not suffer him to be reduced to the necessity of experiencing extreme want; thou canst, if thou wilt, be of some assistance to him. But indeed thou art in thy wisdom the better judge. I could not, however, withhold my too eager hand from writing a word in his behalf. So much for the moment. Farewell, most learned sir. Noyon. 5 September.

Thine from the heart

CALVIN

To Dr. Bucer, Bishop of Strasbourg.[27]

---

[26] The letter has been published by Herminjard, *op. cit.*, III, 201-204, and in *Calvini Opera*, Xb, 22-24. The original manuscript is now in the *Archives et Bibliothèque de la Ville* at Strasbourg.

[27] The letter reads as follows in the original Latin:

Gratia et pax Domini tecum per misericordiam Dei et victoriam Christi.

Scribendi nec ocium erat, nec argumentum neque etiam consilium,

These paragraphs raise the issue: Does this letter prove a previous acquaintance or at least a correspondence between Bucer and Calvin? If so, then, in all probability Bucer had a direct, personal influence upon Calvin's religious development. Those who would answer the question in the affirmative argue from the "familiar tone" of the letter, and the absence of any form of excuse, of any statement of belief, and of any word of praise. They even suggest that the possibility of Calvin's presence in Strasbourg in 1528 lends credibility to the hypothesis.[28] Doumergue declares that a young man like Calvin would not commence so familiarly his first letter to such a well-known reformer as Bucer.[29]

These arguments are not only inconclusive, they are erroneous. The tone of the letter is not so familiar as it seems at first sight, and even the liveliest imagination would not describe it as intimate.[30] Although there are no obsequious forms of excuse, Calvin twice offers a respectful apology for writing. In the first sentence he anxiously explains that only his sympathy for the poor refugee emboldened him to take the liberty of writing a letter which he had no other "warrant"

---

nisi visum esset paucis apud te deplorare miseram sortem optimi hujus fratis, quam mihi per literas significarunt amici quidam fidei et probitatis non dubiae. Sive tamen dolori meo et sympathiae indulgeo, sive ejus negocium procuro, non potui mihi temperare quin scriberem.

. . . .

Oro te, D. Bucere, si quid praeces meae, si quid lachrymae valent, hujus miseriae ut succurras. Tibi derelictus est pauper; orphano tu eris adjutor. Ne patiaris eo necessitatis redigi, ut extrema experiatur; potes, si vis, aliqua illi succerrere. Verum tu melius pro tua prudentia. Non potui tamen manum ultro lascivientem continere, quin aliquid in hujus caussam scriberem. Haec pro tempore. Vale, eruditiss. vir. Noviod, pridie nonas septembres.

Tuus ex animo,

Calvinus

D. Bucero, Episcopo Argentoratensi."

(Quoted from Herminjard, *op. cit.* III, 202, 203-204).

[28] *Calvini Opera,* Xb, 22, n. 1.

[29] Doumergue, *op. cit.*, I, 298.

[30] *Cf.* Lefrance, "D'un bout à l'autre de cette épitre le langage de Calvin a quelque chose de mystérieux" (*op. cit.*, p. 189).

or "good reason" to send.[31] If he had previously made the acquaintance of Bucer, it would have been discourteous for him to have said that he would not have written without this "warrant" and "good reason." Besides, the words, "too eager hand," express a courteous apology and their severity can only be explained on the ground that Calvin considered his action audacious.[32]

Though there is no direct statement of belief, Calvin indirectly established his own orthodoxy when he exonerates the refugee from the charge of Anabaptism. The editors of Calvin's correspondence make an unwarranted assumption if they claim that custom required Calvin to send such a statement of belief in his first letter. Admitting this contention, however, the absence of a confession of faith might be explained not only by the fact that he had sent one in a previous letter, but also by its irrelevance to the subject of the letter. Though there is no overt praise or pretentious flattery, such as is characteristic of the letters of the humanists, especially when writing to men of a greater reputation, there is an evident deference on the part of Calvin. He addresses Bucer by the strange title of "bishop of Strasbourg," calls him "most learned man," and by asking him to aid a man condemned by everyone else, tacitly acknowledges his importance. As has been shown, there is no possibility that Calvin was in Strasbourg in 1528, and this theory cannot be used to bolster up the hypothesis of a previous correspondence.

While the arguments in favor of the theory carry no weight, the evidence against it, though not noticed by historical critics, is very strong. First, Bucer wrote on November 1, 1536, that he had not yet known or spoken to Calvin.[33] Though, strictly interpreted, this may refer only to a speaking acquaintance, it was a peculiar way for him to speak if he had before this corresponded with Calvin. In the same let-

---

[31] "Scribendi . . . erat nec argumentum neque etiam consilium" (Herminjard, *op. cit.*, III, 202).

[32] Herminjard, *op. cit.*, III, 204.

[33] *Calvini Opera*, Xb, 68.

ter Bucer states that Calvin had gone to the home of Capito, who had failed to make them acquainted. If even the slightest acquaintance had existed between them before this, it would have been at least discourteous for Calvin not to have called upon Bucer, and surely such a hospitable man as Bucer would not have waited for an introduction, nor have been ignorant of Calvin's visit, if he had corresponded with him.

Secondly, the letter is replete with indications that Calvin knew Bucer only by reputation. The salutation, "Grace and peace from the Lord be with you through the mercy of God and the victory of Christ,"[34] is a very formal one, and its stereotyped use by French Protestants would make it equivalent to the English expressions of today, "My dear Sir," or "Dear Brother." Calvin never used it in any of his subsequent letters to Bucer, when he was on familiar terms with him. In fact, it is rarely found in all of his correspondence, and only upon formal occasions.[35] The title "Dr. Bucer" proves a lack of acquaintance, for Bucer did not have a doctor's degree at this time, as any friend would have known. The second remaining letter from Calvin to Bucer, written after they had met at the Synod of Bern, uses the phrase "my Bucer," as would be expected in a letter between friends.[36] If Calvin was acquainted with Bucer, and had corresponded with him before he wrote the letter from Noyon, why did he not write "my Bucer" then, as he did in 1538, for in 1538 they had advanced only slightly beyond an epistolary friendship?

In this letter from Noyon there are no greetings sent to Capito or any of Bucer's other colleagues at Strasbourg. Calvin makes not one, personal reference to himself or to Bucer. It is significant that he bases his plea for the unfortunate Frenchman, *not* on any personal influence with the reformer of Strasbourg, but solely upon the pitiful condition of the man. His tears and his prayers are the arguments upon which

[34] Herminjard, *op. cit.*, III, 202 and n. 4.

[35] K. Müller, "Calvins Bekehrung" (*Nachrichten von der Königl. Gesellschaft der Wissenschaften zu Göttingen*, 1905, Heft II, 250).

[36] Herminjard, *op. cit.*, IV, 338-349.

he relies, not the importance of his name to Bucer. Evidently no one else would help the man, and under such circumstances expediency justified Calvin in writing for him a letter of recommendation to a man he did not know. The whole letter is more carefully phrased than a casual note from one friend to another. No one seems to have noticed that the sentence, "To thee is committed the poor; thou wilt be the helper of the fatherless," is a direct quotation from the Vulgate.[37] There it is addressed to God. Only extreme veneration could excuse its application to a man. "So much for the moment," is not so familiar as it seems at first sight, for it is a stereotyped phrase found frequently in the correspondence of the period.

Third, it is certain that Calvin and Bucer met at the Synod of Bern, 1537. On January 12, 1538, Calvin wrote to Bucer his opinion of the latter's conduct at the Synod.[38] Since this letter is the first one written after it is certain that an acquaintance was established between the two men, it may be taken as a model of what a "familiar" letter from Calvin to Bucer should be. A comparison of this letter with the one from Noyon shows some remarkable differences and a distinctly warmer tone. The high-sounding address, "To Dr. Bucer, Bishop of Strasbourg," has melted into a brief, "To Bucer." The incorrect title "To Dr. Bucer" has been replaced by "my Bucer." He sends greetings to Capito, and makes personal references both to himself and Bucer. Thus in spite of the seemingly "familiar tone" of the opening sentence, this letter to Bucer from Noyon, far from proving that the two reformers were acquainted, indicates clearly that they were not.[39]

Historians have speculated in vain upon the year in which the letter was written. Conrad Hubert, Bucer's faithful secretary, has dated it 1532, but this indicates little for he fre-

[37] Psalm x. 14.

[38] Herminjard, *op. cit.*, IV, 338-349.

[39] The mystery of this "familiar tone" has led Lang to declare, "Vorläufig müssen wir also darauf verzichten, das Dunkel das über dem Briefe liegt, aufzuklären" (*op. cit.*, p. 17). Müller, believing that this

quently made mistakes. Internal evidence gives even less assistance. The letter was written from Noyon on September 4. Calvin is now converted but is still in France, consequently it must be dated either 1532, 1533 or 1534. To say which would be only guess-work. One conclusion is self-evident. If this was the first letter that passed between Calvin and Bucer, and the evidence indicates that it was, then the Strasbourg reformer made no direct, personal contribution toward Calvin's conversion, for by the time this letter was written Calvin had definitely taken his stand with the evangelical party.

The third source of information about the personal relations of Bucer and Calvin before the Synod of Bern, 1537, is a letter written by Bucer to Calvin on November 1, 1536, from Strasbourg.[40] In dealing with this letter, it is first necessary to ascertain the correct date, for Herminjard has questioned the date (November 1) given to the letter by Beza, and declared that it should be dated December 1.[41] Although every writer since Herminjard, who has used this letter, has followed him blindly, there is clear evidence to show that Herminjard was wrong and Beza was right.

The only internal clue to the date is the statement by Bucer that he had recently visited Basel. Therefore, the first step is to follow Bucer's travels in the last months of 1536. During this time Bucer was at Basel certainly twice and probably three times. On September 24, he attended the conference held there to discuss the Wittenberg Concord.[42] The third

---

"familiar tone" indicates a correspondence of which there is no other trace during Calvin's early life, arbitrarily declares that Calvin made a mistake in writing "Noviod. pridie nonas septembres," and suggests that the letter was written from Basel in 1538 (*op cit.*, p. 252). This is a very convenient historical method, but hardly an accurate one.

[40] Herminjard, *op. cit.*, IV, 117-119; *Calvini Opera*, Xb, 66-68. The original manuscript has been lost but the letter is preserved in an edition of Calvin's correspondence by Beza.

[41] Herminjard, *op. cit.*, IV, 119, n. 8, 9, 10, 11.

[42] Schiess, *op. cit.*, I, 822; Herminjard, *op. cit.*, IV, 116, n. 2.; J. W. Baum, *Capito und Butzer*, p. 517; C. Pestalozzi, *Heinrich Bullinger*, p. 194.

visit was on November 14 at another conference.[43] During the last days of October, 1536, Bucer made a rapid journey across the Rhine, where he sought a conference with Ambrose Blaurer and John Zwick. He left Strasbourg shortly after October 18, met Blaurer at Herrenberg, probably on October 25, and may have conferred with Zwick soon after.[44] It is quite likely that his second visit to Basel occurred on his return journey to Strasbourg, and that it is this visit to which he refers in his letter on November 1, 1536. The adverb "lately" would apply more appropriately to this visit, and the fact that Bucer makes no reference to a conference indicates that his visit was not made upon such an occasion. Of course this argument assumes that the date of November 1 is correct, but since this date is clearly given in the only authentic copy of the letter, the assumption is not only justified, but necessary, until this date is proved to be wrong.

Herminjard claims that it is wrong and that the correct date is December 1, but none of his arguments is conclusive and the only strong one is founded on an error. First, he contends that two weeks before the Basel Conference on November 14, 1536, Bucer could not have written, "Truly I wish it were possible for us without neglecting the affairs of the churches, to see our Swiss friends for a short time, even if unbidden!" "How," asks Herminjard, "can this wish of Bucer's be made consistent with the date of November 1, which Beza gives to the present letter? The Strasbourg theologian could not have been unaware on November 1, 1536, that he was invited to the assembly which was going to meet at Basel eleven days later."[45] But it is well to remember that human actions are not always thoroughly consistent or rationally

[43] Pestalozzi, *op. cit.*, p. 194; Herminjard, *op. cit.*, IV, 116, n. 2; Baum, *op. cit.*, p. 517; Schiess, *op. cit.*, II, 828.

[44] Schiess, *op. cit.*, I, 825; Bucer to Myconius, Strasbourg, Oct. 18, 1536, "Thesaurus Baumianus," IX, 241; T. Kolde, *Analecta Lutherana,* p. 281, n. 1; Bucer to John Zwick, Oct. 25, 1536, "Thesaurus Baumianus," IX, 257-259.

[45] Herminjard, *op. cit.*, IV, 119, n. 8.

correct. Granting, however, that they are, would not this wish be even more strange two weeks after the conference? Since the assembly on November 14 had a promising conclusion,[46] why, on December 1, should Bucer wish for another one shortly? That Bucer does not definitely ask Calvin to meet him on November 14 at Basel is not a serious difficulty, for he may have known that Calvin did not intend to be there. Thus, this argument against the date of November 1 is far from conclusive.

Secondly, Herminjard says, "We conclude from this that Beza, to whom Bucer's writing was never familiar, has read the date inexactly."[47] This is an extremely arbitrary argument. The possibility that Beza made such a mistake is very small. It is true that Bucer's handwriting is exceedingly hard to read, but he usually wrote his capital *N* quite clearly.

Herminjard's third argument is at the same time the strongest and the weakest. It is the strongest, because if it were true, the date November 1 would be impossible; and the weakest, because it is not true. He declares, "The first of November, 1536, Bucer was at Marburg (See J. H. Ott, *Annales Anabaptistici*, 1672, p. 89)."[48] The fact is Bucer was not in Marburg November 1, 1536, but November 1, 1538.[49] Ott does indeed say, "Bucer held a colloquy with the Anabaptists of Marburg on the Wednesday after Simon and Jude, 1536,"[50] but "1536" is clearly an error, possibly in printing, for nowhere in Bucer's correspondence or biographies is there found any mention of a visit by Bucer to Marburg in 1536. Moreover,

---

[46] Virck, Wincklemann and Bernays, *Politische Correspondenz der Stadt Strassburg im Zeitalter der Reformation*, II, 693.

[47] Herminjard, *op. cit.*, IV, 119, n. 8.

[48] Herminjard, *op. cit.*, IV, 119, n. 11.

[49] M. Lenz, *Briefwechsel Landgraf Philipps*, etc., I, 46-47, Beilage I, 318, 322, ff.; K. W. H. Hochuth, "Landgraf Philipp und die Wiedertäufer" (*Zeitschrift für die historische Theologie*, XXVIII, 538-644); W. Diehl, "Martin Butzers Bedeutung für das kirchliche Leben in Hessen" (*Schriften des Vereins für Reformationsgeschichte*, XXXVIII, 45).

[50] J. H. Ottius, *Annales Anabaptistici*, p. 89.

the colloquy described by Ott took place in 1538, and the source which he used is noted for its chronological errors.[51]

Thus, not only do Herminjard's arguments fail to prove his point but there are three considerations, unnoticed by him, which show that this letter could not have been written on December 1, 1536.[52] On this day Capito, Bucer's colleague, wrote a letter to Calvin which is similar to Bucer's in that he also requests an interview with the Genevan reformer, but it also contains essential differences. While Bucer offers to meet Calvin at any place he may appoint, even Geneva, Capito declares that it is now impossible to leave Strasbourg, because of previous absences, and requests Calvin to come to him. Capito says that at Basel he and Bucer had planned a trip to Geneva. Bucer says nothing of having considered such a journey, but declares his willingness to do so. The only reasonable explanation of this contrast between the two letters is that Bucer wrote while he and Capito were still contemplating a trip to Geneva, and Capito wrote after it was found impossible to make it. Moreover, Capito makes no mention of Bucer's letter, as his custom was when they both wrote on the same day, nor does Bucer mention Capito's. Finally, on November 26, Toussain wrote to Farel that he had heard that Bucer sought a conference with Calvin.[53] This indicates that Bucer had already written to Calvin for that purpose. Consequently, the date of November 1, 1536 for this letter must be retained.

The date of the letter having been determined, the next point to consider is what Bucer refers to when he says, "For I cannot tell how sorry I am that I was not given an opportunity to know you and to speak to you when you were here."[54] The most natural interpretation of this sentence and the context is that Calvin was at Strasbourg in the latter part of October, 1536. He attended a conference at Lausanne October

---

[51] Lenz, *Briefwechsel Landgraf Philipps*, etc., I, 317 and n. 3.

[52] *Calvini Opera*, Xb, 75.

[53] *Calvini Opera*, Xb, 73.

[54] Herminjard, *op. cit.*, IV, 119.

1-8, and another at Bern, October 16-18, so that he was moving in the direction of Strasbourg. [55] The council of Strasbourg wrote to the council of Basel on November 4, 1536, "The learned John Calvin and Gauchier Farel, both Frenchmen, sent by you and others to negotiate with us on behalf of those persecuted in France for the sake of the holy gospel, have been presented to us by our learned preachers Doctor Wolfgang Capito and Martin Bucer."[56] How can this contradiction be explained? Bucer says he did not meet Calvin and the council says that he presented Calvin to them.[57] The most plausible explanation is that Capito, for some unknown reason, introduced the two envoys to the council in his own and Bucer's name without consulting, or fully informing the latter. Herminjard's proposal that Calvin did not personally accompany Farel to Strasbourg in October, because Capito wrote to Calvin on December 1 requesting an interview,[58] carries little weight, for within a month's time Capito might have discovered urgent reasons for seeing him again.

Thus the question arises, Did Calvin visit Strasbourg in October, 1536? Herminjard and others contend that he did not, and that the visit to which Bucer refers was made during Calvin's first journey out of France in 1534.[59] This is both an unnatural and a probably erroneous interpretation, as a little investigation of the circumstances of Calvin's exile will show. The passage in question indicates that at the time Calvin visited Strasbourg, both Bucer and Capito were there. The probability is that when Calvin passed through on his way to Basel, only one of the reformers was at home. Bucer left Strasbourg October 28, 1534 and though he returned on January 5, 1535, he departed again a month later on February 5

---

[55] Walker, *op. cit.*, p. 201.

[56] *Calvini Opera*, Xb, 68, ff.

[57] Gauchier Farel was at Bern on Nov. 7, 1536, and probably Calvin was with him (Herminjard, *op. cit.*, IV, 99).

[58] Herminjard, *op. cit.*, IV, 96, notes 1-3.

[59] Herminjard, *op. cit.*, IV, 119, notes 9-10.

or 6 and remained away until the end of May, 1535.[60] Capito left Strasbourg soon after Bucer's arrival on January 5, 1535,[61] and did not return until January 28.[62] Consequently, between October 28, 1534, and June 1, 1535, Capito and Bucer were together in Strasbourg for not more than two weeks in all. The chances are few that Calvin passed through at just this time. If he did, then his exile is definitely dated.

It is impossible on the basis of other information to determine just when Calvin first left France and passed through Strasbourg. The general opinion is that he left France late in 1534 and arrived in Basel early in 1535.[63]. If this was the case then it is barely possible that he passed through Strasbourg on January 5 or a day or so later when both Capito and Bucer were there. Doumergue reaches the following conclusion, "Calvin left, that is, began the journey which was to lead him out of France, in 1534; he actually went out during those days which, in the old style are attributed to 1534, but, in the new, belong to 1535; doubtless in February."[64] If Calvin entered Germany in February, 1535, then the chances are very small indeed that he passed through Strasbourg while Bucer was there. Besides, there are indications that Calvin found only Capito in Strasbourg; for example, the latter's undated letter to Calvin,[65] and Beza's statement, "There he had especial friends, those best men, Simon Grynaeus and Wolgang Capito."[66] If Bucer regretted missing Calvin when he passed through Strasbourg in 1534, why did he not seek the young Frenchman during the Basel Conference in February, 1536?[67] The whole implication of Bucer's letter to Calvin on

[60] Schiess, *op. cit.*, I, 591, 593, 638, 699, II, 813, 814.

[61] Pestalozzi, *op. cit.*, p. 181; Baum, op. cit., p. 501.

[62] Bucer to Bullinger, Jan. 29, 1535, "Thesaurus Baumianus," VIII, 28-30.

[63] Beza and Colladon, "Vie de Calvin," *Calvini Opera*, XXI, 57, 124; Lefranc, *op, cit.*, p. 124; Kampschulte, *op. cit.*, I, 246-250.

[64] Doumergue, *op. cit.*, I, 500.

[65] *Calvini Opera*, Xb, 45-46.

[66] *Calvini Opera*, XXI, 124.

[67] Virck, Winckelmann and Bernays, *Politische Correspondenz*, etc., II, 677.

November 1, 1536, is that he had just requested Museau to arrange an interview with Calvin, who had lately visited Strasbourg.

Whether Bucer refers to Calvin's visit to Strasbourg in 1534-35 or not, two things are evident from this letter. No personal acquaintance existed previously between the two men, and it is very doubtful if Bucer had ever written to Calvin before this. Nothing could make this more certain than the highly formal and respectful language in which Bucer expresses himself. Invariably he adopted such a tone in his initial letters, but in subsequent epistles used an easy, familiar style. The dignity of his first letters to Luther,[68] and Zwingli[69] contrasts strikingly with the intimate familiarity of his later correspondence.[70] The formality and deference of Bucer's language is heightened by the fact that he is here addressing a young man of far less reputation and influence than himself. If Calvin had been acquainted with Bucer, he would have come to him at Strasbourg,[71] or at Basel in February, 1536.[72] Likewise, Bucer would not have waited for Capito to introduce him or thought it necessary to arrange an interview through Morelet du Museau.[73] Capito, who was acquainted with Calvin before December 1, 1536, wrote to him on that date in a familiar tone which brings out by contrast the formality of Bucer's letter.[74]

Secondly, this letter shows that Calvin and Bucer were not in agreement, especially upon the Supper and the proper

---

[68] Jan. 23, 1520 (E. L. Enders, *Dr. Martin Luthers Briefwechsel*, II, 298-304; Kolde, *op. cit.*, p. 11).

[69] *Corpus Reformatorum, Zwinglis Werke*, VII, 454-456; *cf.* also his first letter to Spalatin (Kolde, *op. cit.*, pp. 437-440), and Bucer to J. Jonas (*Corpus Reformatorum*, V, 122-124).

[70] *E.g.*, his next known letter to Calvin (*Calvini Opera*, Xb, 218-220; Herminjard, *op. cit.*, 62-66). Even Doumergue declares that in this letter Bucer is "presque respectueux" (Doumergue, *op. cit.*, I, 218).

[71] Herminjard, *op. cit.*, IV, 119.

[72] *Cf.* Virck, Winckelmann and Bernays, *op. cit.*, II, 677.

[73] Herminjard, *op. cit.*, IV, 118-119.

[74] *Calvini Opera*, Xb, 75.

method for overcoming the controversy about it. This seems the most plausible explanation of Calvin's failure to meet Bucer, for it indicates that he avoided a conference with him as did all the rest of the Zwinglian and Swiss theologians. It is perfectly clear that Bucer sought this interview to overcome Calvin's opposition. He used the same arguments in defending the validity of conferences on religion which are common in his letters to Blaurer, Bullinger and others,[75] thus indicating that Calvin sided with them in opposing such meetings. In addition to this letter there are numerous indications that Calvin did not approve of Bucer's beliefs and methods.[76]

It has been proved that Calvin could not have been the youth of Noyon who studied under Bucer in Strasbourg in 1528. It has also been shown that Calvin's letter to Bucer on September 4 from Noyon proves that they were not personally acquainted. Thus all basis for believing that a friendship or correspondence existed between them prior to the Synod of Bern, 1537, has been removed. In addition, it has been demonstrated that Bucer first wrote to Calvin on November 1, 1536; that he had not yet made Calvin's acquaintance; and that Calvin was unfavorable to his attitude on the Supper. The conclusion is unavoidable that Bucer made no direct, personal contribution to the conversion of Calvin and, although Calvin may have read his books, his disagreement with their teaching on the Supper and other subjects[77] indicates that they did not impress him altogether favorably. Those seeking the origins of Calvin's religious development must search elsewhere than in his personal relations with Martin Bucer.

Paoli, Pa. HASTINGS EELLS

[75] *Cf.*, Schiess, *op. cit.*, 641-648; *Corpus Reformatorum*, X, 138.

[76] Herminjard, *op. cit.*, IV, 356, n. 11; *Calvini Opera*, Xb, 124-125, 139-143.

[77] *Cf.* paragraph above and note 76.

CALVIN AND BUTZER

WILHELM PAUCK
Chicago Theological Seminary

CALVIN belonged to the second generation of Protestant reformers. It does not necessarily follow from this fact that he was an epigone; that he was not, is proved by the existence of the type of Protestantism which is generally called Calvinism. But it cannot be doubted that he owed decisive stimuli to anti-Catholic predecessors and that, in the development of his theological and ecclesiastical system, he was not entirely original. It is the general opinion of historians that Calvin depended—at least in the first years of his career as an evangelical theologian—largely upon Luther; particularly the latter's idea of justification is, it is claimed, better understood by no one than by Calvin. Neither will one go very far astray, if one assumes that Melanchthon and especially Zwingli exerted some influence upon the reformer of Geneva. During the last decades, one has begun to pay attention also to another man with whom Calvin is known to have entertained a cordial and close friendship: Martin Butzer of Strassburg. With this relationship we intend to deal in this article.

It is the merit of Seeberg and of Lang to have first related Butzer to Calvin. They were preceded by Usteri,[1] who dealt with the ideas and customs of baptism, common to Strassburg and Geneva; by Erichson,[2] who proved that the Genevan order of worship which, later on, became of world-wide importance by the expansion of the calvinistic sects, is of Strassburgian origin; and by Scheibe,[3] who called attention to the

[1] *Studien und Kritiken* (1884), p. 417.

[2] *Die calvinische und die altstrassburgische Gottesdienstordnung* (Strassburg, 1894).

[3] *Calvins Prädestinationslehre* (1897), pp. 17 ff.; 69 ff.

identity of Butzer's and Calvin's doctrine of predestination. Seeberg[4] claims that "Butzerianism was the preparatory stage for Calvinism," and Lang declares that without Butzer the roots of Calvin's religious system cannot be clearly understood.[5] He also stresses the fact that the most significant ideas in Calvin's theology, namely those on predestination and on church organization, show a direct influence of Butzer.[6] That the latter has nearly been entirely forgotten as an original thinker in comparison to Calvin is explained by the statement that Calvin deepened the thoughts of the Strassburg reformer not only by including them in a clear and consistent theological system, but also by making them effective in a successful practical application. The findings of Lang were emphasized by Anrich, who wrote the first, short biography of Butzer. He asserts boldly that "the triumphant course of Calvinism throughout the world signifies to a continuous influence of the ideas of Butzer," who must be called "the father of Calvinism before Calvin."[7] All these suggestions were finally found fruitful by O. Ritschl in his discussion of Butzer and Calvin in the *History of Protestant Dogma.* He not only gives a full representation of Butzer's theology, but in his chapters on Calvin he refers also very frequently to the influence from Strassburg to Geneva, and to the identity of Calvin's and Butzer's thoughts.[8] He even goes so far as to declare that the latter was superior to the former in "theological originality."[9]

[4] *Dogmengeschichte* (Leipzig, 1898), II, 254; now IV, 2, 556.

[5] *Der Evangelienkommentar Martin Butzers* (1901), p. 373.

[6] A. Lang, *Calvin* (Tübingen, 1909); *Reformation und Gegenwart* (Gütersloh, 1918), p. 176; cf. E. Doumergue, *Calvin,* IV, 401 f., V, 23 f.

[7] G. Anrich, *M. Bucer* (1914), p. 144.

[8] *Dogmengeschichte des Protestantismus* (Göttingen, 1926), III, 122 ff. In respect to the theological relationship between Butzer and Calvin cf. also Joh. Adam, *Evangelische Kirchengeschichte der Stadt Strassburg* (1922), pp. 217 ff., and the remarks of H. Strohl in his interesting study on "Martin Butzer, précurseur du Christianisme social en Alsace du XVIe siècle" in *Le Christianisme social* (1922), pp. 993–1011.

[9] *Ibid.*, p. 125.

The proof of such assumptions, however, is somewhat difficult. It must be achieved by a more or less indirect conclusion; to a large extent one must be satisfied with the demonstration of similarities. This becomes most evident in connection with the doctrine of predestination, which stands in the foreground of the interest. The community of thought seems to exist since Calvin's first Protestant publication, the *Institutes* of 1536. Mr. Van den Bosch,[10] who made a careful investigation of Butzer's concepts of predestination before the appearance of Calvin, before the Protestant public, reaches the conclusion that "in the first edition of the *Institutes* Calvin attributes to the doctrine of predestination the same religious significance as Butzer." It is interesting to note that he feels unable to claim a direct dependence of Calvin upon Butzer.[11]

In order to avoid the difficulties involved, it has been attempted to eliminate Butzer entirely. Scheibe,[12] and especially Holl,[13] have pointed out that in order to understand Calvin, it would suffice to refer to Augustine and Luther, from whom also Butzer received the first stimulus to pay attention to God's "Alleinwirksamkeit." But in contrast to such an opinion, which, at the first glance, seems to be quite conclusive, one must seriously consider the interpretation of Lang, who calls attention to an original trait in Butzer's and Calvin's idea of predestination. The idea of election is to them of the same value as the idea of conversion to the Pietists and the Methodists.[14] It explains to them why a great number of men accept the Gospel and why others do not.

The practical sociological observation of the religious status of a human group, of the fact that there seem to be non-religious individuals, led Butzer to develop his doctrine of predestination. Only later he was compelled to accept its full

[10] *De ontwikkeling van Bucers praedestinatie-gedachten* (Amsterdam, 1922).

[11] Scheibe takes a similarly careful attitude; p. 73.

[12] *Op. cit.*, p. 146.

[13] *Calvin* (Tübingen, 1909), p. 47, n. 15. Cf. E. Doumergue, *Calvin*, IV, 424.

[14] A. Lang, *Calvin*, pp. 78 ff.

theological consequences. It is noteworthy, however, that he never admitted that the predestination idea excluded the possibility of belief in free will.[15] Although a considerable change took place in his theological development, he never surrendered those features of his theory of predestination which he exhibited in his earliest writings. His predestination dogma was based on his idea of the spirit, an idea which gives to all his thoughts a characteristic, regulative note and which distinguished him particularly from Luther, while it related him closely to Zwingli. It is not at all impossible that Butzer is here indebted to the reformer of Zurich. The elect are those who have the spirit, and those who have the spirit are enabled to believe in the word and to express it by good works in a virtuous life according to the Scripture. The foundation of the church is not the word, but the spirit, which renders the word effective.[16] Both supplement each other since both emanate according to the order and the will of God from Christ, to whom he has given all power. The Kingdom of Christ is his rulership over those whom he has elected, i.e., those to whom he has given the spirit so that they can gather around the word, preach, and do it. In this respect the Kingdom of God is identical with the church. The same interest prevails in Calvin's thought; not only his doctrine of predestination, but also that of the word and the spirit are first to be found in Butzer.

But in spite of this community of thought in connection with these leading phases of their theology, a dependence of Calvin upon Butzer could hardly be maintained, if there were not indications of an actual relationship between them. A literary influence of Butzer on Calvin cannot be doubted. The latter expresses his gratitude to the Strassburger in most complimentary words in the Prefaces to his commentaries on the

[15] Cf. his discussion in *Metaphras. et Enarrat. in Epistolam ad Romanos* (Strassburg, 1536), pp. 358 ff.

[16] Cf. Richard H. Grützmacher, *Wort und Geist* (Leipzig, 1902), pp. 116–122; O. Ritschl, *op. cit.*, pp. 129 ff.; W. Pauck, *Das Reich Gottes auf Erden* (Berlin, 1928), pp. 5 ff.; 13 ff.

Epistle to the Romans,[17] on the Psalms,[18] and on the gospels.[19] Lang supposes also that Calvin used Butzer's works already in preparation for the first edition of the *Institutes*.

To what degree Calvin can have received a knowledge of the Strassburg reformer during his years of study in France, cannot be made out with certainty. The traditional opinion refers frequently to the famous discourse of Nicolaus Cop (All Saints Day 1533, Paris), which Calvin wrote for his friend, the rector-to-be. Lang[20] has shown that the author used a sermon from Luther's church postil in Butzer's latin translation. But, of course, that does not prove anything about the kind or even the possibility of Calvin's acquaintance with Butzer's books. Pannier[21] thinks that young Calvin heard his cousin Olivétan, who seems to have studied in Strassburg, speak of Butzer (in 1528)[22] and that, at Bourges, his professor Volmar fully introduced him to the work of the latter. The first certain indication of Calvin's knowledge of Butzer, which is in our reach, is given in a letter of Calvin to Butzer, which Herminjard[23] dates on September 4, 1534, and which is written from Noyon to the "Bishop of Strassburg," imploring him for help in favor of a poor minister. In conclusion, Calvin writes: "Hoc pro tempore. Vale erudissime vir"[24] as if he had

[17] *Calv. opp.*, 10, p. 404. Published in Strassburg, 1539. Cf. Scheibe, *op. cit.*, pp. 69 ff.

[18] *Calv. opp.*, 31 (1557), p. 13.

[19] *Ibid.*, 45 (1555), p. 4. *Bucerum praesertim sanctae memoriae virum et eximium ecclesiae doctorem sum imitatus.* Cf. Paul Wernle, *Calvin* (Tübingen, 1919), pp. 34, 81. Lang mentions an influence of Butzer's book: *De vera cura animarum.* Cf. *Ref. und Gegenwart*, p. 183. Opposing view: Doumergue, *Calvin*, IV, 39.

[20] *Calvin*, p. 21.

[21] Paul Pannier, *Calvin à Strassbourg* (Paris, 1925), pp. 11, 13.

[22] This assumption is based on a letter of Butzer to Farel, dated May (most probably 1528), which Kampschulte used for his theory that Calvin was a student of Butzer. Herminjard refuted this theory, suggesting that Butzer speaks of Olivétan. Cf. H. Eells, "Martin Butzer and the conversion of John Calvin," *Princeton Theol. Rev.* (1924), p. 402.

[23] Herminjard, III, 201 ff.

[24] *Ibid.*, p. 204. Cf. the discussion by Eells, *op. cit.*, pp. 407 ff.

had previous connections with Butzer. It is much more probable that he was on friendly terms with Butzer's fellow-pastor Capito, as the first letter from Butzer to Calvin (Strassburg, November 1, 1536)[25] seems to suggest it. It is written in a tone of respect which very significantly contrasts itself with the familiar language of Capito.[26] Its purpose is to arrange for a meeting with Calvin (now at Geneva) at a place of his convenience where all mutual and common problems shall be discussed until an agreement of opinion is established. The last sentences read as follows:

> Farewell, most learned and holy man, and do not despise my request, giving me thereby new cause of sorrow. For it cannot be said how much I regretted that I was not privileged to make your acquaintance and to speak to you when you were here. At other times, Capito shared everything with me. I do not know which dark spirit made him so forgetful that he did not think of introducing you to me. Now he himself is very sorry about it.

These words refer to Calvin's visit in Strassburg at the end of 1534,[27] or, what is more probable to that of October, 1536.[28]

It is most probable that the two reformers did not become personally acquainted with each other until the synod of Bern, which took place in 1537. Calvin refers to this meeting in his letter to Butzer of January 12, 1538,[29] written under the impression of the dismissal of Megander from the church of Bern, while the lutheranizing pastors Peter Kuntz and Sebastian Meyer, whom Calvin despised, were retained. He felt that Butzer's efforts toward a union between the Swiss and the Wittenbergers on the basis of the Wittenberg Concord of 1536 were responsible for this upheaval at Bern. He addresses Butzer in a way that continued to be characteristic of his attitude toward the busy and famous man from Strassburg even after their relationship had developed into a cordial friendship. He

[25] Herminjard, IV, pp. 117 ff.; cf. the correction of the date (not *Dec.* 1) by Eells, pp. 412 ff.

[26] *Ibid.*, p. 119.

[27] *Ibid.*, p. 119, n. 7, 9, 10.

[28] Cf. Eells, pp. 415 ff.

[29] *Calv. opp.*, 10, pp. 137 ff.

reviews the opinions of Luther and of the Swiss from an impartial point of view, asserting that he is vitally interested in a church union. However, he still favors the Swiss in contrast to the Lutherans. He appeals to Butzer that he attempt to bring the obstinate, narrowminded Wittenbergers to their senses. He himself takes—with some superiority—the position of an impartial although interested observer. As such, he, a man of twenty-nine years, has the courage to extend a severe admonition to the renowned theologian and church-man, seventeen years his senior. Butzer is criticized for his diplomatic carefulness in theological discussion, which originated out of a desire to provoke no one. Calvin writes to him:

> If you want a Christ, who is acceptable to all, you must not fabricate a new gospel for that purpose. . . . . After you have said that the veneration of Saints is produced in human superstition rather than founded in God's word, you add at once, that one must, nevertheless, consider the writings of the church-fathers, and that a veneration, recommended by them, ought not to be entirely condemned. Thus you re-introduce constantly that authority by which every error can be represented as truth. But does it mean to keep God truly holy, if one grants so much to man, that His truth does no longer rule over us?[30]

The letter shows the royal freedom and superiority of Calvin. He was willing to co-operate wherever, without danger of sacrificing fundamental views, he could see a promise of success. This emphasis upon clarity in theological purpose and this impartiality are characteristic of him in his relationship to Butzer to the end.

Butzer does not seem to have been offended by the severity of the criticism—he was accustomed to such a treatment! For when Calvin was forced to leave his position at Geneva during the year 1538, he and Capito stretched every nerve to persuade Calvin to come to Strassburg. Butzer's forceful appeal was finally successful.[31]

While in Strassburg, Calvin was exposed to the full influ-

[30] *Ibid.*, p. 142 f.

[31] See Calvin's own account in *Opp.*, 31, pp. 25 ff. Cf. Doumergue, II, 225 ff

ence of Butzer. In his letters to his friends,[32] one discovers an attitude much friendlier than before toward the man who bore not only the burden of the ecclesiastical reform of Strassburg and of Hesse, but also that of the upbuilding of a Protestant consciousness throughout the European world. Although he still emphasizes differences of opinion between them and his unwillingness to follow Butzer in every respect, he defends him with a cordiality and with the forcefulness that indicates clearly that their acquaintance has become close and intimate. This was the more important as Calvin spent a highly formative period of his life in this attachment to Butzer. It is, therefore, quite right that Pannier, in his admirable study on Calvin in Strassburg, stresses the possibility that Calvin became, during the years from 1538 to 1541, in many regards butzerian.[33] He had many precious experiences; he deepened his theological views; and he made valuable observations of practical church-organization. His views on predestination and on the Lord's Supper became more precise. In regard to these doctrines, he was, when he left Strassburg, a pupil or follower of Butzer. Furthermore, there can hardly be a doubt that, in Strassburg, Calvin was introduced to the idea of a universal Protestantism, for the cause of which he worked so enthusiastically and ceaselessly during the last years of his life. It was Butzer who called him to Frankfurt and asked to be accompanied by him to the memorable religious peace-conferences, synods, and disputations of Hagenau and Regensburg in 1541. Through the mediatorship of Butzer, Calvin came into contact with German Protestantism and especially with Melanchthon. From that time on, he was almost another Butzer in his interests for a union of the Protestant churches.[34] In

[32] *Calv. opp.*, 10, pp. 341; 344 ff.; 348.

[33] Pannier, *op. cit.*, pp. 9, 54 f. Cf. also the fascinating accounts of Doumergue in *Calvin* (1902), II, 293 ff.

[34] Cf. Bohatec in *Calvin-Studien* (Tübingen, 1909), p. 440; Lang, *Calvin*, pp. 78, 192. Compare also the articles of Prof. McNeill on "Calvin's Efforts toward the Consolidation of Protestantism," *Journal of Religion* (1928), pp. 411, and on "Catholic Protestantism," *Canadian Journal of Religious Thought* (1928), pp. 449 ff.

many respects, he brought to Butzer's plans at least a partial realization. However, he never became butzerian in the sense of losing himself entirely to his cause. He always refused to attempt a church union at any price. He became rather more himself. Pannier has well said:[35] "Calvin was, when he left Strassburg, more himself; he was more calvinistic—and that due to the nearness of Butzer." Whatever he took away with him, he had made fully his own. Indeed, one cannot say that he transplanted thoughts or institutions into his world without correcting or improving them. Whether it is baptism, the Lord's supper, predestination and the whole type of theology for which it stands; whether it is the idea that the school is most significant for an effective church-discipline, and the picture of the Strassburg Academy; whether it is the order of worship or church-organization itself, and the idea of a united, world-wide Protestant church—he made them all calvinistic when he accepted them for himself and took them to Geneva. But nevertheless in all this lives Butzer. What he thought out and planned and recommended and inspired in all these respects becomes real through the understanding mind and the efficient hands of Calvin.

The type of church which we call, in our day, calvinistic or reformed, is really a gift of Martin Butzer to the world, through the work of his strong and brilliant executive Calvin. The very peculiar relationship between the two men becomes quite clear in connection with this institution of ecclesiastical organization. Gustav Anrich has just published a study[36] on this very subject and shown very convincingly indeed how strangely the two worked hand in hand. Being of a fundamentally equal religious disposition—both of them were under the influence of Humanism—thinking and acting, therefore, more or less in the same direction, tied to such cities as Strassburg and Geneva, so similar in character and need, they finally

[35] *Op. cit.*, p. 55.

[36] *Strassburg und die calvinische Kirchenverfassung* (Tübingen, 1928).

found themselves. What the elder wanted to see fulfilled in plans that had busied his life, the younger eagerly made his own, erecting a building which he could rightly call his own property, but which never could have been thus built without the enhancing, stimulative, productive thought of the other.

As we describe the building and its growth we represent the arguments of Professor Anrich: When Calvin returned to Geneva in 1541, he proposed at once to the city-magistrate a new church organization, and within a few weeks, he had won his case in the "Ordonnances ecclésiastiques." Their most characteristic feature is the instalment of the four offices of pastors, teachers, elders, and deacons. The pastors are combined in the Congrégation, later on called the Vénérable Compagnie. The soul of the whole organization is not this pastoral group, but the Consistoire, consisting of the ministers and the elders. Its task is the execution of church discipline, which it may independently put into practice even unto excommunication. Only for these two outstanding offices the method of appointment and election is clearly stated: A pastor is selected by the Vénérable Compagnie, presented to the magistrate, and, if accepted, elected by the congregation, this election being ratified by the magistrate. The twelve presbyters are appointed upon the proposition of the pastors; all are members of the city-council. If one asks for the origin of this order, one is inclined to follow Calvin, who points to the New Testament. In the 1543 edition of the *Institutes* he has given the scriptural proof by using the enumerations of the offices and gifts of the spirit in I Cor. 12 and Eph. 4. But after a careful study and examination of these references, it becomes evident that not the early Christian situation has been applied to the conditions of Geneva, but rather that the needs of the Genevan situation have been projected into the New Testament. Since a scriptural origin of the church order seems not possible, it might be found, one thinks, in Calvin's own proposal for church discipline of 1537. But therein one does not encounter the term "elder," nor the doctrine of the four offices as jus divinum, nor collegial ecclesiastical magistrates. Neither do the *Institutes* of 1536 or 1539 present the case differently, nor is the hint at other cities where church discipline had been introduced before, e.g. Basel, of value, since the characteristics of the Genevan order are lacking. One has to turn to Strassburg.

Begun in 1531 under the leadership of Jacob Sturm as the representative of the magistrate, church discipline had been fully constituted in the church order of 1534, with the collaboration especially of Butzer. Three Kirchenpfleger or elders assist the pastor of each parish in his work of discipline. All pastors and three of the helpers, who take turns in attending the meetings, form the church assembly, convening twice a month. Pastors are called in the following way: After having passed an examination, the candidate preaches before the congregation, and the elders of the parish with twelve members of the congregation undertake the election, which has to be ratified by the magistrate.[37]

This order was developed in protection of the church against the anabaptist sects. It resulted from a practical necessity. It is most interesting to note that Butzer devised the theological theory for these institutions. In the Strassburg Catechisms of 1534, 1537, and 1543, in his book "De vera cura animarum" of 1538 and especially in his church-order for Hesse (accepted at Ziegenhain in 1538, published in 1539), he deduces from I Cor. 12 and Eph. 4 the theory of the divinely ordered offices of pastors, presbyters, deacons and also that of the teachers, although they became never so prominent as in Geneva. That these Strassburg offices were not installed upon the authority of the Bible, but that this biblical author-

[37] The old Butzer seemingly wanted to exclude the congregation in this respect. According to *De regno Christi*, the ministers elect the elders, in contrast to the order of Strassburg, where he had the presbyters elected by the congregation, which led to the formation of conventicles. (Cf. W. Sohm, *Die Schule Joh. Sturms und die Kirche Strassburgs* [München, 1912], p. 163.)

ity was applied to a more or less accomplished organization is seen in the fact that deacons as city-officials had been at work since the twenties, when the city had undertaken the restoration of reorganized poor relief. Ecclesiastical poor relief was really never established in Strassburg, in spite of Butzer's theory.

These orders, it is true, were not fully realized. Butzer could never attain to the full co-operation of the magistrate—only in Hesse, he was quite successful. But there can be no doubt that Calvin was introduced by him to the Strassburg system of discipline. From Butzer he learned the theory of the jus divinum of ecclesiastical offices, especially that of the presbyters. So far Anrich.

It is, then, quite evident that the so-called calvinistic type of church organization originated very largely in Strassburg and in Butzer, whose ideas Calvin could put into practice. The growth of this organization illustrates better than anything else the fact that Calvin was butzerian in order to be himself. Professor Von Schubert has rightly said:[38] "What the contact with the spirit of Rome was to the founder of the order of the Jesuits, the contact with the spirit of Strassburg and of Butzer was to Calvin." If one adds to the community of all those theological and ecclesiastical attitudes which we have mentioned also their identical estimation of social ethics, which Klingenburg has fully investigated,[39] the affinity of the two reformers appears as truly astonishing. But whether that minimizes the originality of Calvin or of Butzer, is a question that cannot be answered. One will have to be satisfied with the fact that there existed in them a very close relationship of viewpoint. "Bucer et Calvin," says Pannier,[40] "étaient bien faits pour se comprendre."

[38] *Calvin* (Tübingen, 1909), pp. 13 f.

[39] Georg Klingenburg, *Das Verhältnis Calvins zu Butzer auf Grund der wirtschaftsethischen Bedeutung beider Reformatoren* (Bonn, 1906). Cf. Doumergue, *Calvin*, V, 688 f.; compare also R. H. Tawney, *Religion and the Rise of Capitalism* (New York, 1926), pp. 105 ff.

[40] *Op. cit.*, p. 12.

We know that since their Strassburg days, this friendship was cordial. But its expression in correspondence is largely unknown to us, because only a few of their letters are preserved. It is characteristic of both of them that, when Calvin was about to return to Geneva, Butzer wrote to Bern that Calvin was needed in Strassburg for the French congregation and the Academy as well as for the great tasks of Protestantism,[41] and that Calvin wanted Butzer to accompany him to his city.[42] A few examples of the intimacy that marked their relationship are still existing. On October 15, 1541, Calvin wrote to Butzer in a letter of thanks for his reception in Strassburg:[43] "If I should not live up to your expectations, you know well that I am in your power. Admonish, chastize, do all that a father is permitted to do to his son." And Butzer, who held Calvin's brilliance equalled only by that of Melanchthon,[44] and who longed for Calvin just as much as for Capito, who had been taken by the plague of 1541,[45] was no less intimate in his letters to Calvin. Thus he ends a hearty letter of consolation and encouragement:[46] *"Sed tu meum cor, meus animus* (thou, my heart, my soul), *semper tuo, imo Christi bono, omnium omnia mala vinces, quo ad licuerit . . . Tuus totus* (thine wholly) *Bucerus."*

The few letters of Butzer, written during the following years, which are still in existence give chiefly information about political and ecclesiastical affairs.[47] Only with the year 1547, the letters become more frequent and also more imme-

[41] Herminjard, VI, 242 f. [42] Doumergue, II, 701.

[43] *Calv. opp.*, 11, p. 299: *Et si qua in re spei vestrae non respondeam, scis me sub tua protestate esse. Admoneas, castiges, omnia facias quae patri licent in filium.*

[44] Herminjard, VI, 235 (letter to O. Myconius of Basel [Sept., 1541]: *Datis ergo operam ut juvete virum certe eximium, et cujus perfecto parem, excepto Philippo, nullum habemus, ardore, eloquentia et judicio).*

[45] To A. Blaurer; T. Schiess, *Briefwechsel der Gebrüder Blaurer* (Freiburg, 1910), II, 133.

[46] Herminjard, VIII, 150 f.

[47] E.g., *Calv. opp.*, 10, pp. 414 ff. (July 7, 1542); pp. 456. (Oct. 28, 1542); pp. 634 f. (Oct. 28, 1543); *ibid.*, 12, pp. 152 ff. (Aug. 29, 1545); pp. 162 f. (Sept. 8, 1545).

diate and open in tone and emotion. The dark days of the Emperor's warfare against the Protestants and of the Interim were approaching. Butzer saw his life-work endangered: God's avenging hand was stretched out over his unfaithful people.[48] God himself was demanding the supreme sacrifice for the sake of faith. Butzer was willing to give it.[49] In these years, he proved that he was a man of firm, courageous decision. But his heart was trembling, and in his sad letters he deplores the situation of the German church, beseeching his friends for their prayers, so that the vain, faint hope for a victory of the Gospel might perhaps be fulfilled.[50] He prepared himself for the exile. He feared that he would have to leave the city which he loved with all his heart, in order to dwell in a foreign land. But in the fall of 1548, he expressed the hope that in such a case the Lord might give him an opportunity to see the churches of Geneva.[51] When his fate became more certain and when he had probably already decided to go to England, he had still the wish to bid farewell to the friend personally.[52] Evidently Calvin was again close to his heart, for he signs his letters again: Tuus totus Bucerus.[53] His hope was not to be fulfilled; he fled to England, never to return, on April 6, 1549.

None of Calvin's letters of this period are preserved. But we can still read a few which he wrote to England. They are examples of his fine, noble sensitiveness and tact, for it cannot have been easy to deal with Butzer, who was broken in health and in spirit and who saw his course ended. But Calvin's affection was still strong and fresh.

Butzer was homesick in London and in Cambridge. He

[48] Cf. *Calv. opp.*, 12, pp. 507; 520 f., 555 f.

[49] *Ibid.*, 13, p. 5.

[50] *Ibid.*, pp. 147 ff.; 181 f.; 197 ff.

[51] *Ibid.*, p. 56: *Tum forsan dabit, ut quod expetii toties, videam vestras ecclesias.*

[52] *Ibid.*, p. 199.

[53] *Ibid.*, pp. 350, 358, 574.

longed for his family and for his friends, and he suffered because they did not write to him. He suspected that they had left him, turning to the Zurichers under the leadership of Bullinger, who saw in him a menace to the cause of the Gospel, blaming him for having obscured the doctrine of the Lord's Supper. The Swiss animosity against Butzer had turned into hatred. Already in 1546, referring to the death of Luther (February 19, 1546), Bullinger had written to A. Blarer,[54] who was not only his but also Butzer's friend:

> But I would begin to hope for the better, if Butzer also would be called by the Lord; for there lives no other man in our days, who gives more hopes to the Papists and who disputes about the Lord's supper in an obscurer way than this Butzer. . . . . So much is certain: Now that Luther is dead, Butzer will dive deeper into his union efforts, because until now he was miserably afraid of Luther, in his cause.

About Butzer in England he wrote:

> Butzer is in England and remains fully himself. What Germany had accepted from him, England will also accept. May the Lord protect her from evil and may He give him a better mind or a better end *(meliorem mentem vel meliorem metam)*. In such an ungrateful and bad time, however, there must be instruments of anger and corruption. The Lord Jesus may have mercy with his people![55]

Calvin knew all about this. He not only consoled Butzer, but he defended him also. He requested Bullinger,[56] informing him of Butzer's complaints, that he should tell Hooper, who was taking Bullinger's side, to treat Butzer as he, one of the foremost servants of Christ, deserved. He assured Bullinger constantly of his friendship with Butzer: "I should do wrong to the church of God, if I should hate or despise him, not to say

[54] Schiess, II, 442 f.

[55] August 11, 1549 to A. Blarer; Schiess, III, 56. Note the following verses of a satirical poem on Butzer (communicated by A. Erichson in his little book *Martin Butzer, der elsässische Reformator* [Strassburg, 1891], p. 33): *Butzer der butzt auch am Rhein, Nimmt zuletzt ganz England ein.*

[56] *Calv. opp.* 13, p. 489. To Farel he wrote (August 18, 1550, *ibid.*, pp. 624 f.) that he would not mention the Zurichers again in his letters to Butzer, in order not to hurt his feelings.

anything about his merit for me personally."[57] Or: "Of course, I am sometimes of another opinion than you, but my heart is not at all estranged from you; just as I keep friendship with Butzer, although, in all freedom, I think sometimes otherwise than he."[58] To Butzer himself he wrote cordial letters, not quite as intimate as one might expect. He wrote to Edward VI and to the Lord of Somerset,[59] assisting Butzer in his efforts for a reformation in England. He expressed his regret that he could not have asked Butzer's advice in connection with a letter to Melanchthon.[60] He advised him—the best council to a homesick man—to write books in order to make his wonderful gifts useful to the church.[61] And what was probably of more value to Butzer than anything else: He succeeded in having the Consensus Tigurinus accepted. Not without having asked for Butzer's opinion and not without praising his assent,[62] he pursued a work that was dearest to Butzer's heart. When he announced the friend's death (February 28, 1551) to Bullinger he said that he felt lonesome like an orphan.[63] No doubt he loved him much. If we remember that Butzer had been one of his chief teachers, we know why.

[57] *Ibid.*, 12, p. 729: *Sed obsecro te, mi Bullingere, quo iure nos a Bucero alienaremus quum huic nostrae confessioni quam posui subscribat? Ego virtutes et raras et permultas, quibus vir ille excellit, in praesentia non praedicabo. Tantum dicam me ecclesiae Dei gravem iniuriam facturum, si hunc vel oderim vel contemnam. Taceo ut de me privatim sit meritus.*

[58] *Ibid.*, 13, p. 165.

[59] To Seymour: *ibid.*, 13, pp. 16 f., 18 f., 64 ff., 528 ff. To Edward VI: *ibid.*, 13, pp. 669 ff.; 14, pp. 30 ff., 38 ff., 341 ff.

[60] *Calv. opp.*, 20, pp. 401 f. This letter was written a few days before Butzer's death. Butzer never read it.

[61] *Ibid.*, pp. 393 f.

[62] *Ibid.*, 13, pp. 424, 457, 534 f.

[63] *Ibid.*, 14, p. 106: *Nuncius de Anglia nondum rediit. Sed interea de Buceri morte certior factus magnum accepi dolorem. Quod nollem, brevi sentiemus quantam ecclesia Dei iacturam fecerit. Satis dum vivebat reputabam quam praeclaris dotibus excellerit: quam utilis adhuc nobis foret, melius nunc demum ex orbitate ipsa agnosco.* To Viret he writes a few weeks later (*ibid.*, pp. 121 f.): *Moeror quem ex Buceri morte concepi sollicitudinem ac metum auget. . . . . Quam multiplicem in Bucero iacturam fecerit, quoties in mentem venit, cor meum prope larcerari sentio.* And still a few weeks later to Farel (*ibid.*, p. 133): *De Buceri obitu nihil attigeram, ne vulnus meum scinderem.*

After having observed this friendship and the indebtedness of Calvin to Butzer, one wonders why the latter never received the proper credit for his contributions and how it could happen that Calvin so entirely overshadowed him. An answer to this question can be found by a comparison of the goal that the two men had set to themselves and to their work.

During the controversy of 1544 between the Lutherans and the Swiss, Bullinger once used the expression *bucerisare*[64] (*verbutzern* or *butzern*), having in mind Butzer's method of reconciling the divergent views on the Lord's Supper. By coining that word, he testified to the fact that Butzer represented an original type of Protestant theologian. It was because of this very fact that the Strassburger had so many enemies and that even his friends disagreed with him. He himself was well aware of the animosity his activity and viewpoint caused, but although he grew sometimes weary, he never ceased to pursue his ends. He was driven on by a decision which he had clearly defined to himself and which was the heart of all his work. Its note is prominent in all his writings, in commentaries, pamphlets, and letters. For our purpose it may suffice to concentrate our attention on the correspondence with the Blarers, of whom at least Ambrosius (of Konstanz) always understandingly tried to take his side.

Butzer was blamed for conceding too much to the Lutherans or to the Catholics. But he declared:[65] "I condemn the Erasmian caution and the Saxon ambition; I seek the simplicity of Christ." What he meant by this he explained at another occasion:

> My aim is, although I pursue it not always with the necessary warmth and broadmindedness, that the Christians recognize and embrace each other in love; for all defects in customs and judgment result from the fact that because of weak concord the spirit of Christ misses its effect. . . . . How well do I understand now, since my attitude toward Luther, Philipp (Melanchthon) and others is purer, their pious writings at which I had before so much to criticize.[66]

[64] Schiess, II, 308. [65] *Ibid.*, I, 721. [66] *Ibid.*, I, 742.

He intentionally wanted to overcome the differences in theology, because a theological faith as such did not seem to comprehend all the essence of Christianity. "In true theology," he wrote,[67] "everyone knows so much rightly as he expresses in life." The same principle is described in the gospel Commentary in these beautiful words:[68] "True theology is not theoretical or speculative. Its aim is rather action, i.e. a godlike life." Through a faith that was effectively expressing itself in love, he wished to see the realization of the *communio sanctorum*.[69] "Communion"—that was his great ideal. Everything had to serve to this end.

> For nobody truly knows Christ who does not feel the necessity of a communion, of mutual care and discipline among his members. . . . . Christ suffered and taught for no other purpose but that we should be one and embrace each other with the same love with which he embraced us, and that we should seek our mutual salvation with the same eagerness with which he sought ours.[70]

Hence his emphasis upon church discipline. No communion of love could exist, he thought, without discipline.

Such an ideal was new and original in the compass of Protestant theology. It is interesting to note that Butzer attributed the ideal of communion now to the local congregation and then to the church at large. In this latter respect, he was still under the powerful impression of medieval ecclesiasticism and universalism. Christ, the head of the one church, the corpus Christi—to this medieval church concept he gave a Protestant flavor. He pointed out:

> Christ, the head, is working in one body which is connected with him and consists of well connected and cooperating members. O pernicious blindness, that even the best Evangelicals do not recognize what it means

[67] *Ibid.*, I, 648: *In vera theologia tantum quisque rite novit quantum vita exprimit.*

[68] *Enarr. in quat. Ev.* (Basel, 1536): *Vera theologia non theoretica et speculativa, sed activa et practica est. Finis siquidem ejus agere est, hoc est vitam vivere deiformem,*

[69] Schiess, I, 774: *Religio nititur fide efficiente communionem sanctorum.*

[70] *Ibid.*, II, 131 f.

to believe in a catholic church and in a communion of saints, and to be members of Christ.[71]

These are terms and words in which the medieval Catholics used to define their universalism.[72] When Butzer spoke or wrote them, he filled them with a new passion, described by "faith and love,"[73] which he had learned from Luther and Zwingli. For him, this passion culminated in the doctrine of predestination and thereby he broke medievalism. But one senses still the atmosphere of the Dominican order, in which Butzer received his education, and one hears, if ever so softly, the great Thomas, when one reads:[74] "The Kingdom of God is the church of Christ"; but the Protestant explains: "It lies in nothing that is external *per se*, but in faith and justice, and in such a use of external things as faith dictates." Butzer was a Catholic with a Protestant heart.

As such he desired to be a Paul to his contemporaries; and he also had the wide-open heart of the great apostle.

If we cannot agree *(congredi)*, we are neither against nor of Christ. He promised that he would be in the midst of those who gather together in his name; if we cannot come together in his name, we cannot pray to him either.[75] All who read Paul, must know how Paul and all true Christians promoted the protection and the development of the communion of saints and their agreement *(consensus)* in all things. By the ministry of the word faith is born and nourished; that is why the apostle traversed land and sea and sent out his (pupils) with such eagerness; now another spirit is at the helm, which flees all union *(congressum)*.[76]

The same passion that sent Paul restlessly around the world was driving him on to make Christ the ruler "to whom the

[71] Schiess, II, 119.

[72] It is most interesting to observe how often the judgments of Gierke, Maitland, Figgis apply also to Butzer. Cf. O. Gierke, *Genossenschaftsrecht*, III (Berlin, 1887). English translation by F. W. Maitland, *Political theories of the M.A.* (Cambridge, 1900); F. N. Figgis, "Respublica Christiana," in *Transactions of the Royal Hist. Soc.*, 3d series (London, 1911), V, 63 ff.

[73] "Fides et caritas" is another slogan in Butzer's theology. Note how F. W. L. Baum (*Capito and Butzer* [Elberfeld, 1860]) emphasizes it in his representation of B.

[74] Herminjard, VI, 20. This is the theme of his last work, *De regno Christi.*

[75] Schiess, I, 773.

[76] *Ibid.*, I, 772 f.

Father has given not only some regions of Germany but the whole globe."[77] One is almost tempted to say, that like the apostle, he desired to be a Jew to the Jews and a Greek to the Greeks, in order that Christ might become true king of all his believers.

But another Paul was claimed by Luther and by Calvin, a Paul that knew no compromise. If Butzer stressed the words "love" and "communion" most of all, Calvin emphasized, one may say, "faith" and "faithful." The famous saying of Hundeshagen: *"Die Dogmatik ist bei den Reformierten nur ein locus in der Kirche, bei den Lutheranern umgekehrt die Kirche nur ein locus in der Dogmatik,"*[78] is more appropriate in regard to Butzer than to Calvin.

Butzer—if it is permitted to speak in very general terms—thought of religion first of all as ministering to man's salvation, while Calvin related it primarily to the eternal God. Butzer was a humanistic, social biblicist, Calvin a theocentric biblicist. Calvin could always hold fast to one steady firm pole, which he called *majestas Dei,* but Butzer was shifting and changing for the sake of the *communio sanctorum.* That is why the doctrine of predestination finds a clear logical place in Calvin's theological system, while Butzer started out to use it as a means to analyze and to command a practical, sociological situation, later on compelling himself to think it out to its full theological consequences. That is why Calvin could afford either to differ from others in his opinions and yet keep friendship or to differ and break radically, while Butzer could neither stop to seek in friendship also some agreement of opinion nor radically break with anyone. Calvin could be cruel; Butzer could not and he was no less energetic than Calvin!—for the *cura animarum* came first.

All this leads us to understand why Butzer was barely remembered by the side of Calvin. And yet—he was the father of Calvinism.

[77] *Ibid.,* I, 641.

[78] G. O. Ritschl, *op. cit.,* p. 129, n. 26.

THE EDUCATION OF CALVIN

I

CALVIN's collegiate[1] preparation was both prolonged and varied. He had no proper Alma Mater, inasmuch as he studied at several universities. It was on the benches of Paris that he first took his seat, enrolling in the Collège de la Marche at the age of fourteen. Calvin was chiefly indebted to Mathurin Cordier, professor of rhetoric, for the education he received there. Cordier was one of the pioneer leaders in the movement towards educational reform; indeed he has been called the true founder of secondary education. For the dryness and dreichness of the old teachers, with their monotonous and mechanical instruction, he substituted intelligent methods of tuition by means of lessons full of life and interest, special attention being given to the furtherance of classical studies on this plan.[2] Cordier was the implacable enemy of routine and cut-and-dry rules, recognizing that education meant more than the filling of the memory with facts and words and phrases, being indeed of little value unless it opened up the mind to the spirit distilled into a language and also developed the faculty of perception and the power of independent judgment. That view, a commonplace now, was a novelty then, and the merit of bringing it into the sphere of educational practice largely belongs to Cordier. But for the preparation Calvin received from him, it is doubtful if he would have profited as he did from the famous masters in the higher branches of learning under whom he afterwards studied. Cordier laid a sound foundation for his whole subsequent education. He found serious gaps in the school training Calvin had received and had practically to give him a fresh start. He taught him to think in Latin, while with equal care training him in the correct use of the French language. Calvin felt the liveliest gratitude all his life for what he owed to this remarkable man. Cordier sided with the Reformers, and found refuge ultimately in Geneva beside his old pupil, where he died at the age of 85, having been a professor for sixty years.

[1] Calvin received his schooling proper along with the son of a noble family, in whose house he resided during that time. Through this experience he early acquired a certain fineness and distinction of manners, in striking contrast to those of Luther, and was prepared to play his part worthily with princes and nobles. (*Doumergue*, I, 35.)

[2] A book of Latin exercises compiled by Cordier was in almost universal use in the parish schools of Scotland up till a century ago. (Lindsay, *Hist. Reform.* II, 93, note.)

From the Collège de la Marche Calvin passed to that of Montaigu, whose atmosphere, unlike that of the former, was strongly ecclesiastical. The celebrated Scotchman, John Major, was one of its professors. Rabelais, who had been a student there, gives it a sinister reputation for the manner of its life, " unsavoury, unhealthy, and inhumane ". " If I were king at Paris ", he declares, " the devil take me if I would not set fire to it and burn up principal and regents who tolerate such inhumanity before their eyes." The use of French was here strictly prohibited. The régime was hard and exacting, no provision being made for recreation. From four in the morning till eight at night in winter and nine in summer, the mind was kept on the strain without intermission, except for unappetizing and debilitating meals.[1] As a result, Calvin's health was undermined and the train laid of that complication of ailments which so seriously handicapped him in later life and brought him to a premature grave at the age of 55. His stay here provides one of these dramatic historical coincidences in which the mind takes a curious pleasure. Ignatius Loyola, the founder of that Jesuit Order which did so much to stem and reverse the work of the Reformation, entered the College about the time when Calvin left it, and these two arch-antagonists may have sat side by side on its benches.

Whatever other benefit Calvin received at this college, at least his mind was given that sharpness of edge and practised agility which made him the matchless controversialist of after days. Disputation was carried on there incessantly; in the programme of the day, a large part was given to argument and discussion: to these exercises an hour in the morning and another at night were consecrated, but the students far exceeded the provision made by the authorities. They disputed before dinner, during dinner, and after dinner, writes one of them in 1531; they disputed in public, in private, in every place and at all times. If argument did occasionally wax fast and furious over such problems as whether a led pig was held by the string or by the man, other more weighty themes were discussed as eagerly. As Barnard says, the habit of discussion, thus developed, was not a mere weapon for parade, but became one under

[1] Erasmus describes the horrid conditions of life at some of these colleges, the sleeping rooms filthy and swarming with fleas, the food unwholesome, rotten eggs and mouldy wine being often provided. It is not to be wondered at that scarcely any left without carrying the germ of some disease. Brutal whippings, too, were administered frequently.

whose blows the scholasticism, which forged it, at last itself succumbed. Calvin's success in his studies drew attention to him, his prodigious memory and the amazing ease with which he mastered his subjects putting him head and shoulders above all his fellows.

Having completed his course of grammar and philosophy (which included the science of the day), Calvin left Paris in 1527 and matriculated at Orleans. As the result of differences with the clergy of his town, his father had relinquished his original ecclesiastical ambitions for his son, and projected for him instead a legal career, " seeing that it is a better means of arriving at wealth and honours ". For Calvin himself, the law had little attraction, but with filial obedience he submitted to his father's will and settled down with his habitual application to legal studies. Orleans boasted of one of the most distinguished lawyers of the day, one who enjoyed a European fame, Pierre de L'Estoile. Students came from all parts to hear him. Unlike Cordier, he was still in bondage to old ways and ideas, and, in spite of the stimulus of the judicial revolution set afoot by his rival Alciati, he lacked courage to break with the past. Towards Reform he was consistently hostile, and helped to draw up the decrees pronounced against heretics by the provincial council of Sens (1528). That however did not hinder Calvin from taking advantage of his rare talent and gratefully acknowledging his debt to him. The university itself as a whole was strongly tinctured with sympathy for the new religious tendencies. According to a tradition, it was at Orleans that the assembly gathered in which the Protestants first resolved to celebrate their worship in public, and so it gained the name of " le boulevarde de calvinisme ". Unlike the College of Montaigu, the University of Orleans was characterized by a gaiety which constituted one of its chief attractions. The manners of its students manifested the emancipation from scholastic ideals and ways which it was amongst the first to assert. Calvin was not impervious to the influence of the place and proved himself capable of indulging in innocent frivolities.

At Orleans Calvin devoted himself specially to the prosecution of legal studies. It is evidence of the respect in which his abilities were held that he was elected " procureur de la nation de Picardie ", the attorney who represented in case of need those who hailed from his native province of Picardy. In that rôle he took a leading part in an action for the assertion of certain rights they claimed. Such an impression did he leave behind that Beza, who studied there some years after, found his memory still green, the recollection of his devotion to work and what was there regarded as his excessive sobriety of life being specially fresh. One of those who can do with scanty sleep, he was always awake at dawn, but remained in bed for some time, conning over what he had studied the night before. Such rapid progress did he make that he soon came to be regarded not as an ordinary scholar but as one of the ordinary Doctors conducting classes in the absence or illness of any of the Professors. His agility and resourcefulness in debate excited the admiration of all his masters. Specially were they surprised that such a sobersides, one ordinarily so grave and composed, should exhibit such powers of sarcasm, badinage, and fancy as well as such a lofty eloquence. Indeed the Professors unanimously proposed to bestow upon him the degree of Doctor of Laws without examination, but Calvin declined to accept such a flattering distinction. Already he had gained the degree of Licentiate of Laws, and it may be that his native scrupulousness of conscience would not allow him to regard himself as yet worthy of the higher diploma. By his inordinate industry here he aggravated some of the bodily maladies which Montaigu had started.

II

From Orleans Calvin was drawn to Bourges by the fame of Alciati, an Italian jurisconsult, the great rival of L'Estoile. The course of instruction given by him was something very different from that which Calvin had received at Orleans. Alciati was the Cordier of law, repudiating dry-as-dust study, seeking to breathe the spirit of life into its abstractions, treating it as an organism whose origins and relationship of parts he discussed with the aid of philology and archæology. The interest thus infused into the subject was heightened by the elegant and chaste language of which he was master. But the principal influence exerted on Calvin at Bourges proceeded from an entirely different quarter. His heart had all along been in his humanist studies, and he found a teacher exactly to his mind in Melchior Wolmar, a scholar of German birth, a man "adorned with the rarest virtue, whose firmness was inflexible, . . . and of a calm and equable temper", as Calvin described him when proposing him for a model to a newly appointed professor of law. Aware of his deficiencies in classical culture, he gave himself under Wolmar's direction to their correction with an enthusiasm which had never been inspired by law. A warm friendship sprang up between teacher and pupil, based not only on respect for each other's abilities but also on spiritual affinities and religious sympathies. What Cordier did for his Latin, Wolmar did for his Greek and in part for his Hebrew. It happened that during his stay here, his father died and that event determined him to abandon the study of jurisprudence prosecuted up till then only out of respect to his father's wishes. Henceforth he devoted himself exclusively to the humanist and theological studies that were most congenial to him.

Thanks to his paternal legacy, he now possessed independent means and with their aid he decided to return to Paris, the centre of the humanism of which he was a whole-hearted disciple. But the study of law, irksome and uncongenial though it had been and joyfully forsaken, had been of a value to him which only the future disclosed. Apart from the knowledge which it furnished, it had contributed to give him that force of dialectic and that keenness and quickness of judgment which stood him in such good stead in the incessant controversies of later days.

Francis I had established lectureships in languages in the capital, ambitious to make it the "hearthstone of humanism". Needless to say, those who held them were amongst the most eminent scholars of the day. They also proved to be amongst the most broad-minded, not seeking to dissimulate the sympathy they had with the revolutionary views abroad. Calvin took full advantage of their tuition, and had his mind not only furnished but profoundly influenced. The College of Fortet at Paris then contained a professor worthy of such a pupil in Pierre Danès, a man of encyclopædic learning, of whom it is said that "he embraced at the same time Greek and Latin philology, rhetoric, mathematics, philosophy, medicine and theology, having one of the most profound and powerful minds of that Renaissance which created so many universal geniuses." Under his guidance and inspiration, Calvin pursued his favourite classical studies, receiving at the same time tuition in Hebrew from Vatable. That there is truth in the assertion that Reuchlin,

Erasmus and Lefèvre, princes of humanism, were his models and inspirers rather than Luther and Zwingli, finds support from the nature of his first published volume issued at this period, the Commentary on the two books of Seneca's De Clementia. In this work the interest of the philologist is predominant, combined however with that of the political moralist. It embodies a vigorous plea for legislative reform and the correction of administrative disorders. There is nothing to regret in this continual absorption in classical studies. He was perfecting himself in that equipment which made him the authoritative Biblical Commentator of later days and also conduced to the amazing rapidity and volume of his work.

Calvin left Paris for a time, taking perhaps a second course at Orleans and paying a brief visit to his native town. He is back again in the capital within a year, and speedily finds himself embroiled in the affair of Nicolas Cop, the Rector of the University, with whom he had struck up a close friendship. At the Feast of all Saints, it fell to the Rector to pronounce an oration in L'Église des Mathurins before the university and the professorial staff. For some reason Cop invited Calvin to compose the speech for him and the result was an unexpected bombshell dropped into the camp of the Sorbonne, the College citadel of Catholic orthodoxy. Calvin had now at last fully wakened up to the condition of things in the religious world, and with a cold fury he made a violent attack on the prevalent abuses which revolted his soul, appealing to those present no longer to support " heresies which were an insult to God ". In proportion to the distinguished nature of the occasion and the daring of the attack was the immensity of the scandal caused. The Parlement took up the matter resentfully, and both Cop and Calvin had to fly, the real culprit escaping through a window of his room with the aid of a rope made of his bedclothes.

In the obscure period that follows, Calvin found temporary asylum at Saintonge in Angoulême[1] with his friend Louis du Tillet, curé of Claire. There he passed several months engaged in researches for which he found rich material in a library of

[1] Here and at Poictiers, which he visited later on, he was brought into contact with Roman Catholicism at its worst. The behaviour of the bishops at Angoulême was a public scandal. Poictiers was a perfect museum of relics, and supplied Calvin with rich store of material for his treatise on them, in which he made such a crushing attack on the silly superstitions associated with their worship. This treatise had a wide vogue. Before 1600, it had passed through five or six editions in French, a still larger number in Latin, most of all in German. It was also translated into English and Dutch.

2,000-3,000 volumes and MSS. put at his disposal. His private studies were agreeably and profitably diversified by conferences at a neighbouring village with du Tillet, the prior of Bouteville, and the Abbot of Bassac, whose favourite study was Greek. We are told that Calvin, who took the lead, was accustomed to introduce the subject of discussion with the characteristic words, Trouvons (not cherchons) la verité. Certainty, assurance, was ever his aim. His interests were now largely theological, and here he did the work of preparation for the writing of the Institutes. It is possible that in Angoulême also he met Rabelais, whose acquaintance he must already have made in Paris, seeing that they frequented the same circles. There was little real sympathy between the future Reformer and the mordant satirist who lashed out so pitilessly at the Roman Catholic Church. Rabelais proved to have little of the true Protestant in him, being more a literary freelance, an irresponsible sniper. Calvin denounced Pantagruel as an obscene work, recognizing behind its sarcasms and jests a profane and sacrilegious spirit hostile to all things high and holy. Rabelais was not slow to return the thrust, with the genial frankness of the times speaking of "the demoniacal Calvin, the impostor of Geneva".[1]

From Angoulême, Calvin moved to Nérac where he spent some time with Lefèvre d'Étaples, the patriarch of humanists and pioneer of reform, receiving from him, along with much enrichment of mind and stimulus of soul, the parting advice (according to Florimel de Raymond) to take Melanchthon as his model. From one place to another he moved, always in virtue of character and capacity received as the natural leader of whatever company he fell among, storing and developing his mind, and exercising it upon the first theological treatise he published, the Psychopannychia. This was designed to refute the Anabaptist belief in the sleep of the soul between death and resurrection, and the eager and intense spirituality of the man glows through in the aversion he manifests to any cessation or disruption of fellowship with Christ. Back again in Paris, the folly of the Protestant placards against the mass, fixed up all over the city and on the very doors of the king's residence, precipitated

[1] *Lefranc, La Jeunesse de Calvin*, p. 119. "Rabelais was curé of Meudon, but was in strong sympathy with Protestantism, though disagreeing with its leaders on many doctrinal points, e.g. original sin (he preached the goodness of human nature) and predestination. He was one of the fathers of 'conditional immortality', holding that there were two sorts of souls, the intellectual and the rest—'the rest', who are not separated from matter, perish with it." (*Schneegans*, quoted by Doumergue, I, p. 612f.)

a second hasty flight. Under the pseudonym of Martianus Lucianus, he took up residence in Basel and plunged again deep into his studies. Here he perfected himself in Hebrew, probably putting himself under the tuition of Sebastian Münster, the best Hebraist of his day, himself a pupil of a converted Jew who was a celebrated Hebraist.[1] The people used to ask curiously about this young stranger wandering solitarily through the street, sunk in meditation. It was no fruitless thought to which Calvin was giving himself. Basel has the honour of being the birthplace of the *Christian Institutes*, which in their first form were completed here on August 23rd, 1535. "That is a capital date in the life of the Reformer," says Lefranc.[2] "The savant and the humanist have definitely given place to the apostle. With this book begins the great religious mission of the leader of the French Reformation."

III

Calvin's education was not yet complete, recognized as he already was in spite of his youth as a leader among leaders. Leaving Basel, he once more became a wanderer, and amongst other places found welcome shelter in Ferrara with the Duchess Renée, a daughter of Louis XII of France, who had constituted herself protectress of many refugee Protestants. In the stimulating atmosphere of her court, brought into contact with other high and emancipated intellects, Calvin's mind must have had its outlook enlarged, its grasp of principles strengthened, and its perception of the situation sharpened. Seeds that afterwards bore abundant fruit in the psalmody of the Reformed Church were dropped into it by his association with Clement Marot, the poet of the Reformation, a protégée of Renée's at this time.

It was in the course of his flittings from place to place during this period that his dramatic settlement in Geneva took place. His first ministry there, if it left him little time for anything but the organization of the church and the discharge of his pastoral duties, at least initiated him into the sphere of administration, providing him with instruction in its difficulties and with knowledge of the qualities requisite for success. But his education

[1] Doumergue, I, 504f.

[2] *Op. cit.*, p. 125.

for the position he was destined to occupy left still something to be desired. He lacked the experience and the wisdom only to be gained by work in a settled charge. Nothing better could have happened to him than the exile from Geneva which resulted in his becoming minister of the French congregation in Strassburg. While diligently preaching and faithfully prosecuting his pastoral work as well as delivering lectures on theology, he laid the coping stone of the edifice of his studies by receiving tuition from Martin Bucer and Capito, men of the highest erudition, whose friendship he had formed at Basel. Capito, author of a widely used Hebrew grammar, was the third eminent Hebraist by whom Calvin had been instructed, a fact which inspires confidence in the equipment of thorough scholarship which he brought to the exegesis and elucidation of the Old Testament. Perhaps no one exercised a more profound and lasting influence upon Calvin than Bucer.[1] He frequently expresses his admiration for his old teacher and acknowledges his deep indebtedness, often quoting him as a recognized authority in support of views he is putting forward. Indeed many of the developed views which are identified with the younger man and styled specifically Calvinistic are little more than echoes of those set forth by Bucer. Calvin's doctrinal system had certainly been thought out and crystallized in the first edition of the *Institutes*, but the mode of expression and the greater prominence given to certain of its doctrines which came to bulk so largely in the later editions may be confidently ascribed in no small degree to the influence of this last of his teachers. Spiritually as well as intellectually Calvin received the impress of Bucer, and whatever may be thought of the wholesomeness of the doctrinal influence, Bucer's spiritual influence was of the healthiest. Staunch to his convictions, firm without severity, more concerned to adorn the doctrine of Christ than to impose his views upon all and sundry, he symbolized the spirit of his life and the source of his inspiration in his last dying act, when, exile in England, he pointed his three fingers towards heaven and murmured, "He reigns and guides all."

[1] The leading Strassburg minister and theologian, who played a highly important part in the Reformation. He sought to mediate between and reconcile Lutheranism and Zwinglianism, but without success. Because of the refinements he indulged in, Bossuet called him "the great architect of subtleties". His refusal to sign the Interim proposed by the Emperor led to his accepting Archbishop Cranmer's invitation to England, where he became King's Professor of Divinity at Cambridge. He was a man of great learning and blameless life, bearing himself always with a singular modesty. He died in England in 1551, and was buried in St. Mary's, Cambridge, but his remains were exhumed during Mary's reign and burnt in the market place. (v. Prof. Lang's article in *The Evangelical Quarterly*, 1936.)

But Calvin's education again received its chief addition from the intercourse he had with many other eminent men gathered here. Strassburg provided an asylum for numbers of refugees from France, Germany and Switzerland. One of them in a letter to Calvin calls it " the Antioch of the Reformation ", and the French exiles who enjoyed its safe hospitality " considered it a new Jerusalem ". Here were to be met many men of light and leading. Many shades of Protestant opinion were represented, from Lutheranism to Brethrenism. Calvin industriously gleaned all the information and instruction they had to give, as we gather from the instance of the Bohemian Brethren, with whose history, ideas, rules, and the terms in which they expressed their faith he made himself familiar.

One somewhat surprising defect in Calvin's education may here be mentioned. Though in more or less constant touch with German-speaking people, either in Germany itself or in Switzerland, he never took the trouble to learn that language. His ignorance of it must have handicapped and embarrassed him considerably at times, and limited his usefulness and opportunities at conferences such as that which took place at Ratisbon during his stay at Strassburg, in which he was invited to co-operate with the German Protestant leaders, Melanchthon, Bucer and others. One of the obstacles which prevented his marriage to a German young lady suggested for his consideration was that she knew no French while he knew no German. He had to get translations made of German volumes sent to him for perusal. " As I am unacquainted with the German language ", he writes to an author, " I gave your book to a friend of mine to peruse and let me know the contents of it."[1] Bullinger, on the other hand, leader of the Zwinglians, knew as little French. We find Calvin apologizing for sending him a pamphlet in French, telling him that he will no doubt find translators who would explain the principal points to him.[2] This common unfamiliarity of scholars in those days with any foreign tongue is of course to be explained by the universal use of Latin as the medium of scholarly intercourse, not merely in writing but also in speech. In academic or ministerial circles, at any rate, in which Calvin almost exclusively moved when absent from Geneva, his mastery of the classical tongue would enable him

[1] Letter, August 1st, 1557.

[2] Letter, October 1st, 1560.

to carry on intercourse with perfect ease and fidelity to his thought.

IV

In the city of Strassburg, too, Calvin was given a useful insight into the working and worth of established civic institutions of a democratic cast. The tradesmen and artisans of the city were divided into corporations or guilds and every burgess had to become a member of one or other of them. Both duties and privileges were attached to membership. Ordinarily it seems that men of letters, pastors, advocates and such as had no trade, chose the corporation of the occupation of their fathers, or that in which they had most friends. Calvin joined himself to that of the tailors, perhaps because their headquarters were near his church. The entry in the records of the corporation runs, " Jean Calvin a acheté le droit de bourgeoisie et sert chez les tailleurs."[1] Every experience of this kind helped to prepare him for the important legislative work which Geneva subsequently entrusted to him.

His pastorate at Strassburg provided him with the necessary field for putting into testing operation his ideas of how congregational services and work should be carried on. He proved the importance of that regular visitation of the flock which afterwards he laid down as essential in the ecclesiastical ordinances of Geneva. He thought out and drew up the methods and forms of worship which seemed to be most conducive to edification. He compiled a Liturgy and became a pioneer in fostering congregational singing, providing both metrical Psalms and tunes for their musical rendering. The liturgy was not intended to be compulsory or for stated and regular use, though Calvin himself was fond of using stereotyped forms of prayer at certain points in the service. He gave every encouragement to extempore prayer, desiring only that it be informed, reverent, sincere, and scriptural. Perhaps most important of all, he gave the sermon the central and large place it has ever since held in Presbyterian churches, because he believed that in the mouth of a true preacher it embodied a message fresh from the heart of God.

Calvin could not have come to a better place to be educated in appreciation of the political conditions of the times. The situation of Strassburg was such as to command a comprehensive

[1] Doumergue, II, p. 350.

view of the march of events and to promote an understanding of the profound meaning of the struggle in which Christendom was so fiercely engaged. Calvin's mind was anything but provincial; like John Wesley, his parish was the world. Those qualities of statesmanship which were afterwards so brilliantly displayed and which would have made him a Foreign Secretary of no mean calibre, must have here received that stimulus and education which equipped them for the large and urgent demands subsequently laid upon them. Strassburg indeed might be said to have completed his education and preparation for the great work of his life.

Here too Calvin won his spurs in the field of controversy, in which he soon proved to be without an equal. It was a redoubtable antagonist with whom he crossed swords, no less than one of the most astute, learned, and estimable Cardinals of the Roman Church. Taking advantage of Calvin's absence from Geneva, Sadoleto addressed an open letter to the inhabitants of Geneva, cunningly contrived to flatter them back into the "one and only true fold". "He contrasted the unity, the inerrancy, the antiquity, and the universality of the Church of which they had been members, with the recent origin, the uncertain doctrine, and the distressingly fragmentary condition of Protestantism, and he closed by picturing the poor appearance which a Protestant as compared with a Catholic would make at the bar of Divine judgment."[1] A copy reached Calvin via Berne. He was disposed to ignore it, in spite of unmistakable, though veiled, depreciatory allusion to himself, but under pressure from Bucer, Capito, and others, he was persuaded to undertake an answer. The result was a literary achievement which he never excelled, written off in a few days and published within a month of his receipt of the copy.[2] Already he proves himself past-master in the art of controversy. There is a self-control and grave courtesy about the work which is sometimes lacking later. He uses polished weapons and his cuts are clean. He passes swiftly and effectively from defence to attack, evades no point of moment, and without difficulty demolishes all his adversary's

[1] Reyburn, p. 92.

[2] It is worthy of remark that the French of this work is reckoned to be "harsh and disagreeable"; Calvin was yet in the early stages of that gradual progress towards the mastery of that language which he afterwards attained. Kampschulte, the Roman Catholic biographer, reckons the work to be "one of the most brilliant that came from his pen. In the defence of his faith, Calvin develops a force of speech, a skill in discussion, a wealth of thought, which put in a very sad light the rhetoric, the sentimentality, the emptiness and feebleness of the phrases of his opponent."

positions. The answer is notable for the evidence is affords of Calvin's consciousness of leadership. He feels the eyes of the world already upon him, and he does not think it irrelevant or gratuitious to offer an apologia of his own career and position. He professes no false modesty about the abilities he possessed. "If I had wished to consult my own interests", he declares, "I would never have left your party. I do not say the road to preferment would have been easy to me, but I certainly know not a few of my own age who have attained eminence, and there are some of them whom I could have equalled, if not outstripped. But I will say that I would have had no difficulty in reaching the summit of my desires, if these had been for a life of leisure and an honourable position." It is evident that Calvin had reached the stage when he was no longer the pupil or the follower, but the teacher and leader. The days of his preparation were ended, and when the call came soon to his life's work, the man was ready for it as few men have ever been.

We cannot do better than review the course of his education in the words of Doumergue.[1] "Calvin has seen Italy; he has seen Switzerland; he has seen Germany. Progressively, slowly but continually, the little scholar of the Capets at Noyon has become the pupil of Mat. Cordier at the College of La Marche, the student of the great universities, Orleans, Bourges, Paris, the lawyer, the humanist, the theologian, the guest of the court of Ferrara, the colleague of Farel at Geneva, the colleague of Reformers at Strassburg, the intimate friend of Melanchthon, the respected counsellor, desired by conferences, by diets, by princes . . . Vires acquirit eundo!"

V

Of no man could it be more truly said that he illustrated his own doctrines of predestination and providence.[2] Unconscious of his destiny, fighting against it when first summoned to his appointed task, he followed a course of study and passed through experiences than which nothing could better have prepared him for the future that awaited him. Master of Latin, Greek and Hebrew, his legal mind fully furnished with legal knowledge,

[1] Doumergue, II, p. 71.

[2] "Whilst my one great object was to live in seclusion without being known, God so led me about through different turnings and changes, that He never permitted me to rest in any place, until, in spite of my natural disposition, he brought me forth to public notice." (Pref. to Psalms.)

profoundly versed in Scripture, with the whole field of patristic literature at his command, saturated with the principles of the Reformation, aware of its conflicting cross-currents, instructed in the views of the many sects and parties to which the spirit of revolt had already given birth, with clear ideas as to pastoral duties and the qualifications requisite for fruitful congregational life, expert in the weapons of controversy, he returned to Geneva to stamp his name thereon indelibly and write it in large characters upon the face of the whole world.

A. MITCHELL HUNTER.

Edinburgh.

A French Humanist's Chef-D'Oeuvre: *The Commentaries on Seneca's "De Clementia"* by John Calvin

TODAY, A YOUNG scholar, anxious to achieve immediate acclaim as an authority in his field, probably thinks in terms of receiving a Doctorate, locating a post at an Ivy League institution, and publishing a book. In the era of the Renaissance the requisites for admittance to the inner circle of scholars were not exactly the same —Erasmus, for example, was never anything more than a visiting professor at an institution of higher learning— but the publication of an erudite study of classical theme was an almost sure-fire method of attracting the attention of established authors and assuring one's entrance into the world of the literati. It has not been definitely ascertained why John Calvin, in 1532, wrote his *Commentaries on Seneca's "De Clementia."* Earlier historians, such as Papire Masson, Guizot, Henry, and Pannier saw in Calvin's work a plea to Francis I to show mercy in his dealings with Protestants, [1] and even Émile Doumergue in his monumental classic, *Jean Calvin, Les Hommes et les Choses de son Temps,* echoed that theory. More recent studies such as those by Quirinus Breen, Basil Hall, or Ford Battles have suggested an entirely different explanation. They see Calvin, not as a Protestant reformer in that period of his life, but as a humanist à la Erasmus or Budé who thus designed his work on Seneca to be a humanist's chef-d'œuvre which would transform the author overnight, as it were, into a master of repute. However, there is still a general tendency among those who write of Calvin to ignore entirely, or almost entirely, his career as humanist and, specifically, his *Com-*

[1] The *De Clementia* was addressed by Seneca to the young emperor Nero to urge him to be merciful in his relations with his subjects.

mentaries on Seneca and their significance as a preparation for Calvin the Reformer. M. Lecoultre had commented on this in an article appearing in 1891 and noted that the *Commentaries* had never been translated from Latin[2] — they still have not. Professor Basil Hall remarked that it is a well-known fact that Calvin's effect was so earth-shaking as to transform "the religion of half Western Europe." Yet people fail to realize that Calvin was a "humanist lawyer before he was a theologian."[3]

What is the evidence which would indicate that Calvin was a humanist, at least until the fall of 1533? First, it has been demonstrated that Calvin's training was humanistic, his interests were inclined in that direction, his motive for writing the *Commentaries* was in keeping with the typical aspirations and conduct of a humanist, and finally, the work itself was a typical Renaissance study of the North of Europe.

Calvin, as most students of the Reformation must be aware, was sent in August of 1523 to the College of La Marche at Paris where he received excellent instruction in Latin and French under the humanist, Mathurin Cordïer. Later, but in the same year, Calvin transferred to the College of Montaigu where instruction was thorough and where a professor of some note, the Scottish nominalist, John Major or Mair, lectured. Finally, it was here that religious liberals, such as Roussel, Olivétan, and Nicholas Cop, the son of Francis I's physician, were to become his friends.[4]

In 1528, Calvin's studies at the University were interrupted by his father's decision that his son's career lay in the study of law rather than theology. This choice may not have been a second-best one, as far as the father was concerned. Calvin, later, in his *Commentary on the Psalms* asserted that his father chose that profession for him on the basis of its profit-making expectancies. At any rate, Calvin went first to the University of Orléans and, later (the following year), to that of Bourges to study.[5] One of those who influenced him strongly at Orléans was Melchior Wolmar who taught him Greek, and Calvin also found a friend in François Daniel with whom he corresponded later with regard

[2] H. Lecoultre, *Calvin d'après son "Commentaire sur le 'De Clementia' de Sénèque (1532)* (Lausanne, 1891), p. 4.
[3] Basil Hall, *John Calvin: Humanist and Theologian* (London, 1956), p. 7.
[4] *Ibid.*, p. 9.
[5] *Ibid.*, p. 11.

to the Seneca *Commentaries,*[6] as well as Nicholas Duchemin, whose *Antapologia* would contain a preface composed by Calvin.[7] Furthermore, Calvin studied under Pierre Taisan de l'Estoile, the most noted instructor of law. This training, Professor Breen maintains, provided Calvin with "the background for appreciating the critical work of Budé and ... Alciati."[8] In 1529 Calvin, now having enrolled at the University of Bourges, continued his study of law under Andrea Alciati, the only Italian instructor that Calvin was to have, who had "brought with him the atmosphere of the trans-Alpine Renaissance."[9]

In 1531, on the death of his father, Calvin returned to Paris to study at the Royal College (Lecteurs Royaux),[12] an institution where lectureships in Latin, Greek, and Hebrew were available. Here Calvin would attend classes in Greek taught by Pierre Danès, a humanist, and one in Hebrew taught by François Vatable, one of the most prominent Renaissance figures in France.[13] Soon Calvin in April 1532, published his first work, his *Commentaries on Seneca's "De Clementia."*[14] His strongly humanist background would explain, not only his interest in classical authors, but his familiarity with and interest in contemporary humanist writers. Thus, Calvin had chosen Seneca over other classical authors on the advice of Erasmus who, in the preface of his second edition of the works of Seneca published in 1529, had written that further editorial comments on Seneca by young scholars were welcomed.[15] Did Calvin believe that if he accepted the challenge offered by the "Prince of Humanists," who had thus placed his stamp of approval upon the name and thought of Seneca, he would be accorded an eager reception by the community of famous writers? It seems so; however, another explanation has been offered — the fact that during the Renaissance there occurred a revival of Stoicism, a philosophy which tends naturally to become attractive in troubled times. Professor Breen sug-

[6] Quirinus Breen, *John Calvin: A Study in French Humanism* (Grand Rapids, Michigan, 1931), pp. 40-43.

[7] *Ibid,*, p. 37.

[8] *Ibid.*, p. 43.

[9] *Ibid.*, pp. 44-46.

[12] Hall, p. 12.

[13] Breen, pp. 62-63.

[14] *Ibid.*, p. 65.

[15] The earlier edition of Seneca's works, the one of 1515, appeared under the name of Erasmus, but the latter disclaimed the honor of having undertaken that task by explaining that only the preface was his. The job of publication was that of a friend. See Lecoultre, p. 6.

gests, too, that Stoicism may have been revived as a counterforce against the growing popularity of another Hellenistic philosophy, Epicureanism. Humanists in France fell into various classifications, but those who belonged to the cult of Erasmus were fond of searching the classics, especially the writings of the Stoics, as Cicero or Seneca, for instruction in moral law. In this circle would also be found those who, like Calvin, were students of Roman civil law. [16] But what of the theory that the *Commentaries* were written in order to recommend Protestants to the mercy of Francis I? There is no evidence to support such a view. Nowhere is the French King given mention; the work is not even dedicated to him, and, as M. Lecoultre points out, for Calvin to have compared Francis with Nero, to whom Seneca addressed his work, would have been a gross miscalculation. Francis, at that time, was not given over to persecutions. Neither is there anything of a specific nature that might be described as Protestant. [17] As Professor Breen shows, Calvin could not have been interested in Protestantism at that time. [18] Did Calvin, himself, provide any clue to his decision to produce the *Commentaries?* All that appears is a very brief explanation in his dedicatory letter in which he lamented the fact that Seneca, although he enjoyed the reputation of being one of the best writers of classical Rome, had not proved especially popular in Calvin's day. Therefore, he (Calvin) had looked forward for some time to the coming of a famous champion of Seneca's name. [19] Theodore Beza (Bèze), later to be Calvin's successor in Geneva and the author of a biography of him, had merely this to offer: soon after the death of his father, Calvin returned to Paris where he wrote his commentary on Seneca, "a great favorite with him (Beza)" because he was "obviously in accord with Calvin." [20]

Was there any reason why Calvin, when he returned to Paris in 1531, should have chosen to attend the Royal College rather than the

[16] Hall, p. 7.
[17] Lecoultre, p. 24.
[18] Breen, p. 80.
[19] Jean Calvin, *L. Annaei Senecae...libro duo De Clementia...Jo. Calvini Noviodunaei Commentariis illustrati...* in *Ioannis Calvini Opera quae supersunt omnia,* eds. Guilielmus Baum, Eduardus Cunitz, Eduardus Reuss, vol. V (Brunswick, 1863-1900) in *Corpus Reformatorum,* vol. LV, p. 7. This is hereafter cited as *Comm.*
[20] John Calvin, *Tracts relating to the Reformation by John Calvin with His Life by Theodore Beza,* trans. Henry Beveridge (Edinburgh, 1844), vol. I, p. xxiv.

University of Paris? Since the Sorbonne by 1526 had begun its condemnation of "dangerous" books, including the writings of Erasmus, only one answer seems likely. Calvin must have been a humanist, and in keeping with the sentiment of other humanists, preferred to shun the University of Paris and attend lectures delivered by humanist professors in a college founded through the efforts of Budé, the foremost French humanist, to combat the conservative tendencies of the scholastics of Paris.[21] Therefore, Calvin in 1532 could hardly have been a Protestant, but a young man of the Renaissance seeking to make his mark in the world.

Any examination of the *Commentaries* makes it clear that we have before us the kind of classical study which an Erasmus or a Budé would have produced. First of all, Calvin revealed that he was a Latinist of a superb order, as he explained and analyzed Seneca's *De Clementia* from the standpoint of grammar, philosophy, and history.[22] Furthermore, Calvin displayed in this work a wide range of knowledge of Greek and Roman classical authors, as well as an acquaintance with other humanist writings of his day. What is more, Calvin expressed his approval and praise of such secular writings. Professor Ford Battles, who has made a study of the sources used by Calvin in his *Commentaries,* has shown that Cicero was cited more often than any other author; there are approximately sixty references to his *Letters,* ninety five to the *Speeches,* eighteen to the rhetorical writings, and eighty to his philosophical treatises.[23] However, Calvin also referred to Horace, Juvenal, Lucan, Ovid, Plautus, Terrence, Virgil, Suetonius, Tacitus, Plutarch, Livy, Sallust, and others.[24]

Special eulogies were paid by Calvin to two contemporary humanists, Budé and Erasmus. The former was described as the "first glory and support of literary affairs, thanks to whom our France claims today the palm of erudition";[25] it is his *Annotations* which have revealed to us what is "equitable and good."[26] On the other hand, Erasmus, heralded elsewhere as the chief of humanists, was rated as second-best, although still one of the "first delights" of the realm of letters.[27] It

[21] See Breen, p. 35.
[22] *Ibid.,* p. 14.
[23] Ford Battles, "The Sources of Calvin's Seneca Controversy," *John Calvin,* ed. Gervase Duffield (Appleford, Abingdon, Berkshire, 1966), p. 49.
[24] *Ibid.,* p. 53.
[25] *Comm.,* p. 54.
[26] *Ibid.,* p. 119.
[27] *Ibid.,* p. 6.

has been ably demonstrated by Professors Battles and Breen that of these two, it was Budé who exerted the greater degree of influence upon Calvin in that his (Budé's) *Annotations on the Pandects of Justinian* provided Calvin with the technical terms and concepts of Roman law, as well as other aspects of Roman society, for Calvin believed that to understand the *De Clementia* he needed an understanding of the whole of Roman history, and, more specifically, the history of the reign of Nero.[28] Professor Breen also suggests that another influence upon Calvin must have been derived from Budé's *L'institution du Prince* which consists of apophthegms from Plutarch's work of that name which, as was true of the *De Clementia,* offered advice to a young king. Thus, this work and Calvin's *Commentaries* had essentially the same purpose, and it is interesting to note that the first sentence of Calvin's *Commentaries* came from the apophthegms of Plutarch.[29]

Calvin also utilized a work by another humanist, this time an Italian, Lorenzo Valla, who in his *Elegantiae,* had laid the foundations of modern classical philology. That Calvin should be impressed by Valla's work is not surprising, especially in the light of Budé's recommendation of him in his *Annotations.*[30]

Professor Battles indicates one more contemporary influence on Calvin, that of Philippus Beroaldus the Elder, whose Commentaries on Suetonius' *Lives of the Caesars* were studied closely by Calvin.[31]

As for Erasmus, there are several references by Calvin to the *Adagia,* one to the Panegyric of Philip, and it is highly probable that Calvin was familiar with the *Education of a Christian Prince.*[32]

Though under the spell of classical letters and the thought of contemporary humanists, Calvin demonstrated his mettle as a humanist scholar in his own right by the painstaking and exacting manner in which he carried through his task of explaining and expounding the ideas of Seneca. Here also, Calvin displayed the marks of a questioning spirit by his refusal to swallow whole the philosophy of Seneca. However, this was not all. Even the great Budé and Erasmus were not spared his critical eye; nor were the judicial and educational systems of his time immune from attack. For example, Calvin, taking exception

[28] See Breen, pp. 119-120 and Battles, pp. 42-45.
[29] Breen, p. 120.
[30] *Ibid.*, p. 104.
[31] Battles, pp. 46-47.
[32] *Ibid.*, pp. 40-41.

to Erasmus' acrimonious assault in his preface of 1529 upon some of the ethical and religious beliefs of Seneca, as well as his literary merits,[33] rose to Seneca's defense in the Preface to his *Commentaries* by praising him as "a man of great erudition and of remarkable eloquence ...; the first after Cicero, he is a pillar of philosophy and Roman eloquence."[34]

Hereafter, Calvin referred only rarely to "errors" of Erasmus in interpretation and word-usage.[35] In several passages, however, Calvin continued to exhibit this critical tendency in his attacks upon the venality of the judges of his day[36] and in his censure of teachers whom he termed "cruel tyrants" to whom the name "pedagogue" would be an insult.[37] Even Seneca was not allowed to escape reproof. Calvin decried his verbosity, absence of order, and his occasional inaccuracies in historical references.[38] Calvin was also prepared to reject any thoughts which were not in harmony with his own religious or ethical convictions. Thus, Seneca's references to the operation of Fortune or Chance prompted Calvin to remark that he (Seneca) should have written, "Providence."[39] The impersonal clemency extolled by Seneca appalled him also, and, in support of his own position, he cited St. Augustine and Cicero.[40] In another commentary Calvin reproved Seneca for declaring that he was not preoccupied with the thought of his reputation, but was content with the witness of his conscience.[41] And when Seneca referred to souls which are "ambitious," Calvin raised an objection to the use of the word, "ambitious." "Here, Seneca," Calvin commented, "shows clearly what those eminent virtues of the pagans were."[42] Thus, to Calvin the virtues of the ancients were tainted with the evils of self-centeredness and vain-glory.

Such evidences of a critical disposition in Calvin were in keeping with the mood of the Renaissance, but, alas, the thrusts of a young unknown against the great Erasmus, mild though they were, may have been regarded amiss, and could well have proved responsible, or partly responsible, for the failure of Calvin's first publication to reach the best-seller list of the day.

[33] See Lecoultre, p. 7.
[34] *Comm.*, pp. 6-7.
[35] See *Ibid.*, pp. 32, 159.
[36] *Ibid.*, p. 23.
[37] *Ibid.*, p. 115.
[38] *Ibid.*, p. 7.
[39] *Ibid.*, p. 18.
[40] *Ibid.*, pp. 156-157.
[41] *Ibid.*, pp. 111-112.
[42] *Ibid.*, p. 45.

It should be kept in mind, however, that Calvin's censures were infrequent, and, when they occurred, delivered in a courteous and somewhat apologetic manner. [43] As might be expected of a book authored by a humanist, eulogies of classical antiquity and contemporary scholarship abounded. Generally speaking, Seneca's advice to the Emperor Nero was viewed favorably, and, as we have seen, Erasmus and especially Budé, were accorded lavish praise.

What was the political theory of Seneca which attracted the attention of young Calvin? First of all, Seneca's prince —and Calvin's too— is absolute in power — for in the *Commentaries* Seneca is quoted as maintaining the principle that the emperor's powers are subject to no law save that of the gods, and Calvin echoes this proposition by declaring that the prince is indeed free of the law and responsible alone to divine authority. It must be added, however, that Calvin does modify this principle somewhat, for he states that it would be better for the well-being of the state or people if the ruler submits to the law instead of placing himself over it and refers to a passage in Cicero's *De Officiis* in which the author compares administrators to the protectors of the republic. [44] In another passage Calvin writes that it is the duty of the prince to minister unto the "health and care of men"; of those good things which God has given to them, they distribute a portion to their subjects and a part they retain for themselves. He then proceeds to quote the passage from Romans XIII in which subjects are admonished to obey the powers —that— be. [45] Thus, Calvin attempts to show that there are some postulates which Christians and pagan Stoics share in common.

Of all the qualities possessed by princes none is more impressive in the eyes of Seneca and Calvin than that of clemency. Once again Seneva invokes the principle of natural law to support his contention, for in the natural kingdom, Seneca notes, the ruler of the bees is more impressive than the rest, but has no sting. [46] The human prince should conduct himself in the same manner, since that man is truly great who,

[43] As an illustration of this, Calvin in his Preface (p. 6) stated: "a number of points failed to be observed by Erasmus ... a criticism which may be made without ill-will."

[44] *Comm.*, pp. 23-25.

[45] *Ibid.*, p. 18.

[46] Lucius Annaeus Seneca, *The Stoic Philosophy of Seneca; Essays and Letters of Seneca*, ed. Moses Hadas (Gloucester, Mass., 1965), p. 158.

though wronged and in possession of unlimited power, is able to keep his temper in check and knows the meaning of the word "magnanimous." [47] In another passage, Seneca once more finds a parallel in nature. This time, the cruel king is compared with a stormy day. Since a king finds it easy to take vengeance on those who have offended him, he is to be awarded unqualified praise when he exercises, instead, gentleness and restraint. The king who is, by his very position, elevated above the crowd and hence most apt to be noticed, must be doubly aware of his reputation, for people are watching him. [48] Calvin observes that Seneca's remarks on the restraint which a ruler must exercise indicate that a condition has been imposed on kings. For them, intemperance and license are an abomination. When we refer to the ruled, we may speak of a man's angry disposition, but in the case of a ruler, the harshest terms of disapprobation such as "cruel" and "proud" are in order. [49] In the matter of the dispensation of acts of mercy, Seneca points out that clemency is of value to both the innocent and the guilty; if applied properly it will make a large portion of mankind innocent again. On the other hand, pardon, if general, ends in chaos and an "eruption of vice." Thus, moderation should be employed with the object of separating the "curable from the hopeless." [50] Calvin concurs with this view, [51] and later refers to the picture which Gregory the Great painted in his *Moralia* of the impartial judge who, with scales in hand, extends both justice and compassion. . . . Through justice he pronounces the sentence of sin and through compassion he tempers the penalty of sin. . . ." [52]

According to Seneca, the clement ruler will discover that his subjects are much more likely to render loyal service to him than would be the case if he attempted to rule as a cruel tyrant. Of the power of a ruler, Seneca wrote, is indeed directed toward promoting the well-being of his subjects, the latter will know that their prince is on their side and will willingly sacrifice their own lives, if need be, in the defense of their monarch. [53] Calvin agrees that clemency is a "heroic virtue without which princes are not able to rule." Such a quality does not

[47] *Ibid.*, pp. 159-160.
[48] *Ibid.*, pp. 145-146.
[49] *Comm.*, p. 65.
[50] Seneca, p. 140.
[51] *Comm.*, p. 35.
[52] *Ibid.*, p. 37.
[53] Seneca, p. 141.

constitute a sign of weakness. Indeed, a king may be powerful; it is permissible for him to be so. However, he will discover that if he does not tone down his immoderate actions, affairs of state will not run smoothly. "All things will lose their charm unless he takes upon himself the qualities of gentleness and graciousness. He will then find that all his words and deeds will be accepted without opposition if he has conciliated the favor of the people ... by this virtue (clemency)." [54] In this manner, a king's reign is a stable one if the ruler becomes a "veritable shepherd of his people," ministering to the best interests of those placed in his charge. On the other hand, the prince who rules as a tyrant reaps his own destruction. [55]

Calvin also approved Seneca's assertion that the prince is to the state as the soul is to the body. For as the soul rules over and moderates all functions of the members, so are those placed under the rule of a prince nurtured and guided and governed. [56]

Did the practice of clemency enjoined by Seneca and Calvin mean that the prince must rid himself of rod and sword? Hardly. Seneca and also Calvin were in accord that all men are sinners and that sins need to be punished. Why? Seneca cites three reasons: (1) to reform a man; (2) to set an example for other men; (3) to lock up the criminal so that the rest of society will be protected from him. In the first case, the lighter form of punishment is preferable, believed Seneca. If a man has something worth saving he "will live more heedfully." It is otherwise with the individual who has already lost his reputation. As for the state, it benefits also if sparing use is made of punishment. [57] A ruler's clemency has the effect of making men ashamed of wrong-doing and "punishment seems more grievous if it is inflicted by a kindly man." [58] On the other hand, overly-harsh forms of punishment may lead to outbursts of violent indignation, and Seneca cites, as an example, revolts of private citizens and slaves against those who invoked the extreme penalty of crucifixion. [59] Frequent punishments also lead to internal dissension, for if a king punishes frequently, he may prevent a few from hating him, but the hatred of all is aroused since antagonisms

[54] *Comm.*, p. 41.
[55] *Comm.*, p. 41-42.
[56] *Ibid.*, pp. 42-43.
[57] Seneca, p. 161.
[58] *Ibid.*, p. 162.
[59] *Ibid.*, p. 164.

have a way of multiplying. One execution provokes the many relatives of the executed to become the sworn enemies of the prince.[60]

Another recommendation which Seneca makes is that a state to be moral must be led to think of itself as a good state. He illustrates this by referring to the occasion when a motion was made in the Senate to create a distinctive dress for slaves and freemen, and then the danger of this procedure was realized. The slaves would begin counting the number of freemen. Thus, if no one came to be pardoned, we would soon note that the worst element was in the majority.[61]

Seneca's arguments for light and infrequent punishments were carefully noted and sanctioned by Calvin who deplored the cruel, tyrannical actions of a prince, who, free from all checks upon his authority, gives full reign to the basest of emotions, meting out punishments with the heavy hand of vengeance.[62] Sometimes a king must execute, he maintained, but only when public welfare necessitates it.[63]

Should a ruler fail to heed the advice of Seneca and rule tyrannically, was there no way for his subjects to find release? Was there a theory of right of revolution in the thought of Seneca and Calvin? No, but their propositions led them close to the threshold of Lockeian ratiocination, for it will be recalled that Seneca had observed that a cruel ruler bears within himself the fruits of his own debacle in that revolutions somethimes break out in opposition to the cruel deeds of a despot. Calvin notes that they who are cruel and tyrannical are cursed while they live and are often destroyed by the sword. Subjects may, then, take comfort in the thought that though the rule of a wicked prince may be a 'stormy' one it will also be a brief one.[64]

Seneca sees yet another effect of tyranny. This time it is not the reaction of the populace to deeds of cruelty or the physical harm which may befall a prince that concerns him, but the question of the effect of evil deeds upon the soul of the man who commits them. What are the psychological changes which accompany the tyrant's acts? Seneca paints a picture of the progressive deterioration of a man's character. One crime leads to another and another as the cruel ruler finds that he cannot call a halt to his evil actions. Faces of death are

[60] *Ibid.*, pp. 146-147.
[61] *Ibid.*, p. 162.
[62] See *Comm.*, Book I, chaps. VIII, XXIII and XXIV.
[63] *Ibid.*, p. 104.
[64] *Ibid.*, p. 89.

at every hand and, for once, the ruler knows the meaning of fear, but the new emotion merely leads him on to further acts of violence. Gradually, he reaches the stage where he is unable to trust anyone and is frequently tormented by fears of death, or more often, the desire to die.[65] Calvin adds that tyranny is that "miserable state" which serves only to "horrify both gods and men."[66] And there is also the "mirror of conscience" which reveals that "reflection of the vermin within."[67]

Thus, Calvin observes two results of tyranny: outwardly, revolutions or riotings may occur; and, inwardly, the tyrant becomes, in the end, a sniveling coward afraid to approach his most intimate friends and is filled with a fear of, or even longing for, extinction. In rebelling against the cruel tyrant, the subjects may not be exercising a right of revolution, but they are fulfilling a role which the natural law dictates, for rebellion in the *De Clementia* appears as the natural consequence of the evil deeds of a prince. If in Stoic philosophy, 'virtue is its own reward', then injustice brings its own reward, too — revolutions, and rioting and inner throes of conscience.

Calvin's prince is, thus, a ruler with no limitations upon his own powers save those of his own devising. These self-imposed restraints he has learned to exercise, for he knows that for his own good and the well-being of his state he must rule in justice, temperance, and clemency. Is he not the antithesis of the Renaissance ideal of princehood? Certainly, Calvin's ruler is no Machiavellian prince who has been advised to take upon himself the ways of the fox and lion. Nor has he been told that it is not necessary to be clement and humane; all that is demanded is that he just appear to possess those qualities. On the other hand, Calvin's prince is remarkably similar to the ideal princes which are depicted in Erasmus' *Institutio Principis Christiani* and Budé's *L'Institution du Prince*. In the former work, the prince, just as Calvin's, considers the welfare of his people and shows mercy in dealing with violators of the law. In Budé's book, the ruler is likewise presented as humane and just, as he strives to set a good example for his subjects.

[65] Seneca, p. 153.
[66] *Comm.*, p. 87.
[67] *Ibid.*, p. 102.

Calvin's *Commentaries,* even with respect to their political content, are thus found to be congenial with other political writings which were produced by the Northern Renaissance.

University of Alabama, Huntsville LOUISE SALLEY

CALVIN'S *PSYCHOPANNYCHIA*: ANOTHER LOOK

Timothy George

It is a curious fact that Calvin's first theological writing as a Protestant has received relatively little attention from his many interpreters. Originally directed against the somewhat obscure heresy of soul sleep, the *Psychopannychia* has suffered from its proximity to the *Institutes* of 1536, which all of the biographers have recognized as Calvin's real first work of genius. Moreover, the specific origin and provenance of the treatise have been matters of dispute since the first modern critical edition appeared in the *Corpus Reformatorum* in 1866. Indeed, the term "psychopannychia" itself is fraught with ambiguity, and there is no scholarly consensus concerning the identity of Calvin's original opponents.

Despite these difficulties, the *Psychopannychia* is an important document both for our understanding of Calvin's development and for our assessment of early Reformed polemics. In this treatise we see Calvin wrestling for the first time with what might be called the "eschatological tension" in his thought--the effort to hold in balance a fervent eschatological hope with a realistic commitment to history. Here he also broaches certain christological and soteriological concerns which he will treat *in extenso* in his later theological writings. The purpose of this essay is first to review the bibliographical problem related to the

Psychopannychia, then to suggest several sets of opponents who may have attracted Calvin's attention, and, finally, to measure the significance of the treatise for Calvin's developing theology.

I.

The first printed edition of Psychopannychia of which we have an extant copy appeared in Strasbourg in 1542 published by Wendelin Rihel, who three years earlier had also published the first edition of Calvin's Commentary on Romans as well as the famous epistola to Cardinal Sadolet.[1] This edition carried the title, Vivere apud Christum non dormire animis sanctos, qui in fide Christi decedunt. The same printer brought out a second edition three years later in March, 1545, but with a revised title: Psychopannychia, qua refellitur quorundam imperitorum error, qui animas post mortem usque ad ultimum iudicium dormire putant. The edition also bore as a subtitle the following ascription: "Libellus ante septem annos compositus, nunc tamen primum in lucem aeditus." This statement is puzzling for two reasons. The proposed date of composition--"seven years earlier"--would have fit more accurately the 1542 edition, judging from the two prefaces which were attached to each edition; further, the claim that this was the editio princeps was clearly false since, with only minor variants, the identical treatise had been published by the same printer in the same city only three years before. Perhaps this is merely an example of sixteenth-century "book talk"--the ruse of a publisher trying to dress up an old product with a new, flashier title for a showing at the Frankfort book fair!

Several subsequent editions of the Psychopannychia are worthy of note. A French translation was made in 1542, but published only in 1558 by Conrad Badius in Geneva. The editors of the Corpus Reformatorum were aware of only one extant exemplar of this edition, although it was reprinted in the Bezae corpus gallicum in 1566.[2] A possible explanation for the long delay in publication of the French translation was the appearance in 1544 of Calvin's Briève Instruction contre les Anabaptistes, which dealt at length with the issue of soul sleep and incorporated much material from the Psychopannychia.[3] The first English translation of the document appeared in 1581 translated by T. Stocker under the title: An Excellent Treatise of the Immortalyte of the Soul. A second English translation, made by Henry Beveridge, appeared in 1844, published by the Calvin Translation Society in Edinburgh. A Hungarian translation was published in 1906. Two critical editions of the Latin text have been published: the first in the Corpus Reformatorum, Vol.5 of Calvini Opera; the second, and far superior, by Walther Zimmerli, a German Old Testament scholar. Zimmerli's edition was published at Leipzig in 1932 as volume 30 in the series "Quellenschriften zur Geschichte des Protestantismus."[4]

Having survey the printed editions of Psychopannychia, we must now turn to the controverted question of its original Sitz im Leben. All of the editions we have mentioned contain two prefatory letters by Calvin, the first addressed "to a certain friend" and dated "Orléans, 1534," the second "to the readers" dated "Basel, 1536." On the basis of these prefaces the editors of the Corpus Reformatorum assumed that two early editions of Psychopannychia had in fact been printed. They guessed that the 1534 edition had been published by some unknown printer in Paris, while (they assumed) that of 1536 must have come from the press of Thomas Platter at Basel. They admitted that they had not been able to find any exemplars of these editions, though they expressed hope that they might yet be discovered in "some dark corner of a French library" (in obscura quadam interioris Galliae bibliotheca).[5] In support of their theory was Beza's statement, supported by Colladon, that Calvin had first published the Psychopannychia before he was forced to withdraw from France.

However, on the basis of his careful study of Calvin's correspondence, A. L. Herminjard was able to show that, in all likelihood, the first drafts of Psychopannychia circulated only in autograph form. Of great importance here is a letter of Wolfgang Capito addressed Martianus Lucanius, one of Calvin's pseudonyms. Herminjard argues that the letter was sent to Calvin during his sojourn in Basel "toward the end of

1534."[6] In this letter Capito says that he has been pleased by Calvin's book, although he complains that he has not been able to read it thoroughly "because of the small characters"--perhaps a reference to Calvin's handwriting? He counsels against publication because that would only give greater notoriety to the teaching Calvin is seeking to refute. Moreover, there are certain autores splendidi, whom the Lord has allowed to fall into the same error, who would only be further exacerbated by Calvin's attack. Nonetheless, the fruit of Calvin's labors are not lost, for they can be revised and used at a more favorable time.

We must return to the question of the identity of the splendidi autores whom Capito is so wary of offending. However, at this point it is well to note that Calvin seems to have taken Capito's advice to heart. The preface of 1536 opens with at least a half-hearted apology for his rather "severe and harsh expressions which have perhaps given offence to delicate ears." Apparently Capito was not alone in upbraiding Calvin for his blunt polemics, for in the same preface he defends himself against those who "charge me with stirring up fierce contests about nothing, and of making trifling differences the source of violent dissensions." He responds that the issue at hand is more significant than many suppose: "it is certainly no trivial matter to see God's light extinguished by the devil's darkness."[7]

In fact, by the time Calvin wrote the preface of

1536, he had apparently already completely re-worked the original draft. This can be deduced from a letter of 3 September 1535 addressed to his friend Christopher Fabri who had been among the critics of the first draft. Calvin informs his friend that he has thoroughly revised this "little book" changing the order of presentation, taking out some things, adding others, so that the copy he is now sending is really a "novum librum."[8] Apparently, Calvin intended to submit this revised edition to the press, and accordingly wrote the 1536 preface to introduce it afresh. For some reason, however, this intention was not fulfilled. On 1 October 1538, settled now in Strasbourg following his expulsion from Geneva, Calvin wrote to his former classmate from Orléans, Antoine Pignet: "At present you will receive nothing from me against the lethargic hypnosophistas. I hope the booklet I wrote against them three years ago will very soon be published. For Bucer, who had advised against its publication before, encourages me now."[9] One year later the work remains unpublished, for on 4 October 1539 Pignet writes to Calvin from Geneva urging him to send the work against soul sleepers. As we have seen, it would be nearly three more years before the first imprint of 1542.

II.

Against whom was the Psychopannychia directed? Who were Calvin's opponents? This is perhaps the most difficult question we face in seeking to reconstruct the life setting of the document. Before suggesting several possible sets of opponents, we should look briefly at the preface of 1534. In his first sentence Calvin tells us that he is taking up the pen against the soul sleepers at the urging of certain "pious men." Emile Doumergue makes a great deal of the word "pridem" (long ago), or in the French version, "dejà de long temps." Doumergue thinks this word supports an early dating of Calvin's conversion since "depuis long temps" he had been regarded "comme un défenseur, comme un chef des idées evangeliques."[10] More to the point, Calvin indicates that this heresy, which he had hoped would simply vanish of its own accord, had in fact grown into a rather virulent movement. "These babblers have so strenuously exercised themselves, that they have already drawn thousands into their insanity." How well informed Calvin was about the size or even the nature of this sect is quite dubious. He claims never to have seen their writings. Indeed, he says that he has only received "some notes from a friend" who had transcribed what "he had heard from their lips, or collected by some other means." Nonetheless, he is convinced that there is a clear and present danger to the faith, for this sect is "gaining ground daily" and "eating in like a cancer."[11]

Once in the preface of 1534, and once again in that of 1536, Calvin refers to his opponents as Anabaptists: in the former he calls them "dregs of Anabaptists" (ex anabaptistarum faece), in the latter "the nefarious herd of Anabaptists." Apart from these two references, the name "Anabaptists" appears only once in the body of the text, and that in the very last paragraph. More commonly, he refers to his opponents in pejorative terms such as "these soul slayers" (isti animicidae), "dreamy sleepers" (somniatores), hypnologists, vain dreamers, etc. Moreover, Calvin distinguishes clearly two levels of heresy among his opponents: first, those who allow a real existence to the human soul after death, but who teach that it sleeps in a state of insensibility until the Day of Judgment; secondly, those who claim that the soul cannot exist without the body, that in fact it perishes along with the body, until the day when the whole person is raised again. The former view, psychosomnolence, Calvin regarded as an error which had to be corrected; the latter, thnetopsychism or, more popularly, mortalism, he saw as a serious heresy which "ought to be repressed."[12]

Calvin believed that he was faced with the recrudescence of an ancient heresy which had recurred at intervals throughout the history of the church. In the preface of 1536 he locates the origin of the error with certain Arabs who, according to Eusebius, taught that "the human soul dies and perishes with the body" to be rejoined with it again at the resurrection.[13] Calvin then mentions the case of Pope John XXII (1249-1334) whom he classifies as a mortalist, although apparently John had only taught that the beatific vision was withheld from the faithful departed (including the saints and the Virgin Mary) until after the Last Judgment. To be sure, this was a serious enough departure from orthodox eschatology. Under pressure from the theologians at Paris, John was forced to embrace the standard view.[14] This false doctrine, Calvin avers, then "lay smoldering" for some years until its recent revival by "some dregs of Anabaptists."

While blaming this teaching on the Anabaptists, Calvin admits that is "has been spread abroad far and wide" (longe et lateque pervagatae).[15] Indeed, there were multiple sources for psychopannychist sentiment in the sixteenth century. We must speak not only of the polygenesis of Anabaptism, but of the polygenesis of psychopannychism as well. Let us now look at several diverse streams of psychopannychist thought which may possibly have had some bearing on Calvin's situation.

III.

1. Italian Philosophical Speculation. The problem of the natural mortality of the soul had been a topic of lively debate among several Italian philosophical schools in the decades prior to the Reformation. The Averroistic interpretation of Aristotle, for example, found no place for individual souls, but only for an eternal rational soul, in which each individual transiently participates. Within this context immortality meant merely the absorption of the individual in the universal Intellect. Another challenge to orthodox catholic eschatology was put forth

by Pietro Pomponazzi in his daring analysis of Aristotle's anthropology, published in 1516 as On the Immortality of the Soul. Therein he sought to demonstrate by natural reason that human beings were possessed of dignity and individuality despite the mortality of the soul.

Pomponazzi believed that these speculations, deduced from mere human reason, posed no threat to ecclesiastical doctrine, based as it was on the higher norm of divine revelation. This, however, did not prevent Pope Leo X, in the first year of his pontificate (1513), from condemning at the Fifth Lateran Council all views which denied the philosophical probability of the natural immortality of the soul.[16].

In a striking comparison George H. Williams has suggested that psychopannychism should be considered the Italian counterpart of German solafideism and Swiss predestinarianism in contributing to the dismantling of the medieval structures of sacramental grace, thus weakening the grip of the papacy on human souls at the very outset of the Reformation.[17] Among Calvin's possible opponents at Orléans, Williams, following Henri Busson, suggests certain "French Paduans" who presumably had been infected with the views of Italian Averroists, Pompanazzi, or both. Admittedly the identity of such heterodox dissenters remains shadowy at best. Nonetheless, the persistence of psychopannychist ideas (of both the mortalist and psychosomnolent variety) is a distinguishing trait of most, if not all, of that heterogeneous group of radical reformers Williams refers to as "evangelical rationalists". Most of them were Italians or had strong contacts with Italian radicals; to mention only three of the most prominent in this grouping--Michael Servetus, Camillo Renato, and Lelius Socinus, all of whom had extensive personal contact with Calvin. We know, for example that Calvin had planned a rendezvous with Servetus in Paris in 1534, about the time he would have written the first draft of Psychopannychia. It has been suggested that Calvin's depiction of his opponents' view of the soul as "merely a vital power derived from arterial spirit on the action of the lungs" (ex spiritu arteriae aut pulmonum agitatione) echoes Servetus' theory of the pulmonary circulation of the blood.[18] In any event, the intensity of Calvin's hostility toward Servetus is better understood when we remember that the latter was not only an anti-Trinitarian but also an Anabaptist and a psychopannychist.

The psychopannychist ideas attacked by Calvin, however, were not the sole domain of university-trained academics such as Socinus or eclectic intellectuals such as Servetus. They had also gained wide acceptance among radicals of the rank and file. For example, the famous synod of Venice, which met for forty days in 1550 and summoned delegates from as far away as St. Gall, declared that there was no hell except the grave, and that the souls of the elect slept from death until the Day of Judgment. Carlo Ginzburg has shown how these radical eschatological doctrines trickled down to a common miller of the Friuli, a certain Mennochio, who was condemned to death by the Inquisition for holding, among other things, that "when the body dies, the soul also dies and returns to God who gave it to us."[19]

2. Evangelical Anabaptism. Among the radical reformers the doctrine of soul sleep seems first to have been taught by Andreas Bodenstein von Karlstadt and his brother-in-law, Gerhard Westerburg, both of whom had studied at Italian universities--Karlstadt at Siena and Westerburg at Bologna. In 1523, while both were serving as peasant preachers in the village of Orlamünde, the two men published two attacks on purgatory, which also included a positive affirmation of the transient sleep of the soul pending resurrection. Westerburg's eight-page tract, Vom Fegfeuer und Stand der verschiedenen Seelen: Eine christliche Meinung, was so popular that it earned him the nickname of "Dr. Fegfeuer." In 1524 Westerburg was in Zürich conferring with Conrad Grebel and Felix Manz. In a letter to Vadian (14 October 1524) Grebel writes that Westerburg had stayed with them six days and claims to have read Westerburg's libellum on the slumber of souls.[20] By 1529 Westerburg had embraced Anabaptism and become the leader of the Anabaptist movement in his native city of Cologne.

The first Protestant reformer to defend immortality of the soul against sectarian psychopannychism was Heinrich Bullinger. In 1526, while serving as "Schulmeister" at Kappel, Bullinger wrote a little pamphlet entitled, Quod Anima a Corporibus Separatae, Non Dormiant, sed cum Christo in Coelis Vivant. This was written at the request of a certain Paul Berkius who had complained that the common people in his area were being swept away by this false doctrine.[21] Some five years later Zwingli picked up the same theme in his Elenchus(1529), claiming that "the Catabaptists teach that the dead sleep, both body and soul, until the day of judgment, because they do not know that the Hebrews used the word 'sleeping' for 'dying.'"[22]

Over against this, Mennonite historians have denied vehemently that sixteenth-century Anabaptists advocated any form of the soul sleep doctrine.[23] Whatever may be said of Calvin's original opponents, it seems clear that later editions of Psychopannychia were indeed directed against certain French-speaking Anabaptists who held some form of psychopannychism. In the early 1540s there was an outburst of Anabaptist activity in the area of Neuchâtel. The first Anabaptist to be arrested at Neuchâtel was a woman from the parish of Cornaux who reportedly had said that "the soul of a person dies with the body, and that there was no difference between the soul of a beast and that of a person."[24] Writing to Calvin in early 1544 Farel, then the pastor at Neuchâtel, suggested that a French translation of Psychopannychia would greatly help in his efforts to counteract the principal doctrines of the Anabaptists. In lieu of such a translation (which did not appear until 1558) Calvin added to his Briève Instruction a separate chapter comprising nearly one-third of the entire work dealing with psychopannychism.

3. Lutheran Soul-Sleepers. We have noted already Capito's advice against publication of the first draft of Psychopannychia lest certain "autores splendidi" be offended. And, in the preface of 1536, Calvin concedes that there are some "boni viri" who have fallen into this error either, as he imagines, "from excessive credulity or from ignorance of the Scriptures." He does not wish to offend these pious brethren since his main target is "the nefarious herd of Anabaptists."

Who were the "autores splendidi" and the "boni viri" whom both Calvin and Capito are so wary of offending? Herminjard suggests that Capito was alluding to Caspar Schwenckfeld and Martin Cellarius; the editors of the Corpus Reformatorum suggest Karlstadt as a likely possibility. Even more likely, however, is the reformer of Wittenberg himself, Martin Luther. Luther had strongly condemned the decree of the Fifth Lateran Council on the natural immortality of the soul. This was partly in keeping with his blast against "whore reason"; it was another example of philosophy intruding into the realm of faith. But it also reflected his suspicion of the inherited Catholic view of the afterlife. In a sermon of 1524 he declared that the soul sleeps until God awakens both it and the boy at the Last Judgment. In another sermon (1533) he proclaimed: "We shall sleep until he comes and knocks on the grave and says, 'Dr. Martinus, arise!'"[25] His clearest statement on the issue is from his Commentary on Ecclesiastes, published in 1532, two years before Calvin penned the first draft of Psychopannychia. Commenting on the text, "there is no work, nor desire, nor knowledge, nor wisdom in the grave whither thou goest,"(Eccl. 9:10), he writes:

> Solomon judges the dead are asleep, feel nothing at all. For they lie there accounting neither days nor years, but when they are awakened, they shall seem to have slept scarce one minute.[26]

Luther's psychopannychism was picked up by his English disciples. William Tyndale and George Joye, who proceeded to defend its basis in Scripture against the attacks of Sir Thomas More.[27]

Calvin, then, directed Psychopannychia against the Anabaptists, although he was aware that the heresy of soul sleep had also been advanced by more reputable reformers. We cannot identify with precision the "hypnologi" who elicited the first draft of 1534. While we cannot rule out the influence of Italian philosophical speculation on various streams of radical dissent, Calvin's opponents seem to have been thoroughgoing biblicists who were possessed of an acute apocalyptic eschatology. Despite the paucity of primary evidence for the teaching of soul sleep among evangelical Anabaptists, it seems certain that some of their number had in fact embraced this view and that Calvin was not entirely off base in ascribing it to them. Whoever the original soul sleepers may have been, Cardinal Sadolet felt justified in attributing their teaching to Protestants in general. Was it not a logical step for those who had denied prayers for the dead, invocation of saints, and purgatory to also deny the sentient existence of the soul after death? Here then is a major apologetic motive which may well have prompted Calvin to write the Psychopannychia: his desire to dissociate himself and the true evangelicals from this pernicious error. We must now turn to a brief review of the central theological themes touched upon in Psychopannychia.

IV.

1. Immortality of the Soul. Psychopannychia contains Calvin's first extensive treatment of the nature and origin of the human soul. Over against his opponents, psychosomnolents and mortalists alike, Calvin maintains that the soul is a true substance (substantia) endued with both sense and understanding which are not abrogated by the death of the body. Calvin had been preoccupied with the issue of the soul as early as his Commentary on Seneca's De Clementia where he had reviewed the various philosophical opinions as to the location of the soul--Herephilus had located it in the brain, Plato in the entire head, Strato between the eyebrows, Diogenes in the heart, etc.[28] In the Psychopannychia, while referring approvingly to both Plato and Aristotle's discourses on the soul, Calvin

asserts that the true nature of the soul cannot be derived from philosophical inquiry. He proceeds to identify the human soul with the imago dei: "Whatever philosophers or these dreamers may pretend, we hold that nothing can bear the image of God but spirit, since God is a spirit."[29] In contrast to animal life which is derived from the general creative process, the human soul is a special creation of God. "The soul of man is not of the earth. It was made by the mouth of the Lord, i.e., by his secret power."[30] Calvin opts for the creationist rather than the traducianist theory of the origin of the soul.

Despite Calvin's claim to be following a strictly biblical view of the soul, many of his interpreters have criticized him for being too heavily influenced by the Greek, especially Neoplatonic, philosophical tradition. Heinrich Quistrop, for example, charges Calvin with not taking seriously enough the corporeal connotations of the Hebrew word nephesh and the Greek word psyche. More recently, Suzanne Selinger has argued that Calvin's disparagement of the body together with his overly spiritualized view of the soul resulted in "a continuous and significant conflict between dualism and orthodoxy" within his entire thought.[31]

There is no question but that Calvin's depiction of the soul in the Psychopannychia is laden with Neoplatonic imagery. He stresses the sharp distinction between soul and body, quoting Jesus' statement in John 2:19, "Destroy this temple, and in three days I will raise it up," to prove his point.[32] Significantly, this was also Nestorius' favorite proof text in his disputes with the Monophysites. The soul he describes as the "bona pars hominis" which is contained in a vessel of clay. Again, the soul is that "better part" held captive by bodily chains (anima corporis viniculis captiva). The body is the "prison of the soul," a "kind of fetters," which decays, "weighs down the soul, and greatly limits its perception."[33] At death the soul will shake off all kinds of pollutions and return, as it were, to its true spiritual condition.[34]

Calvin's doctrine, however, is much more than an echo of the Fifth Lateran Council's decree on the philosophical provability of the soul's natural immortality. Calvin, no less than Luther, would not have accepted philosophical proofs of natural immortality. He in fact plainly disavows the natural immortality of the soul.

> For when we say that the spirit of man is immortal, we do not affirm that it can stand against the hand of God, or subsist without his agency. Far from us be such blasphemy!

He then quotes Irenaeus who says, "Let us not be inflated and raise ourselves up against God, as if we had life in ourselves," [for] God alone is immortal.[35] Calvin also distances himself from the Neoplatonic world view by insisting on the corporeality of the resurrection. To be sure, he does not enlarge upon this theme in the Psychopannychia since it was a tenet which he held in common with the soul sleepers. The reality and futurity of the bodily resurrection will emerge as a major theme in Calvin's polemic against the libertins spirituels whose overly realized eschatology he vehemently opposed.[36]

In the Psychopannychia, then, Calvin, while making liberal use of Neoplatonic imagery, shies away from the notion of the natural immortality of the soul. At one point he does go so far as to deny that the imago dei has any reference to the body, a position he will later qualify in the Institutes.[37] For the most part, however, his emphasis is on the biblical/parasitic idea of the soul's constant sustenance by the power of God.

2. The Intermediate State. Calvin's primary concern throughout the treatise is to show that the soul in its posthumous state is conscious, vivid, and filled with awareness. In order to make this point against the soul sleepers he uses a variety of theological arguments. We observe briefly his appeal to exegetical, Christological and soteriological concerns.

a. Exegetical. He appeals throughout to a number of Old Testament exempla to illustrate the active, vigilant state of the soul after death. For example, Jesus likened his own death to Jonah's stay in the belly of the fish, whence the wayward prophet cried unto the Lord and was heard. Further, in an imaginative allegory, Calvin compares Isaac, who was offered on the altar but did not die, to the soul while the ram, sacrificed in his place, represents the body. In his

Commentary on Genesis, published in 1563, Calvin seems to have abandoned this use of the Isaac story declaring that "subtle allegories" have no foundation in the text."[38] In another, somewhat strained analogy Calvin compares the soul prior to its release at death to the wanderings of the children of Israel in the wilderness before their entrance into the Promised Land.[39]

However, Calvin's primary exegetical support for his refutation of soul sleep comes from several well known loci in the New Testament. The first of these is the story of the rich man and Lazarus in Luke 16:19-31 which Calvin insists on interpreting as a "vera narratio" rather than a parable. He cites Ambrose, Tertullian, Gregory, Irenaeus, Origen, Cyprian, Jerome, and Augustine in support of this view. Even Chrysostom, who did view it as a parable, saw it as proof of the sentient state of the dead, which Calvin's opponents deny. Abraham's bosom is the place where the faithful "enjoy God fully without weariness." It is that special condition of rest,

> a heavenly Jerusalem, i.e., a vision of peace, in which the God of peace gives himself to be seen by his peace-makers, according to the promise of Christ.[40]

Abraham's bosom, then, is not a dormitory, a sleeping room, but rather a repository, a waiting room; the souls therein are neither slothful nor drowsy, but tranquil and vigilant, freed as they are from the warfare of this world.

Calvin also makes use of Jesus' words to the

penitent thief, "Today shalt thou be with me in paradise" (Luke 22:42) and the cries of the souls of the martyrs under the altar in Rev. 6. These latter souls are said not only to have cried out loudly, but also to have received white robes. With a touch of sarcasm, Calvin asks: "O sleeping spirits! what are white robes to you? Are they pillows on which you are to lie down and sleep? You see that white robes are not at all adapted for sleep, and therefore, when thus clothed, they must be awake."[41] Calvin also draws on apocryphal writings such as Ecclesiasticus, Wisdom, and Esdras to which his opponents have appealed. These books, while not canonical, "ought to have some weight" as ancient pious writings.[42]

b. Christological. The very fact that Calvin chose to focus so much attention on the somewhat obscure doctrine of soul sleep indicates that for him something of tremendous theological import was at stake. In the 1536 Institutes he declares that "the whole sum of our salvation and also all its parts are comprehended in Christ," and "by faith we possess Christ and all that is his."[43] It is therefore not surprising that in the Psychopannychia Calvin appeals to the Christological focus of redemption to buttress his argument against soul sleep. There is an inviolate nexus between Christ and the believer. When Paul proclaims that we have been made conformable to Christ's death, Calvin draws a precise parallel.

> Now, O dreamy sleepers, commune with your own hearts, and consider how Christ died. Did he sleep when he was working for your salvation? ... Let any one of you now put on a supercilious air, and pretend that the death of Christ was a sleep--or let him go over and join the camp of Apollinaris! Christ was indeed awake when he exerted himself for your salvation; but you sleep your sleep, and buried in the darkness of blindness, give no heed to his awakening calls![44]

However, it is not only the death of Christ but also his resurrection, ascension, and session at the right hand of the Father which is the focus of the believer's hope.

> If, therefore, the life of Christ is ours, let him who insists that our life is ended by death, pull Christ down from the right hand of the Father, and consign him to the second death. If he can die, our death is certain; if he has no end of life, neither can our souls ingrafted in him be ended by any death![45]

c. Soteriological. The believer's union with Christ is not abrogated but rather enhanced by the death of the body. Indeed, if at death believers were to lapse into a state of unconscious slumber, their constant communion with Christ would be severed. This would mean, in effect, that we would enjoy greater bliss now than after we have departed this earthly life. "If, as they maintain, our souls are at death overwhelmed with lethargy, and buried in oblivion, they must lose every kind of spiritual enjoyment which they previously possessed."[46]

While Calvin devotes most of his attention to the

state of elect souls after death, he does not shrink from speaking plainly about the fate of the reprobate as well. They too are reserved in a chamber of waiting; but, unlike the elect who rest in the felicitous care of Abraham's bosom,the reprobate anticipate the dreadful judgment and are tortured by that expectation. Calvin is reluctant to spell out precisely the nature of the torments experienced by the damned--that would be "to plunge into the abyss of the divine mysteries."[47] Later, in his commentary on the rich man and Lazarus, he seems to have demythologized certain features of the medieval conception of hell ("For souls have not been endowed with fingers and eyes, nor are they tormented with thirst .... The Lord is painting a picture which represents the condition of the future life in a way that we can understand.") while retaining a literal enough view to speak of the reprobate as terror-struck by the incomprehensible vengeance of God, enduring the "terrifying torments" which have been prepared for them.[48] Calvin has no developed doctrine of predestination in the Psychopannychia, but even here he speaks of those "whom God has condemned and doomed to destruction," those reprobate spirits who in their lamentable posthumous state despair because they know themselves excluded from the redemption in Christ.[49]

3. The Consummation. Calvin has defined the rest or peace of the elect in terms of three distinct stages. First, there is the rest into which believers enter upon receiving the gospel. The effects of this initial

evangelical experience are described in almost Lutheran categories: God the dreaded Judge becomes now a gracious Father; instead of children of wrath, believers now see themselves as children of grace. At the same time, this rest remains partial, incomplete in this life. Human life on earth is a warfare, and those who are beset by the "stings of sin and the remains of the flesh" (simul iustus et peccator) must feel depression in the world even while they find consolation in God.[50] The second stage of rest is the peace which awaits the believer after death, the experience of Abraham's bosom. The release of the soul at death does bring about a qualitative change in the "rest" of the elect: they will then "see" their future reward from a distance, and rest in the sure hope of a blessed resurrection."[51] Yet even this rest is by its very nature also provisional. Indeed, Calvin says, our blessedness is always in progress (in cursu) up to that day which shall conclude and terminate all progress, the final consummation, the apocatastasis when, as St. Paul has it, "God shall be all in all" (I Cor. 15:28). This third, consummate stage of rest Calvin identifies with the Parousia of Christ and the resurrection of the dead.

One major objection which Calvin's opponents had levelled against traditional eschatology was that it reduced the resurrection to an anticlimactic event at the end of the age.

> How will the elect be then called to the possession of the heavenly kingdom, if they

> already possess it? How can they be told to come, if they are already there? How will the people be then saved, if they are safe now?[52]

To forestall this kind of objection, Calvin emphasizes the incompleteness of the beatific experience prior to the resurrection. At one point he suggests that elect souls continue to progress during the interval between death and the resurrection. He supports this idea with a quotation from Augustine which he only half endorses, realizing perhaps the fine line between this notion and the Catholic conception of purgatory.[53]

For Calvin the Kingdom of God is present here and now; it may "in some measure be beheld," he says. And yet we continue to pray "Thy kingdom come," because it will only properly come when it is completed.[54] In the meantime, the church is (as Calvin points out several times in the Psychopannychia) "still a pilgrim on the earth," called to live out its mission in the tension between the "no longer" and the "not yet."[55] At this point individual and corporate eschatologies converge. For Calvin the way one viewed life after death had important implications for the way one lived life before death. The regnum Christi consists both in the progress of believers (profectus fidelium) and the building up of the church (aedificatio ecclesiae). The church as a community of pilgrims, and itself a pilgrim community, is often enough the church "under the cross," ecclesia militans, the church at war with the principalities and powers of this present age. This is the church which is sustained amidst all its struggles by the assurance of its union with Christ, which not even death can sever, and by its expectation of the ultimate victory of that kingdom not made with hands. Such are the people, Calvin says, who sing and celebrate the goodness of the Lord, for he delivers and restores the hopes of those who are "afflicted, bruised and in despair."[56] Perhaps these were among Calvin's thoughts as he fled the persecution in his native France, and trudged along the road toward Basel.

And now, a brief postscript. This year, 1986, is the 450th anniversary of the first edition of Calvin's Institutes and of the official acceptance of the Reformation in Geneva. It is also the 100th anniversary of the birth of the Reformed theologian, Karl Barth. In the winter term of 1934-1935, Barth's theological students at Bonn gathered for their seminar in the home of their professor. Their text: Calvin's Psychopannychia, in the Zimmerli edition which had just been published. However, the seminar was never able to complete its study of the treatise due to the expulsion of Barth from Germany. Like Calvin 400 years earlier, Barth too found refuge in Basel. Perhaps in our own apocalyptic times Calvin's eschatology can be studied with profit by a church which, in the midst of turbulence, dares still to hope.

NOTES

[1]On Rihel see Miriam U. Chrisman, Lay Culture, Learned Culture: Books and Social Change in Strasbourg, 1840-1599 (New Haven: Yale University Press, 1982), pp. 13-25.

[2]The French translation bears the following title: Psychopannychie. Traitte par lequel est prouvé que les ames veillent + vivent apres qu'elles sont sorties des corps, contre l'erreur de quelques ignorans qui pensent qu'elles dorment iusques au dernier iugement. This translation is reprinted in Oeuvres Françoises de J. Calvin, ed. P.L. Jacob (Paris: Librairie de Charles Gosselin, 1842), pp.25-105. Jacob refers to a French edition of 1556 and suggests that Calvin himself was the translator: "Ce traité, qui avait paru en latin dès 1534, nous semble avoir été traduit par Calvin lui-même, comme un de ses ouvrages de prédilection," ibid., ix. An extant copy of the 1558 imprint is located in the rare book collection of the University of Aberdeen.

[3]It has been suggested that the section on "the state of the souls after death" in the Briève Instruction may have been the original draft of Psychopannychia. Cf. the introduction and English translation of the Briève Instruction in John Calvin: Treatises Against the Anabaptists and Against the Libertines, ed. Benjamin W. Farley (Grand Rapids: Baker Book House, 1982). Cf. also the helpful discussion by Willem Balke, Calvin and the Anabaptist Radicals (Grand Rapids: Eerdmans, 1981), pp. 25-38, 169-208.

[4]Joh. Calvin, Psychopannychia, ed. Walther Zimmerli (Leipzig: A. Deichertsche Verlagsbuchhandlung, 1932).

[5]Joannis Calvini Opera quae supersunt omnia, ed. Guilielmus Baum, Eduardus Cunitz, and Eduardus Reuss (Brunsvigae: C.A. Schwetschkte, 1863-1900), vol. 5, xxxv. Thomas F. Torrance, Kingdom and Church (Edinburgh: Oliver and Boyd, 1956), p.90, posits two early published editions before the "third" one at Strasbourg in 1542.

[6]Correspondance des Réformateurs dans les Pays de Langue Française, ed. A.L. Herminjard (Geneva: H. Georg, 1870), III, pp. 242-45 No. 490. In his Bibliotheca Universalis, published in 1545, Conrad Gesner mentions only the 1542 Strasbourg edition of the Psychopannychia.

[7]John Calvin, Tracts and Treatises, ed. Henry Beveridge (Edinburgh: Calvin Translation Society, 1851), III, p. 418. Hereafter cited Tracts.

[8]Herminjard, III, pp. 349-50, No. 527.

[9]Ibid., V, p. 132, No. 749: "Adversus veternosos hypnosophistas nihil habebis a me in praesentia, tum quia longior est disputatio quam ut epistola comprehendi queat, tum quod libellum quem ante triennium adversus eos scripseram propediem editum iri spero. Bucerus enim qui editionem ante dissuaserat nunc est mihi hortator."

[10]Emile Doumergue, Jean Calvin: Les hommes et les choses de son temps (Lausanne: Georges Bridel, 1899), I, p. 467.

[11]Tracts, p. 414-15: "Atque utinam inventa esset alia ratio, quae malum hoc plus nimio pullulascens mature recideret, ne velut cancer magis ac magis indies serpat."

[12]Etymoligically, the word "psychopannychia" means "wakeful watch of the soul" (cf. Greek, pannychios, all night long). Calvin, however, uses it as a general designation for all views, psychosomnolence and mortalism alike, not consonant with his own idea of the soul after death as capable of motion, feeling, perception, etc. Interestingly, the Oxford English Dictionary defines psychopannychia as "the all-night sleep of the soul," and cites Calvin as the first source for this meaning.

[13]Tracts, p. 415; Zimmerli, pp. 16-17: "Siquidem legimus arabicos fuisse quosdam huius dogmatis auctores, qui iactarent animam cum corpore una emori, in die

indicii utrumque resurgere." According to Eusebius, Origen held a public disputation on this subject and won back many of those who had embraced mortalist views. Eusebius: The Ecclesiastical History, tr. J.E.L. Oulton (Cambridge: Harvard University Press, 1932), II, p. 90-91 [bk. 6, ch. 37].

[14]John's views were set forth in a series of sermons preached in 1331-32. Cf. the discussion in Leroy E. Froom, The Conditionalist Faith of Our Fathers (Washington, D.C.: Review and Herald, 1955), pp. 35-37.

[15]Tracts, p. 415; Zimmerli, p. 17.

[16]Pomponazzi's treatise is translated in The Renaissance Philosophy of Man, ed. Ernst Cassirer et al. (Chicago: University of Chicago Press, 1948), pp. 257-381. The famous Apostolici regiminis is translated in part in George H. Williams, The Radical Reformation (Philadelphia: Westminster, 1962), p. 23. The original text is printed in Mansi, Concilia xxxiii, coll. 842f.

[17]Ibid., p. 24.

[18]Ibid., pp. 584-86. Tracts, p. 419; Zimmerli, p. 23.

[19]Carlo Ginzburg, The Cheese and the Worms: The Cosmos of a Sixteenth Century Miller (New York: Penguin Books, 1982), p. 75. The influence of psychopannychism on subsequent radical theologies has been traced by George H. Williams, "Socinianism and Deism: From Eschatological Elitism to Universal Immortality?" Historical Reflections/Reflexions Historiques 2 (1975), pp. 265-90. In a letter written from Louvain on 1 November 1519, Erasmus refers to certain Christian groups with mortalist views: "Quis antem crederent adhuc superesse qui stulticiam Epicuri profiterentur, negantes animas nostras superesse post obitum?" Opus epistdolarum Des. Erasmi Roterdarmi, eds. P.S. Allen and H.M. Allen (Oxford, 1906-1957), IV, No. 1039, p. 114.

[20]The Sources of Swiss Anabaptism, ed. Leland Harder (Scottdale, Pa.: Herald Press, 1985), p. 295.

[21]Bullinger's tract was never published. The original text, in Bullinger's own hand, is housed in the Zentralbibliothek Zürich Ms A 82 f. 116r-119r. Cf. Heinhold Fast, Heinrich Bullinger und die Täufer (Weierhof: Mennonitischer Geschichtsverein, 1959), p. 83.

[22]Selected Works of Huldrych Zwingli, ed. Samuel M. Jackson (Philadelphia: University of Pennsylvania, 1901), p. 252. Cf. Richard Stauffer, "Zwingli et Calvin: Critiques de la confession de Schleitheim," in The Origins and Characteristics of Anabaptism, ed. Marc Lienhard (The Hague: Martinus Nijhoff, 1977), pp. 126-47.

[23]Cf. Christian Neff's article on "Sleep of the Soul" in Mennonite Encyclopedia, IV, p. 543: "There is no convincing evidence that such a belief was held by Anabaptists or Mennonites anywhere."

[24]Quoted by Jules Pétremand in Guillaume Farel, 1489-1565. Biographie nouvelle écrite d'apries les documents originaux par un groupe d'historiens (Neuchâtel and Paris, 1930), p. 536: "... avait nulle différence entre l'âme d'une bête et celle d'une personne." The nature of the soul was one of three topics discussed by Farel and Calvin at a disputation with Anabaptists in Geneva in 1537. Cf. Balke, Anabaptist Radicals, p. 81.

[25]WA, 37, p. 151.

[26]WA, 20, pp. 162-63.

[27]Cf. Norman T. Burns, Christian Mortalism from Tyndale to Milton (Cambridge: Harvard University Press, 1975), pp. 18-41. On Luther's psychopannychism see Paul Althaus, The Theology of Martin Luther, tr. Robert C. Schultz (Philadelphia: Fortress Press, 1966), pp. 410-17. Cf. Luther's hymns, "In Peace and Joy I Now Depart," LW, 53, p. 248, and his letter to his dying father, Hans Luther in Luther: Letters of Spiritual Counsel, ed. T. G. Tappert (London: SCM Press, 1955),

pp. 29-32.

[28]Calvin's Commentary on Seneca's De Clementia, eds. Ford Lewis Battles and A. M. Hugo (Leiden: E. J. Brill, 1969), p. 93.

[29]Zimmerli, p. 29.

[30]Ibid., p. 28.

[31]Heinrich Quistorp, Calvin's Doctrine of Last Things, tr. Harold Knight (London: Lutterworth Press, 1955), p. 64; Suzanne Selinger, Calvin Against Himself: An Inquiry in Intellectual History (Hamden, Conn.: Archon Books, 1984), p. 3.

[32]Zimmerli, p. 35.

[33]Ibid., p. 50, 60; Tracts, p. 425, 440, 454.

[34]Zimmerli, p. 60: "Quamdiu in corpore est virtutes suas exserere, cum ex illo ergastulo egreditur ad deum migrare. Cuius sensu interim fruitur, dum in spe beatae resurredtionis requiescit."

[35]Ibid., p. 95; Tracts, p. 478.

[36]Farley, Treatises, pp. 292-98.

[37]Tracts, pp. 422-24. Cf. Quistrop, Last Things, p. 64.

[38]Zimmerli, p. 48; John Calvin, Commentaries on the First Book of Moses called Genesis (Grand Rapids: Baker Book House, 1984), p. 571.

[39]Zimmerli, p. 82.

[40]Ibid., pp. 43-44. Luther, Zwingli, and Calvin's exegesis of Luke 16:19-31 is compared in Auslegungen der Reformation, ed. Gerhard Friedrich (Göttingen: Vandenhoeck and Ruprecht, 1984), pp. 125-35.

[41]Tracts, p. 445.

[42]Ibid., p. 424.

[43]John Calvin, Institution of the Christian Religion, ed. F. L. Battles (Atlanta: John Knox Press, 1975), p. 77, p. 81.

[44]Tracts, p. 436, p. 439. Torrance, Kingdom and Church, p. 94, points out the Christological character of Calvin's argument in the Psychopannychia.

[45]Tracts, p. 439.

[46]Ibid., p. 443.

[47]Ibid., p. 450.

[48]Calvin's New Testament Commentaries, eds. David W. Torrance and Thomas F. Torrance (Grand Rapids: Eerdmans, 1972), II p. 119.

[49]Tracts, p. 480, p. 429.

[50]Zimmerli, p. 42.

[51]Ibid., p. 81: "Quia et deum agnoscunt sibi propitium et futuram mercedem eminus vident et in certa exspectatione beatae resurrectione acquiescunt."

[52]Ibid., p. 77.

[53]Tracts, p. 470.

[54]Zimmerli, p. 77. Cf. Calvin's exposition of the Lord's Prayer in the 1536 Institutes: "While we pray in this way, that 'God's kingdom come,' at the same time we desire that it may be at last perfected and fulfilled, that is, in the revelation of his judgment. On that day he alone will be exalted, and will be all in all, when his own folk are gathered and received into glory, but Satan's kingdom is utterly disrupted and laid low." Battles, Institution, p. 108.

[55]Tracts, p. 449. Cf. also p. 432.

[56]Cf. Torrance, Kingdom and Church, p. 96.

CALVIN'S FIRST REFORMED SERMON? NICHOLAS COP'S DISCOURSE — 1 NOVEMBER 1533

JOSEPH N. TYLENDA

THE first sermon to come from the pen of John Calvin may have been one written some 440 years ago towards the end of October 1533. At that same time of year, but sixteen years previously, Martin Luther was engaged in drawing up his ninety-five theses which he posted on 31 October 1517. If the sermon be Calvin's, then both Luther and Calvin initiated their careers with short theological compositions; Luther's was an invitation to an academic disputation, Calvin's an academic discourse. Calvin's sermon, however, was delivered by another, Nicholas Cop,[1] a very close friend who had just been elected rector of the University of Paris, 10 October 1533,[2] and who, according to custom, gave his rectorial address on 1 November, the Feast of All Saints, to the assembled faculties of the University.

Over the years, two opinions have grown up relative to the authorship of the sermon; one favors Calvin,[3] the other attrib-

[1] Nicholas was the third son of William Cop physician to Francis I and professor of medicine at the University of Paris. Nicholas was four years older than Calvin but both attended the University at the same time. They passed from fellow students to intimate friends. Nicholas graduated with the degree of Bachelor of Medicine, and in 1530 was appointed professor of philosophy at the Collège Sainte-Barbe, Cf. E. and E. Haag, *La France protestante*, Vol. 4 (Paris, 1884), pp. 615-617.

[2] For a contemporary sketch of the University of Paris, cf. Robertus Goulet, *Compendium recenter editum de multiplici Parisiensis Universitatis magnificentia* (Paris, 1517). English translation by Robert Belle Burke, *Compendium on the Magnificence, Dignity and Excellence of the University of Paris in the Year of Grace 1517* (Philadelphia, 1928). The rector was always elected from the Faculty of Arts; the prescribed term was for three months, and new elections were held in December, March, June, and October.

[3] *E.g.*, August Lang, "Die ältesten theologischen Arbeiten Calvins" in *Neue Jahrbücher für deutsche Theologie*, 2 (1893), 273-300; Emile Dou-

utes it to Cop himself.[4] Neither opinion can root itself in irrefutable documentary proof. The proponents have to be satisfied with arguments of a secondary nature whose sum total results only in probability. In the present case, one wonders whether one will ever pass from the realm of the probable to hard historical fact; perhaps we may have to remain satisfied with what is more probable.

Up to the 1960s the opinion denying authorship to Calvin seems to have been the more popular. On the occasion of the fourth centenary of Calvin's death (1964) M. Jean Rott of Strasbourg published a carefully reasoned re-examination of the question and of the discourse.[5] He argues for Calvin — has he succeeded in tilting the balance in favor of the reformer? This essay intends to present an over-view of the state of the question relative to the authorship of the discourse, note the contribution that Rott has made, and add an element or two which may point to Calvin as the more probable author of the discourse. Finally, at the end of the essay, we offer a new translation of the discourse.[6]

The All Saints discourse has survived in two versions, i.e., as found in the Geneva and Strasbourg archives. The Geneva

mergue, *Jean Calvin, les hommes et les choses de son temps,* Vol. 1 (Lausanne, 1899), pp. 331 ff.; Peter Barth, *Joannis Calvini opera selecta,* Vol. 1 (Munich, 1926), p. 1; Jean Cadier, *The Man God Mastered* (tr. O. R. Johnston [London, 1964]), p. 36.

[4] E.g., Karl Müller, "Calvins Bekehrung," in *Nachrichten der königlichen Gesellschaft der Wissenschaften zu Göttingen; Phil.-hist. Klasse* (1905), pp. 188–255; John T. McNeill, *The History and Character of Calvinism* (New York, 1954), pp. 110–11; François Wendel, *Calvin: The Origins and Development of His Religious Thought* (tr. P. Mairet [London, 1963]), pp. 40–41; Alexandre Ganoczy, *Le jeune Calvin: Genèse et évolution de sa vocation réformatrice* (Wiesbaden, 1966), pp. 67 ff.; Williston Walker, *John Calvin: The Organizer of Reformed Protestantism* (New York, 1969), pp. 68, 100–01.

[5] Rott's study, "Documents strasbourgeois concernant Calvin. 1. Un manuscrit autographe: La harangue de recteur Nicolas Cop," in *Regards contemporains sur Jean Calvin: Actes du colloque Calvin, Strasbourg, 1964* (Paris, 1965), pp. 28–49. This also appeared in *Revue d'Histoire et de Philosophie religieuses,* 44 (1964), 290–311. References are given according to the former.

[6] The first English translation was "Academic Discourse: John Calvin," translated and annotated by Dale Cooper and Ford Lewis Battles in *The Hartford Quarterly,* 6 (Fall, 1965), 76–85.

[G] manuscript, preserved in the Bibliothèque de Genève,[7] is an incomplete copy in Calvin's hand, consisting of only the first page, approximately one fourth of the discourse, and bears the heading *Concio nomine rectoris Nic. Copi scripta cal. novemb. MDXXXIV*, added by Nicholas Colladon, who evidently mistook the year.

The second manuscript, the Strasbourg [S] version, preserved in the Archives du Chapitre Saint-Thomas,[8] is the complete discourse and bears the heading *Est concio nescio cuius* in a hand other than that of the discourse. Always acknowledged as having been written in a contemporary sixteenth-century hand, it has only now been identified by Rott. The writer of S is Nicholas Cop himself;[9] the handwriting of S perfectly matches Cop's letter to Bucer of 5 April 1534, also preserved in the Saint-Thomas archives. The watermark in S, identical with the mark in Oswald Myconius's letter written from Basel to the Strasbourg pastors (9 November 1539), also in the same archives, indicates that the paper of S, came from the Basel area, and very probably from Basel itself.[10] The heading on S, "a sermon by someone or other," is now identified as the hand of Conrad Hubert, Bucer's secretary and arranger of his papers.[11]

The Strasbourg version has the appearance of a rough draft with its additions and cancellations, and this has led some to think that S must have been the actual text used by Cop on the Feast of All Saints.[12] But taking into account that S is a Basel-produced paper, it is more likely a copy of Cop's actual text — a hastily made copy, with Cop at times distracted, omitting es-

[7] Ms. fr. 145, f° 85. The text has been reprinted in *Opera Calvini quae supersunt omnia* (ed. J. Baum, E. Cunitz and E. Reuss), vol. 9, col. 873–875. A facsimile of the ms. was published by Müller, *art. cit.*, pp. 232–233.

[8] N° 174 (*Varia ecclesiastica*) IX, f° 334r°–337v°. Reprinted in *Opera Calvini* vol. 10², col. 30–36; in P. Barth, *op. cit.*, pp. 4–10, and in Rott, *art. cit.*, pp. 43–49.

[9] Cf. *art. cit.*, p. 29.

[10] *Ibid.*, note 8.

[11] *Ibid.*

[12] A. Lang, *art. cit.*, compared both versions and concluded that G is Calvin's original while S was the copy Cop used in delivering the discourse. Of the same opinion are E. Doumergue, *op. cit.*, p. 331, and P. Barth, *op. cit.*, p. 3.

sential words which he had to insert between the lines. It is presumed, then, that Cop made S when he was in Basel after having fled Paris and that he gave it to Bucer when he visited him in early April 1534.[13] In contradistinction, G is a very neat and carefully transcribed version.

In comparing both versions (the G fragment with the first part of S) it becomes clear that they differ only in non-essential details. Rott scrupulously studied the forty textual variants and concluded that G is the better developed discourse, the better all-around version. Where S is more complete, the added words are mere repetitions or synonyms. A careful scrutiny of style, choice of words, emphases, inversions, omissions, additions, etc., indicates that S cannot be a copy of G (otherwise, how explain some interesting omissions in S),[14] nor can G (the better literary version) be a copy of S.[15] If neither G nor S is a copy of the other, then one must postulate a source common to G and to S.[16] This common source could then be the first rough draft, and the difficulty in reading it can explain the differences that exist between G and S.

Because G is the better Latin composition is this sufficient ground to attribute authorship to Calvin?[17] Was the first draft (which may have served as the copy used by Cop on 1 November, but not necessarily so) written down by the reformer or by the rector?[18] If it was in Calvin's hand, then this can explain why he was able to recopy it more clearly and more accurately than Cop. If it was written in Cop's handwriting, then one wonders why his copy is less exact when compared to G. Perhaps we can only say that in copying his text he did it a bit too hastily. On the other hand, if Calvin copied the rough draft

[13] Cf. Rott, *art. cit.*, p. 31.

[14] The more significant omissions will be found in the footnotes accompanying the translation of the discourse.

[15] Rott, *art. cit.*, pp. 32–34.

[16] *Ibid.*, p. 32. In note 24 Rott postulates an intermediate text of Cop between the original first draft and S, but he does not insist on it. It is possible that the text used in giving the discourse may have been the first draft, but since S is on a Basel-produced paper, S more probably was not the first draft nor the text used on 1 November.

[17] Rott does stress this point but this is not his total argument. A. Ganoczy, *op. cit.*, p. 67, does not think the argument that forceful.

[18] Rott thinks it was written down by Calvin, *art. cit.*, p. 42.

written in Cop's hand, then he must have thought the matter through once again and thus produced the neater and better version.[19]

Throughout the years arguments have been repeatedly brought forward to deny to Calvin any part in the discourse.[20] E.g., (1) Cop was an able humanist and capable of composing such a discourse, (2) and as a humanist he was acquainted with the new religious ideas then current in France in the writings of Lefèvre d'Étaples and his followers. (3) As rector he would not have asked an obscure student to write so important an address as his rectorial discourse. (4) The invocation to the Virgin in the discourse would have been unthinkable in Calvin, (5) and the interpretation of Matthew 5:3 is quite different from the reformer's known interpretation in his commentaries. (6) The content of the discourse has nothing extraordinary about it nor does it manifest Calvin's masterly thought; (7) besides, the style lacks Calvin's characteristic persuasive orderliness. (8) Contemporary sources do not speak of Calvin as author, (9) and when his Genevan friends do, they do so erroneously and quite late.[21] (10) Finally, Calvin's flight from Paris indicates friendship with Cop, not necessarily authorship of the discourse.

None of these reasons is exciting, cogent, or overwhelming when we recall that Calvin was not a mere obscure student but the intimate friend of the rector, whose humanist friends and acquaintances were also Calvin's. Like Cop, Calvin too was a young humanist. Nor should the wisdom of the mature reformer, who composed worthy commentaries and worked tirelessly in perfecting his masterwork, the *Institutes,* be the norm for judging the theological value of his first theological composition. The power and force that the reformer gained by his innumerable sermons over a period of some twenty-five years should not be

[19] Rott does not consider the possibility that even if Calvin did write the first draft, he may have wanted to revise it by putting it into better Latin style.

[20] Cf. Rott, *art. cit.,* pp. 34–40.

[21] Only in the final edition of his *Vita Calvini* (1575) did Beza say that Calvin had a part in the address (*Opera Calvini,* vol. 21, col. 123). Beza uses the words *suggessit eam Calvinus,* but how should these words be translated? Did Beza mean that Calvin suggested the topic and treatment, or that he was the author of the address? In his earlier life of Calvin, Beza makes no mention of Calvin's part in the discourse.

expected to be present in his first attempt at sermon writing. To desire such maturity in the twenty-five year old Calvin is to deny him all theological growth. The date of Calvin's conversion to the Reformation, a date actually impossible to pinpoint, is at times operative in this discussion. Those who feel that the discourse is an extraordinary statement of Reformed beliefs usually attribute authorship to Calvin and place his conversion in 1533.[22] Those who put Calvin's conversion at a later date see the discourse as something compatible with a liberal Catholic outlook.[23]

The arguments offered to urge Calvin's authorship are as weighty as those denying it to him. (1) Because of the bond of friendship which existed between Cop and Calvin, it would be neither extraordinary nor surprising, but rather natural, for the former, not trained in theology, to request the latter, inclined towards theology,[24] to help him with his address. (2) Calvin's claim as a humanist is beyond argument — the previous year, 1532, he published his *Commentary on Seneca's De Clementia.*[25] (3) Furthermore, Calvin's friendship with Gérard Roussel, a disciple of Lefèvre d'Étaples, shows that he was indeed acquainted with the new theological thinking in Paris, and capable of including such ideas in the discourse.[26]

[22] Cf. Doumergue, *op. cit.*, p. 338.

[23] Cf. Ganoczy, *op. cit.*, pp. 68–70. The date of Calvin's conversion need have nothing to do with the question of who composed the discourse.

[24] We should recall the fact that after his father's death (26 May 1531) Calvin gave up law and devoted himself to humanistic studies of Greek and Hebrew. When he dedicated his commentary on 2 Corinthians (1546) to his former teacher, Melchior Wolmar, he wrote: "I added to the study of law Greek language and literature with you as guide and teacher. . . . And indeed it was no fault of yours that I did not profit more from this teaching, for of your kindness you were ready to lend me a helping hand until I had completed the course of study and surveyed it from start to finish. And this I should have done, had it not been for the intervention of my father's death, which was the cause of my being drawn in another direction. . ." (*Opera Calvini*, vol. 12, col. 365; Eng. trans. from J. Cadier, *op. cit.*, p. 27). Though enveloped in humanistic studies, Calvin's natural inclination was in the direction of theology, an area he studied prior to his father's decision that he pursue a career in law.

[25] Cf. *Calvin's Commentary on Seneca's De Clementia*, translated and annotated by Ford Lewis Battles and André Malan Hugo (Leiden, 1969), and Quirinus Breen, *John Calvin: A Study in French Humanism* (Hamden, Conn., 1968).

[26] In fact, after Calvin fled Paris he went to Angoulême, then in April

In addition to the above, we may also add that (4) the examination of the textual variants indicate that G, in Calvin's hand, is not only the better version, but that, if the entire discourse had survived rather than a fragment, the result would be still more convincing.[27] (5) If Calvin were merely interested in possessing a copy of his friend's discourse, then he would have made a copy. But since G differs from S to such a degree as to preclude S as being the source of G, it follows that Calvin bettered the rough draft in making G. Would he have bothered to perfect someone else's composition? It seems more likely that he wanted to better that which he himself had a share in. Considering the discourse as his own, he chose to polish it while recopying it.

Further, several ideas present in the discourse can also be found in Calvin's other early writings, i.e., immediately prior to the discourse, or shortly thereafter. (1) The discourse exhorts the audience not to confide in its own power but to distrust self and confide in God alone. This same thought is present in Calvin's letter to his friend François Daniel, in which he tells of the visit he made, together with Cop, to the convent of La Saussaye to see Daniel's sister about setting a date for taking her vows. Calvin writes: "I admonished her not to rely too much on her own resolution, and not to make any rash promises in regard to herself, but rather that she should rely upon God for all the help she needs. . . ."[28] The date of this letter is 27 June 1533, four months prior to the discourse.[29] (2) The passage on peacemakers in the discourse is an exhortation to reconcile discordant elements by the Word of truth and not by threats: "Would that in this unfortunate age of ours we could bring peace to the church by the Word rather than by the sword." Calvin uses this very idea in his letter to Francis I which precedes his *Institutes*. There he notes that in France

1534 to Nérac where Queen Marguerite had her residence. There he visited Lefèvre d'Étaples, now an old man enjoying the Queen's hospitality.

[27] Cf. Rott, *art. cit.*, p. 42.

[28] *Opera Calvini*, vol. 10², col. 10.

[29] In *Opera Calvini* the letter's presumed date is 1531, but Th. Dufour ("Calviniana" in *Mélanges M. Emile Picot*, 2 [Paris, 1913], pp. 51–66) has corrected it to 1533. Cf. Rott, *art. cit.*, p. 41, note 62.

some are disturbing the realm with fire and sword, but he urges Francis to be a true King, to recognize himself a minister of God and govern the realm by God's scepter, i.e., the holy Word.[30] The date of this letter to Francis I is 23 August 1535.

This letter to Francis I contains a few more echoes or possible contacts with the discourse. (3) Both letter and discourse speak of the Gospel as teaching the certainty that God is propitious to us. The discourse: "It is the new Gospel that Paul teaches, which the Law is incapable of surpassing, that is, we are certain that God is propitious to us"; the letter: "What is better and closer to faith than to feel assured that God will be a propitious Father. . . ."[31] (4) The discourse claims that the individual who doubts or denies the assurance of God's mercy towards us overturns the Gospel and buries Christ completely. To King Francis Calvin wrote that "ungodly men have so far prevailed that Christ's truth . . . still lies hidden, buried and inglorious."[32] (5) Both discourse and letter insist that man's good works do not merit eternal life,[33] and (6) both speak of Satan and the "strong one" of Lk 11:21. In the discourse we read: "Satan is either conquered by the Word of God or not at all . . . Christ is the stronger one. . . ."; in the letter: ". . . the light shining from on high . . . shattered his darkness, when that 'strong man' had troubled and assailed his kingdom. . . ."[34] Finally (7) allusion is made to Regulus in the discourse, the Roman who met a cruel death at the hands of the Carthaginians rather than break his promise. Calvin refers to Regulus in his *Commentary on Seneca's De Clementia,* Book I, chapter 25, the humanistic commentary he published a year prior to the discourse.[35]

[30] For the letter as it appeared with the 1536 edition of the *Institutes,* cf. P. Barth, *op. cit.,* vol. 1, pp. 21, 23. For an English translation of the letter as it appeared with the 1559 edition, cf. *Institutes of the Christian Religion,* translated by Ford Lewis Battles (Philadelphia, 1960), vol. 1, pp. 9, 12.

[31] Cf. P. Barth, *op. cit.,* vol. 1, p. 24; Eng. trans., p. 13.

[32] *Ibid.,* p. 32; Eng. trans., p. 11.

[33] *Ibid.,* p. 23; Eng. trans., p. 12.

[34] *Ibid.,* p. 33; Eng. trans., p. 28.

[35] Cf. Battles' edition of the commentary, pp. 320–21. Calvin read about Regulus in Augustine's *City of God* I, 15, and also refers to him in his *Institutes* II, iv, 8.

These several points of contact between the discourse and Calvin's earliest writings indicate that the ideas in the sermon were Calvin's ideas as well. In truth, these examples do not prove, nor are they intended to prove, beyond a doubt that Calvin composed the All Saints discourse. They suggest that the discourse more probably received its ideas from Calvin rather than vice versa. Since Calvin was the more theologically oriented it was he who more probably contributed them. This would then mean that Calvin had some share, greater or lesser, but a share, nevertheless, in the composition of Cop's discourse.

As a conclusion, an attempt to reconstruct the composition of the All Saints discourse. Cop, as newly appointed rector, was unusually occupied with the duties of office especially since the University had come into conflict with the sister of Francis I, Marguerite d'Angoulême, Queen of Navarre. At the end of September, students of the Collège de Navarre presented a satirical comedy in which they made injurious allusions to the Queen and her chaplain, Gérard Roussel.[36] Having been informed of the insulting nature of the presentation, the Queen saw that its run came to an end. Shortly thereafter, the theological faculty of the University included her book, *Le Miroir de l'âme pécheresse,*[37] among the prohibited books. The Queen took the matter up with her brother, Francis I, who intervened in her behalf. He requested of the University an explanation of its action concerning the book, i.e., whether the book had actually been examined and found that it should be included among those of unsound religion, and if so, why. As the rector, Cop had the task of carrying out the royal request. On 24 October he convoked the four faculties and severely rebuked the few who dared

[36] In the play a queen sits spinning when the fury Megaera (Megère, a name chosen because Roussel was known as *Magister Gerardus* — the first three letters of each word *Mag Ger* become Megère) appears attempting to take the queen from her work. When she does yield, he places the Gospel in her hand and immediately she forgets her old self, becomes tyrannical and persecutes the innocent with every form of cruelty. Calvin narrated these events in his letter (27 October 1533) to François Daniel, cf. *Opera Calvini,* vol. 10^2, col. 27–28.

[37] In *The Mirror of a Sinful Soul,* Marguerite speaks poetically of her faults and sins, as well as the graces and blessing granted her by Jesus Christ, her spouse. The book first appeared in Alençon in 1531, and was reprinted in Paris in 1533.

to insult and condemn the Queen and thus initiate an action in the name of the University without having received the authority to do so. He advised the gathered faculties that if they did not desire to incur the displeasure of the King, or to put themselves against the Queen, "that mother of all virtue and of all good learning,"[38] then they should not interfere in a matter so potentially dangerous. The faculties saw the prudence of Cop's words and decided to inform His Majesty that the University did not recognize the validity of the censure brought against his sister.

Within days after Cop had shown himself the determined and successful defender of the Queen of Navarre and the opponent of a certain faction in the University, he had to appear before the faculties once again, but this time on 1 November, to deliver his rectorial address.[39] Being a medical man by training and not a theologian, he asked Calvin, a friend of his who was keenly interested in theology, to help him with the discourse. Cop's recent friction with the theological faculty over Marguerite's book undoubtedly generated the remarks in the discourse against the sophists. Calvin, not only acquainted with the ideas of Lefèvre d'Etaples, but also favorable to them as espoused by Queen Marguerite and Roussel, supplied them to Cop. Together they discussed the sermon and composed it. It seems somewhat futile to try to establish who actually held the pen when the rough draft was being committed to paper. Authorship is not only attributed to the one holding the pen, but also to the one who supplies the ideas. These ideas Calvin willingly offered his friend, the rector.

Taking the first draft, Cop then copied it, perhaps changing it a bit, prior to delivery. Then in Basel, he recopied it, this copy being S. Calvin, on the other hand, copied the first draft, but not being so rushed for time polished it by introducing

[38] Cf. Calvin's letter to Daniel, *Opera Calvini,* vol. 10[2] col. 27–28.

[39] Ever since Beza's *Histoire ecclésiastique des églises réformées au royaume de France,* vol. 1 (Antwerp, 1580), p. 14, it has been said that the discourse took place in the church of the Mathurins. However, C. E. Du Boulay, *Historia Universitatis Parisiensis,* vol. 6 (Paris, 1673), pp. 238–239 says that it was in the church or the Cordeliers. Rott, *art. cit.,* p. 30, note 13, indicates that in view of what happened after the discourse, it could well have been in the church of the Cordeliers rather than that of the Mathurins.

stylistic changes and strengthened its force by additional phrases. In bettering Cop's discourse Calvin was bettering his own work.

Within days after the discourse a deposition was made against Cop, a charge of heresy, and Parlement took up the matter.[40] Cop appeared on 19 November before the University faculties declaring that they alone were competent to judge the alleged heresy of one of its members and at the same time lashed out at his accusers as being guilty of slander. The faculties of medicine and arts agreed with Cop's position, those of theology and law opposed him. The assembly adjourned without coming to a conclusion. One day shortly thereafter, as Cop was on his way to Parlement he was warned that arrest was imminent; he successfully slipped away from his companions, returned home to collect essentials, and fled Paris heading for Basel. Calvin, learning that he too was being sought, left his Paris residence for southern France. When the police did arrive to apprehend the reformer they had to be content with his papers and correspondence.

All Saints Discourse — 1 November 1533[41]

Preeminent and of an excellence greater than words can express or mind and heart can comprehend is Christian philosophy.[42] This philosophy, which unfolds the true and most certain happiness, was divinely given to man alone by Christ, and by

[40] Cf. Doumergue, *op. cit.*, pp. 353 ss.

[41] This translation is based on the Latin text published by Rott, *art. cit.*, pp. 43–49. Rott's text, in turn, is based on that found in P. Barth, *op. cit.*, vol. 1, pp. 4–10, the Strasbourg manuscript, and the facsimile of the Geneva manuscript in K. Müller, *art. cit.*, pp. 232–233. In the footnotes I have indicated the more significant additions made by Calvin to the discourse and not found in Cop's S version. Many of Calvin's stylistic changes, however, disappear in translation, e.g., where S has *a Christo divinitus data,* and G *divinitus a Christo data,* this necessarily becomes "divinely given by Christ." For the complete list of variants see Rott's text.

[42] A. Lang, *Die Bekehrung Johannes Calvins* (Leipzig, 1897), p. 46, has shown that this introductory portion of the discourse is based on Erasmus's preface, *Paraclesis, id est adhortatio ad christianae philosophiae studium,* to the third edition of his Greek New Testament (*Opera* [Basel, 1540], vol. 5, pp. 116–122). Cf. also Pierre Mesnard's "La philosophie chrétienne de Marsile Ficin à Jean Calvin," in his *Erasme: La philosophie chrétienne* (Paris, 1970), pp. 7–23, and J. Bohatec, *Budé und Calvin* (Graz, 1950), pp. 241 ff.

it we know and believe that we are the sons of God. Its splendor and excellence have caused the wisdom of the entire world to grow dim, and those who have become distinguished in it are, I think, raised far above the rest of mankind just as man surpasses the beast. This should cause us no wonder since these men, unlike other men, embrace something greater and more excellent. It is so admirable and holy that God, in order to give it to men, wanted to become a man; though he was immortal, he chose to become mortal.

It seems to me that this point has to be made: by nothing better do we know God's love for us than that he left his Word with us. What more special or more certain relationship could there be? If we praise and admire the other arts, for example, the art of discourse, or of natural science, or of ethical conduct, because of their usefulness, then what could be compared to this philosophy which shows forth the will of God, a will sought after for so long a time by the philosophers but never discovered? This philosophy which remits sin by God's grace alone: which promises the Holy Spirit who sanctifies all hearts and grants eternal life? If there is anyone who does not think this study worthy of praise, then I by no means know what he considers praiseworthy. If you seek the soul's rapture and rest from worries, and look to living well and happily, then Christian philosophy, since it restrains the restless movements of the soul, provides abundantly for it.

Because the glory and the worthiness of the Gospel are so highly esteemed, I am rather happy that an occasion is given me to explain it, and since I am the rector, the duty of office also requires it. But in so abundant and fruitful an area, where will our address find its beginning or its end? Since the field for speaking is more ample than I can encompass in this address, I will expound that powerful passage of the Gospel which, according to custom, is read in church on this day. But before I begin I wish you to join with me in fervent prayer asking the sovereign Christ, who is the one and true intercessor with the Father, to illumine our minds with his rich Spirit, and as he himself is the glory of the Father[43] we ask that our discourse may praise him, be charged with him, breathe him, deliver him.

[43] In G, Calvin added the phrase *omnium bonorum autor*, "author of all good things."

We ask him to enter our souls and deign to diffuse in us the vigor of his spiritual grace. This, I hope, we will achieve if we greet the most blessed Virgin with that solemn greeting: Hail, full of grace.[44]

Blessed are the poor in spirit, Mt. 5 [:3]

From the beginning we must energetically explore the aim of this Gospel, to which we must relate everything, and we can easily get to know it by describing the Gospel and the Law and then comparing both.[45] The Gospel is the good news and the salvation-bearing preaching about Christ, given by God the Father to give strength to and to win eternal life for all. The Law is concerned with precepts: it threatens, it coerces, it promises no benevolence. The Gospel does not deal with threats, nor does it coerce by precepts; it teaches God's utmost benevolence toward us. Therefore, whoever wishes to interpret the Gospel with purity and honesty must consider everything in the light of the above mentioned description; and those who do not follow this method will never successfully engage themselves in the philosophy of Christ.[46] The wretched sophists fall into this error; they continually quarrel about trifles,[47] they squabble and they

[44] G has *solenni illo praeconio longe omnium pulcherrimo*, "with that solemn and by far the most beautiful of greetings" together with Colladon's marginal note *Haec quia illis temporibus danda sunt, ne supprimenda quidem putavimus*. In S, Cop stopped after he wrote *Ave gratia* omitting the final word *plena*. He then crossed out the entire sentence. The ink used in cancelling the sentence is the same as used in the rest of the discourse and in Cop's letter to Bucer. Since both Bucer and Hubert had a different way of cancelling words, it seems that it was Cop himself who wanted to delete the sentence. Cf. Rott, *art. cit.*, p. 31.

[45] A. Lang, *op. cit.*, p. 53, shows that the explanation of Mt. 5:3 follows the exposition Luther gave in his sermon for All Saints in 1522 (*Kirchenpostillen, WA* vol. 10^3, pp. 400–407). The sermon was translated into Latin by Bucer in 1525.

[46] In G, Calvin turned the phrase "Philosophy of Christ" into *christiana philosophia*, thus effecting both balance and emphasis.

[47] The text quotes a Latin proverb, *rixari de lana caprina*, an expression to signify something trifling. Literally, it means to enter into a dispute about goat's wool, *i.e.*, whether the hair of goats could properly be called wool. The proverb is found in Horace, *Epistles*, I, 18, 15 and the verse has been translated as, "Another in dispute engages, With nonsense armed for nothing rages" (cf. *The Complete Works of Horace*, ed. by Casper J. Kraemer, Jr., [New York, 1936]). Erasmus includes the proverb in his *Adages* I, 3, 53 (*Opera* [Basel, 1540], vol. 2, p. 117).

dispute; they do not discuss faith, nor the love of God,[48] nor true works. They misrepresent everything; they undermine everything; they force everything to fit their own sophistic laws. I ask each of you here present, never to tolerate quietly these heresies, these insults to God.

Let us now turn our discourse back to the point whence we digressed. We must examine this passage lest we conclude that Christ has strayed from the Gospel's norm, for it does seem that he speaks of precepts when he commands us to be poor and pure in heart, to be meek and peaceable. He even offers a reward — though no one should be attracted by a prize, but freely devote himself to Christ, seek only the glory of God, and do nothing out of fear of punishment or hell. Those who have read the divine philosophy, as if with smoked glasses,[49] are of this opinion; they have but a superficial knowledge,[50] and have not advanced the Gospel one bit. Of these, I say with Paul "claiming to be wise, they became fools" [Rom. 1:22]. On the other hand, this philosophy disperses the thickest clouds and delivers us from darkness, so that he who once opened the eyes of the body may now open the eyes of the mind. With great clarity he teaches in this passage the prescriptions once obscurely written down by Moses. The Gospel prescribes nothing but it exhibits the goodness, mercy, and favors of God. Now give me your full attention for a while. No one should be amazed that[51] he includes prizes in the word reward: "Rejoice," he says, "for your reward is great in heaven" [Mt. 5:12]. God's favors are usually indicated by the word reward, though they come to us in a different manner, namely, by the grace of God alone and not be-

[48] Calvin added in G *nihil de remissione peccatorum, nihil de gratia, nihil de justificatione,* "nothing about the remission of sins, nothing about grace, nothing about righteousness."

[49] The text reads "who read the divine philosophy as through a net (*per transsenam*)." The image is that of getting a skimpy yield. The use of "smoked glasses" carries the same meaning, and furthermore, does not mix the images.

[50] The Latin proverb *primis labris degustare,* means to taste only with the upper lip, and thus it expresses the idea of "superficial." G has *supernis* in place of *primis,* while S has *supremis.* Erasmus includes the proverb among his *Adages,* I, 9, 92 (*Opera* [Basel, 1540], vol. 2, p. 318) but he uses the word *primoribus.*

[51] It is at this point that the Geneva manuscript ends.

cause of our capabilities or our worthiness. Yet, when our duties extend beyond our capabilities, these favors then make up for them and are included in the word reward. If I may now use a comparison the matter may be made much clearer. The son in a family is intent on pleasing his father with his total being and fulfills all his duties towards him. Of themselves, these actions are not sufficient to merit the inheritance but he, nevertheless, receives it. Now, you may call this a reward, not because it is owed to the son, but because it more than compensates for the son's duties towards his father. This is the way reward is usually used in the sacred writings. Is there anyone who understands eternal life as a reward in any other way? Who is so idiotic as to think and claim that eternal life is owed to our good deeds, or that our good deeds merit eternal life? Let it be generally acknowledged, then, that in this Gospel passage, as in all others, Christ places his grace and his benefits before our eyes, and that we may understand the Law he gives the true interpretation of Moses.

Let us now listen to Matthew: "Seeing the crowds, he went up on the mountain, and when he sat down his disciples came to him. And he opened his mouth and taught them, saying: Blessed are the poor in spirit" [Mt. 5:1–3]. Christian gentlemen, I ask you, direct your attention and reflect on God's singular favor towards us. No longer does he permit us to slumber in darkness but he arouses us from that deep sleep; he takes the rough and the imperfect and polishes it to perfection. The ancients had a precept not to have strange gods; but since they were immersed in the greatest ignorance, and were wanting in spirit, they thought this was to be understood of images, neither to have nor to adore any as God. "The idols of the nations are silver and gold, the work of men's hands. They have mouths, but speak not" [Ps. 135:15–16]. This interpretation of theirs should not be judged as something totally irreligious. It is true and certain, but still it does not suffice because the Lord desires a heart that is attached to no thing, to no creature. He says that he will only enter a heart that is free and unattached; he teaches that all human goods are to be despised and all human honors counted as nothing. But I am afraid that we may prefer the world to God, and that the flesh may win over the spirit. Rare is the man who does not desire to be ranked first among his peers, or who does not study divine philosophy — falsely called divine philosophy — in order to win the esteem of men? Who does not yearn to possess human goods? Who does not prefer to please men with their trifles rather than God with the truth of the Gospel? O the immeasurable stupidity of men! O the vain glory! Have we forgotten that God reads the mind and heart? Are we ignorant of the fact that he can destroy the soul and send it to hell? O brutish and senseless men who, like beasts, are only aware of the present! My brothers, do we not realize that all of us are to stand before the judgment seat of Christ? If we truly understood this, we would devote ourselves exclusively to piety and to the Spirit; we would find joy in the misfortunes, illnesses, afflictions, and tribulations that God sends us. Christ called those blessed who mourn [Mt. 5:4], who despair of their own powers and nevertheless strive after wholeness of life. These individuals undertake all things and direct all their efforts to this: that they be upright and draw others to embrace righteousness and a better way of life. These are "those who hunger and thirst for righteousness," and if God's Word cannot fail us, they "shall be satisfied" [Mt. 5:6].

No wonder then that God's Gospel gives assurance to their consciences with regard to the remission of sins, God's love, and his acceptance of them. Nothing better nor more joyful can happen to a Christian, and if men are unable to comprehend this then they must remain in deepest error. What kind of worship, piety, or religion can there be in a doubting conscience? When Paul wrote to the Romans he wanted to remove all doubt from their consciences, so he showed them by many arguments that reconciliation and righteousness do not depend on our worthiness nor our merit. He quoted the Psalms: "Blessed are those whose iniquities are forgiven, and whose sins are covered; blessed is the man against whom the Lord will not reckon his sin" [Rom. 4:7–8]. And gain, after a long discussion on the righteousness of God: "Then what becomes of our boasting? It is excluded. On what principle? On the principle of works? No, but on the principle of faith. For we hold that a man is justified by faith apart from the works of the law" [Rom. 3:27–28]. And nothing could be expressed more clearly than what Paul wrote at the beginning of chapter 4: "What then shall we say about Abraham, our forefather according to the flesh? For if Abraham was justified by works, he has something to boast about, but not before God. For what does the scripture say? Abraham believed God, and it was reckoned to him as righteousness" [Rom. 4:1–3]. By these words Paul declares, and rightfully so, that we are righteous because of Christ. Otherwise, if everything depended on the worthiness of our works, or our conduct, or our ceremonies, then everything would remain doubtful. It is the new Gospel that Paul teaches which the law is incapable of surpassing, that is, we are certain that God is propitious towards us. The Law does make mention of God's mercy but with a fixed condition — that it be fulfilled — but the Gospel freely promises the remission of sins and righteousness. God accepts us, not because we have satisfied the Law, but only because of the promises of Christ, and if anyone should entertain doubts about this, then it is impossible for him to live in godliness. In fact, he prepares himself for the fires of hell. If the Lord cured the bodily defects of only those who believed, then he will remit the sins of only those who shall believe. If we remain unsure about God's remission of sins then we are the most unfortunate of all living beings. I well know that the unspiritual man does not understand — is he worthy of love or hatred! Paul says, "The unspiritual man does not receive the gifts of God" but "the spiritual man judges all things," knows all things [1 Cor. 2:14, 15]. The individual who denies this overturns the entire Gospel, buries Christ completely, and does away with all true worship. It is impossible to worship God with doubt in one's heart. My study of the Gospel has led me to this opinion: nothing more ungodly can happen to a Christian than to have doubts. And if doubt does sometimes burden and torment us, we must cry out "Lord, help our unbelief" [Mk. 9:24]. Therefore, those who are poor in spirit, who mourn, hunger and thirst for righteousness, who despair of their own powers, are, nevertheless, certain of God's grace, the remission of sins and righteousness.

But to return to the Gospel. "Blessed are the peacemakers, for they shall be called sons of God" [Mt. 5:9]. A worthy goal towards which all Christians should strive! Is there anything better than peace, anything better than harmony? If the Gentile nations, which did not know God, gave such a high value to peace and had a temple built to it with the greatest care, then how energetically should not the Christian work to preserve peace and bring concord among dissidents! The Gentile nations looked for peace in order to live in tranquility, but Christians, knowing that they are the sons of God, look forward to something greater and better. They strive after that spiritual peace without which the world's peace is empty and trifling. The world's peace consists in removing external evils, in living amid material advantages, and in friendship with one's neighbor, but in the meantime, the root of discord by which we are God's enemies remains. How can the world's peace long endure when there is hostility to God? Therefore, blessed are those who bring peace to souls, who remove dissensions from the church, who reconcile everything with the Word of truth, who do not act by using threats. Can those who do not believe in God's Word be moved by torture? Should we not imitate Christ our sovereign leader who, though he could have destroyed all the Gentile nations and all the Jews, nevertheless, preferred to draw us by his Word? Would that in this unfortunate age of ours we could bring peace to the church by the Word rather than by the sword. Satan is either conquered by the Word of God or not at all. "When a strong man, fully armed, guards his own place" etc. [Lk. 11:21]. Christ is the stronger one, and not human reason nor the afflictions of men. Those who choose to disagree with this do not so much follow Christ as they follow the wretched pharisees. We well know that Christ desires a free, obliging, and ready heart. Blessed, therefore, are the peacemakers, who bring peace to dissidents by the Word of truth.

And further, "blessed are those who are persecuted for righteousness' sake" [Mt. 5:10]. The Romans praise their Regulus who endured an extreme and by far the most lamentable of all punishments in order to keep his word. The Athenians cannot admire Socrates enough, who with great constancy of soul did not hesitate to die, having been accused by the judges of despising the nation's gods. But who will ever consider such men happy when they did not know the righteousness of God but sought their own glory and not God's glory? We do have men who suffer persecution because of abuse shown towards good men or insults to princes, but nowhere has the Lord called these men blessed. Rather, blessed are they who, while they seek the righteousness of God, suffer persecution. Those who seek God's righteousness are those who adhere to God's Word and despise the trifles and foolishness of men, who do not depart not even a hair's breadth from the Gospel and its teachings, but diligently follow that saying of Paul: "But even if we, or an angel from heaven, should preach to you a gospel contrary to that which we preached to you, let him be accursed. As we have said before, so now I say again, If any one is preaching to you a gospel contrary to that which you received let him be accursed" [Gal. 1:8–9]. Happy and blessed must they be who suffer persecution on these grounds. Therefore, let us not have so high a regard for reputation or name, that as a result we become ice-cold in our worship of God, in explaining God's will, or in preaching the truth. "Blessed," he says, "are you when men revile you and persecute you and utter all kinds of evil against you falsely on my account" [Mt. 5:11]. Why should we dissimulate rather than speak the truth? Is it right to please men rather than God? To fear those who can destroy the body but not the soul? O the ingratitude of the human race which will not abide the slightest suffering for him who died for the sins of all, whose blood has freed us from the slavery of Satan and everlasting death! Both the world and wicked men are accustomed to give the name of heretics, seducers, imposters, and slanderers to those who labor with purity and sincerity in instilling the Gospel into the hearts of the faithful — in doing so, they think they are serving God. But happy and blessed are those who bear this with serenity, who express gratitude to God in their sufferings and bear misfortunes with great courage. "Rejoice," he says, "for your reward is great in heaven" [Mt. 5:12].

To action, then, Christian gentlemen! Let us strain our every muscle to achieve this blessedness. May God, who by his Word brings to birth faith, hope, and charity in all of us, assist us by his favor and open our minds to believe the Gospel. May we truly come to know that there is one God who alone must be served with all our being, and in whose name we must bear and suffer all. May he fill us with all joy and peace in believing, so that by the power of the Holy Spirit we may be victorious in our hope and finally enjoy an eternal triumph in heaven. Amen.

The Italian Sojourn of John Calvin: 1536

JAMES J. DIVITA

During their early careers all three great Protestant reformers of the sixteenth century—Martin Luther, Ulrich Zwingli, and John Calvin—briefly visited Renaissance Italy. Luther many years later shared his Italian experiences of 1510 with his audience; and Zwingli, who had strong views on the political and military situation in Italy, wrote brief accounts of his observations during his visits from 1512 to 1515. But Calvin differed from the other two reformers in that he never recounted his impressions and experiences during his Italian sojourn. The French reformer, then, created a blank page in his biography which both mythologizers and historians have tried to fill since his lifetime.

Calvin's Italian sojourn poses a long series of questions. What in his background attracted him to Italy? What did he hope to accomplish and with whom did he seek contact on this journey? Why did he decide to travel to Ferrara and not another Renaissance center such as Florence or Rome? What was the atmosphere at Ferrara upon his arrival? Why did he soon leave this city after undertaking the arduous trip over the Alps? Did his Italian experiences affect him at all? And lastly, why, unlike the other reformers, did he not record these experiences? Giving answers to these questions appears possible only if one searches his background intensively and seeks to delineate the political and religious forces at play upon Calvin and his environment during this period.

Calvin's first biographer, a fellow minister at Geneva and an intimate friend of the reformer for twenty years, tells us that Italy strongly attracted Calvin. Writing shortly after the reformer's death, his biographer pointed out that Calvin, after completing the *Institutes of the Christian Religion,* "felt a desire to pay . . . his respects to Italy."[1]

The son of a church lawyer, Calvin received some of the best intellectual training which France could offer in the 1520s and 1530s. He studied Latin at Paris under Mathurin Cordier, reputedly the finest Latinist in France.[2] He studied philsopohy at the college of which Erasmus was an alumnus and at which Ignatius Loyola would later enroll. At Orleans Calvin worked with Pierre de l'Etoile, the kingdom's leading lawyer,[3] and learned Greek under the German scholar, Melchior Wolmar. He sampled at Bourges the method of the Milanese jurist, Andrea Alciati, who had the reputation of brilliantly explicating legal principles and illuminating the law with history and literature.[4] After receiving his law degree, the future reformer studied Hebrew and theology. In 1532 he published a commentary on Seneca's treatise *On Clemency.* Calvin, in his first book, disagreed with Erasmus' harsh conclusions on Seneca which the Dutch humanist had recently published.

Although his direct comments on what Italy meant to him are not extant, one can be reasonably certain that study of classical languages and literature, philosophy, theology, and law could produce within Calvin the desire to see Italy, the land in which much of the work in these fields had originated. The wandering scholar was a common phenomenon of the era, and since Calvin had moved several times within France for the sake of intellectual pursuit, he could easily decide to follow hundreds of other young educated Frenchmen into Italy.

However, the opportunity to visit Italy only resulted from Calvin's possessing unpopular religious views after 1533. Many humanists, after studying the writings of the Church Fathers and delving into the Bible, became dissatisfied with the current practices of the Catholic Church and the concepts developed by scholastic theologians. Questions concerning man's justification before God, the value of good works, and the proper way to correct ecclesiastical abuses intrigued these men.

Some of Calvin's teachers and humanist friends recognized that certain answers to these questions demanded a break with the old church. His Latin instructor, Cordier, died in exile at Geneva. His Greek tutor, Wolmar, first introduced him to the writings of Luther. And the young Frenchman's close friend, Nicolas Cop, rector of the University of Paris, spoke out strongly in favor of reformed doctrine in late 1533.

The authorities reacted swiftly and vehemently to Cop's speech. King Francis I ordered the arrest of the rector and his circle. Calvin considered seeking the protection of Marguerite of Angoulême, queen of Navarre and sister of King Francis, who, "fond of composing spiritual songs for her heart was much given to God,"[5] favored reformed doctrine. But Calvin, fearing that Francis' ire could outweigh Marguerite's influence and protection, decided to leave Paris.

The young lawyer found temporary refuge at the home of Louis du Tillet at Angoulême in central France. He had met du Tillet, cannon and archdeacon of Angoulême, during student days at Paris. One of du Tillet's brothers was registrar at the Parlement of

Paris and another brother was later to become bishop of Meaux.[6]

But this prominent family could not provide the personal security Calvin needed when persecution broke out after the Placards incident in October, 1534. Because religious radicals had circulated throughout Paris posters attacking the Mass, the ire of the king knew no bounds. Calvin and du Tillet, who sympathized with reformed doctrine and had resigned his ecclesiastical positions, fled France for Basel.

The safety of this Swiss city did not turn Calvin's mind away from his quest for an influential patron. But now he sought someone who also could ameliorate the bloody persecution of Protestants in France. After completing a little handbook explaining reformed beliefs called *Institutes of the Christian Religion,* the exile wrote a dedicatory preface to King Francis himself. The king might be the patron of whom Calvin dreamed. And if he were sufficiently persuasive, Calvin would aid in convincing Francis that persecution of the adherents to the reformed religion offended God and should be ended.

Some editions of the *Institutes* date the address to King Francis "Basil, 1st August 1536,"[7] (subsequent to Calvin's Italian sojourn). Since the printing of the *Institutes* was completed in March, 1536 (as stated at the end of the first edition), the dedication could hardly have been written five months later. No break in pagination precludes the printing of the dedication after the text. Actually the address does not bear a year date in the first edition. It simply states "Basileae, X Calendas Septembres"[8] (23 August). When Calvin translated the *Institutes* into French in 1541, he dated the address 23 August 1535.[9] Moreover, since Calvin was at Basel in August, 1535, but at Geneva in August, 1536, the date ought be 1535. The erroneous dates are probably the conjecture of printers in later editions.

Calvin defended the reformed before the king by saying that they were not heretical or seditious. They composed Christ's church while their persecutors were the ungodly. He asked Francis to be aware of the duties of a true ruler: acknowledge God, the source of all authority, and protect His people. Loyal to the reformed-minded humanist tradition, Calvin cited the Church Fathers and the Bible heavily. He concluded with an appeal for royal patronage and an end to persecution.

> . . . though you are now averse and alienated from us, and even inflamed against us, we despair not of regaining your favor . . . . And even if persecution continue because it is the king's will, . . . yet shall we in patience possess our souls and wait for the mighty hand of the Lord, which undoubtedly will in time appear and show itself armed for the deliverance of the poor from their affliction, and for the punishment of their despisers, who now exult in such perfect security.[10]

But the young exile had another candidate for patron and ameliorator of persecution besides the queen of Navarre and the king of France. Either he remembered her wedding shortly after his graduation from Paris in 1528 or someone in Basel reminded him of her friendly attitude toward reformed doctrine. This personage was Renée, duchess of Ferrara, daughter of the late King Louis XI of France and sister-in-law to King Francis.

At the same time, Calvin probably hoped that Ferrara in north central Italy would become an outlet for his new-found missionary zeal. The *Institutes* were by Christmas, 1535, well on the way toward publication and in late January, 1536, Calvin had conferred with the Zurich reformer Heinrich Bullinger on the first Helvetic confession of faith. With the appearance of the handbook and the doctrinal coordination of the Swiss reform movement, the preaching of the gospel must have spread to Italy. Calvin believed he ought try to free the Italians from the blasphemies and idolatrous practices of the Anti-Christ, the bishop of Rome. He could conceive no better activity to undermine papal power than to preach the reformed religion in the pope's own bailiwick. And possibly Renée of Ferrara could not only help reduce official distrust of religious reform in France but also provide a center for Protestantism in Italy.[11]

Evidently Calvin left Basel for Italy in late February or early March, 1536. Any earlier dates conflict with the reformer's beginning publication of the *Institutes,* his probable work on proof, and his meeting with Bullinger described in a letter the Zurich reformer wrote the Genevan reformer in 1557.[12] Also any date earlier than February would mean that Calvin crossed the Alps at a time when the snows would make them impassable.

Calvin persuaded du Tillet to accompany him on his journey through the Grisons and Venetia toward Ferrara (or possibly through Constance and over the Brenner Pass to Ferrara). The two exiles adopted pseudonyms to avoid possible recognition as French Protestants. Du Tillet assumed the name "Louis de Haulmont." And since the *Institutes* bore his real name and not knowing the length of their Italian sojourn, Calvin called himself "Charles d'Espeville," after an area near his birthplace which had paid him a grain tax as part of the income from an ecclesiastical benefice his father had procured for him.

The Ferrara which Calvin and du Tillet visited was a city of 60,000, a city with a strong intellectual and cultural life that could give the humanist in the reformer an opportunity to observe firsthand an Italian seat of the New Learning. The noted Renaissance educator, Guarino da Verona, had instructed many princes, administrators, and other schoolmasters at Ferrara between 1429 and 1460. Its university, founded in 1391, was noted for its faculties in mathematics and astronomy. Nicholas Copernicus had studied here, and the pope would soon consult its faculty on the proposed calendar reform.[13] Surely Calvin recalled that the philosopher Pietro Pomponazzi had taught at Ferrara. Pomponazzi had concluded that the soul dies when separated from the body, a conclusion condemned at the Fifth Lateran Council in 1513. The reformer recalled Pomponazzi's work when in 1539 replying to Jacopo Cardinal Sadoleto, who had studied at Ferrara, he wrote:

> . . . no doubt, you were unwilling to lose the opportunity of repeating the false assertation which charges us with thinking that the soul perishes with the body. That philosophy we leave to your Popes and College of Cardinals, by whom it was for many years most faithfully cultivated, and ceases not to be cultivated in the present day.[14]

Moreover, the great poet Ludovico Ariosto had worked at the Este court until his death in 1533 and there Torquato Tasso would later compose his verses.

The city also had a long religious history. In 1438 an ecumenical council of the church had assembled in its cathedral. Girolamo Savonarola, a native of Ferrara, had influenced Duke Ercole I (1471-1505) to proclaim a general fast to prevent calamity striking Italy and to draw up plans for the establishment of an ideal state.[15] In the early sixteenth century Ferrara was probably as religious (and humanist) a center as contemporary Florence and Rome. But Protestant ideas had penetrated the city because of the presence of a sizeable number of German students at the univrsity. The university library contained heretical books and several of the professors, similar to some of their colleagues in France, were known Lutheran sympathizers and favored religious reform in the city.[16]

Besides its congenial intellectual and religious atmosphere, Calvin probably realized that Ferrara had a history of friendly relations with France. Ever since French power had arisen in Italy, the house of Valois depended on the house of Este. In 1499 Ercole I had asked Louis XII for protection. Alfonso I (1505-34) had sought French support long after the defeat of Venice in 1509, for he feared the aggressive designs of the pope.[17] After the sack of Rome (1527), this friendship was strengthened when Alfonso's son, the future Ercole II, married the Valois princess Renée.

The two French exiles seemed assured of a gracious reception at the court of Ferrara. Renée considered herself the representative of France in Italy and gained a reputation for extending her hospitality to any Frenchmen who passed through Ferrara. Once when asked why she spent so much money on assisting Frenchmen in Ferrara, Renée answered:

> They are poor Frenchmen of my nation, who if God had put a beard on my chin and made me a man they would all be my subjects; and truly they would be so now if that wicked Salic law did not hold me in check.[18]

No wonder then that Calvin considered Duchess Renée a potential patron. Her generosity was so well-known that surely she could give an ear to Calvin's petition for personal security and her becoming his literary patron.

Besides, Calvin visited Ferrara in order to encourage and utilize the religious views of its duchess. Renée was widely known for her personal piety. In France she had aided the poor and endowed churches and hospitals. In Ferrara she once missed a sermon; so she had the preacher sent to her to repeat his message.[19] But this lady had been brought up at Louis XII's court, which anti-papal emotions had permeated because of Pope Julius II's anti-French policies. Also Renée had studied under the old reformed-minded humanist, Jacques Lefèvre d'Etaples, and had been a favorite of Marguerite of Angoulême. Many reformed Frenchmen had already settled at Ferrara. The duchess' former governess and chief adviser, Madame Michele de Soubise, and her family were Protestant sympathizers. The duchess' secretary, the poet Clement Marot, was seventh on the list of suspects drawn up after the Placards incident. With such support for the reformed religion in Ferrara, Renée might be persuaded to use her blood ties with King Francis to plead the cause of the Protestants in France. And undoubtedly Calvin recognized her as the highest-ranking Protestant sympathizer in the Italy of 1536, a woman who believed could succor those who sought to preach the unadulterated Word of God.

The exact date of Calvin's arrival in Ferrara is impossible to fix, but according to tradition he appeared during Lent. Consequently his earliest possible date of arrival is Ash Wednesday, 1 March 1536. Although the "beginning" or "end" of Lent is not traditionally mentioned, this is hardly sufficient reason to state categorically, as some historians have done,[20] that Calvin arrived on 23 March, near the exact middle of Lent.

But when the twenty-seven year old Calvin arrived at Ferrara he probably found the situation inauspicious for the founding of his New Jerusalem. The duke, Ercole II (1534-59), apparently quarreled constantly with Renée because of her free spending. He found it difficult to support a wife of royal blood in the style to which she was accustomed.[21] A struggle ensued between Ercole and Madame de Soubise over who would dominate Renée. The duke was victorious —the governess left Ferrara on 20 March 1536.

Nevertheless, the presence of other French Protestants (whom the duchess supported financially) in his capital embarrassed the duke politically. Ferrara technically was a fief of the pope, who for many years sought an excuse to absorb the duchy into the Papal State (a goal actually accomplished in 1598). In 1482 Pope Sixtus IV had engineered an alliance with the Republic of Venice against Ercole I. Pope Julius II had exerted pressure on Alfonso I to obey papal commands in 1510. And nine years later Pope Leo X had sent an army to take Ferrara from the Este family. Although Popes Adrian VI, Clement VII, and Paul III had confirmed the autonomy of Ferrara, Ercole realized that the Holy Father might use the existence of Protestantism in Ferrara as a pretext for further action against the duchy. And since he controlled the mouth of the Po River and ruled a rich agricultural region (both coveted by the Venetians) and his territories lay between the Most Serene Republic and the States of the Church, continued friendly relations with Rome were imperative.

But past pro-French policies and the French sympathies of his duchess also embarrassed Ercole. When the duke of Milan died in 1535, Francis I had sent an army over the Alps to force the Emperor Charles V to recognize his claim to this duchy. By mid-1536, the French occupied a sizeable portion of the domain of Charles' brother-in-law, the duke of Savoy. Meanwhile the emperor had arrived at Naples from Tunis, which he had wrested from the Moslems. Ercole, who had returned from an imperial audience at Naples just before the beginning of Lent, recognized the difficulty of his position. If the emperor suspected him of favoring the French in this war, he would be at the mercy of the imperial legions. And if he favored the emperor and the French were militarily victorious, his interests might be jeopardized during subsequent peace negotiations.

The presence of Calvin and other reformed Frenchmen in Ferrara prevented Ercole from enjoying court life or even composing Latin verse as he liked to do for relaxation. An incident with religious and political implications soon occurred. Jehannet (Gianetto), a twenty-year old French singer whom Ercole had taken into his service on Renée's recommendation, had stormed out of church at the adoration of the Cross during the Good Friday service, shouting blasphemies against Catholic ritual and practices.

Some historians imply that Calvin was the organizer of the Jehannet incident. The reformer had shown such tendencies when he was arrested for creating a disturbance in the Noyon cathedral in 1534. Non-conformists, they believe, always committed excesses at Easter time. Calvin's arrival during Lent was providential, for he provided them the needed leadership.[22]

No documentation links Calvin with the Jehannet incident. The creation of disturbances does not appear to be one of the reformer's methods. In his address to King Francis, he had defended the reformed by saying that they did not create disturbances. He pointed out that their opponents disturbed the peace by suppressing the adherents of the Truth. The Noyon episode can be explained by recalling that both his father and oldest brother clashed and were unpopular with local church authorities. Couldn't this unpopularity be reflected in Calvin's arrest by these same authorities?

That Calvin as the author of a recently published book sought fame or as a religious zealot sought martyrdom[23] appear unlikely from one who had adopted a pseudonym for safety's sake. The Protestant Johann Sinapius, physician to the Este Court, wrote Calvin several years later that although they had met in Ferrara he never dreamed that this young Frenchman with the quiet mien was capable of writing such a fine book as the *Institutes*.[24] Since Sinapius did not consider Calvin a leader of the Protestants at Ferrara, the possibility that the reformer organized the Jehannet incident seems nil. Jehannet was capable of organizing his own incident. After all, he was twenty-third on the list of suspects drawn up for King Francis after the Placards incident in Paris.[25]

The local inquisitor soon arrested Jehannet, undoubtedly with Ercole's permission since the singer was in ducal service. Within a few days the singer confessed that he as well as most of the duchess' protegés were Protestant. Fear of persecution rapidly spread within the French community at Ferrara. The climax came three weeks later when the Inquisition arrested Jean de Bouchefort, a priest of the Tournai diocese, and charged him with adhering to Lutheranism.[26] The duke apparently was using the Inquisition to eliminate the French Protestants in Ferrara and simultaneously reinforce his influence over Renée. As an enemy of heresy and seditious Frenchmen the duke could ingratiate himself in the eyes of pope and emperor.

According to some historians, the Inquisition incarcerated Calvin himself. While he was being removed from Ferrara to Bologna by order of the pope, an armed band, probably sent by Renée, released him.

No extant documentation supports the legend of Calvin's imprisonment by the Inquisition. Muratori, the source of the story, says: "I am assured by one who has seen the acts of the Inquisition . . .".[27] So even his evidence was second-hand. The acts of the Inquisition of Ferrara cannot be consulted, for they were removed from Ferrara at Napoleon's order during the 1796 campaign and lost. The papal directive of 10 May 1536 removing the heretics to Bologna is extant.[28] It contains but one name—Bouchefort. Calvin's name could not have appeared in any documents because he used a pseudonym. That Calvin also used the pseudonym "Bouchefort" is possible but not probable, since a man bearing the name "Jean de Bouchefort" appeared as chaplain to Renée in the 1560s and 1570s when Calvin either was in Geneva or had died. Bouchefort might have been the prisoner released on the road to Bologna, but that this prisoner was not Calvin is rather clear.

The story of Calvin's release from captivity on the road to Bologna has interesting parallels. St. Peter was released from his chains so that he could continue his work of spreading the gospel. St. Paul became a vigorous Christian missionary after his conversion on the road to Damascus. Even Calvin's contemporaries, Luther and Zwingli, were "miraculously" saved to continue their work. Luther avoided the clutches of the emperor by being kidnapped on the road out of Worms after the diet of 1521. And Zwingli survived the plague which carried off a sizeable portion of the population of Zurich in 1519. At this rate something similar must have happened to Calvin!

Calvin probably left Ferrara between the arrests of Jehannet and Bouchefort, sometime between 14 April and 4 May 1536. The reformer had no reason to leave before 14 April, for no fear of persecution existed at that time. He still could fulfill his aims in coming to Ferrara. In the first French translation of Calvin's earliest biography we are told that the reformer returned directly to Basel from Ferrara.[29] On 2 June 1536 Calvin was in Paris to sign a power of attorney giving his brother Antoine the right to sell their parents' land.[30] At this time it took a minimum of fifteen days to travel from Ferrara to Basel, and probably a similar period to reach Paris from Basel. At that rate Calvin could hardly have remained in Ferrara beyond 4 May if he met his brother in Paris on 2 June.

This chronology conflicts with the story that the reformer stopped and preached at Aosta on his return from Ferrara. Supposedly he made many converts there and strengthened the local Waldensians in their faith. But when he was accused of plotting to detach Aosta from Savoy and unite it with the Swiss cantons, he fled the city. A procession in which the bishop, nobility, and people participated was held to thank God that the area had been delivered from Calvin's heresy.[31]

The minutes of the estates of Aosta show that on 28 February 1536 the estates voted to remain loyal to the duke of Savoy and Catholicism. It ordered on 22 March that an annual procession be held commemorating this decision. This procession was conducted on 1 January 1537.[32]

Since Calvin surely did not abandon Ferrara before 14 April, he can scarcely be the cause of the Aosta estates' decision of 28 February. And since the procession also was ordered before 14 April, it is impossible that Calvin's preaching was its cause.

That Calvin ever passed through Aosta is doubtful, despite a recent biographer's assertion to the contrary.[33] On 3 April 1536, the French army occupied Turin, southeast of Aosta, and between Ferrara and Aosta. To pass through a scene of French and imperial military action was impossible. Calvin found this the case when a few months later he tried to reach Strasburg from Paris and had to detour through Geneva to avoid the military contestants. Even emissaries from Ferrara to the French court at Lyon avoided the Aosta-Turin region and reached Lyon by way of northern Switzerland.[34]

To complicate this episode, a monumental cross was erected before the Waldensian church in Aosta. It bore the inscription, "Hanc Calvini Fuga erexit anno MDXLI." In that year the local estates repeated their 1536 decision to support their duke and Catholicism in anticipation of renewed military conflict between Francis and Charles.[35] The simultaneous erection of a marker honoring a Protestant reformer is inconceivable. Moreover, that Calvin's visit would be memorialized in 1541, at a time when he was in disgrace at Geneva and had been exiled from that city for three years is unlikely. Probably the reformer's contemporaries did not even erect this cross. More likely those who much later desired to use the story of Calvin's flight to link the great reformer with the local reform movement were responsible for its construction.

On the surface Calvin's sojourn in Italy was a dismal failure. His first biographer wrote that he said farewell to "Italy, whose territories he entered, to use his own language, only that he might leave them."[36] His fear of arrest by the Inquisition had permitted him to spend too brief a time in Ferrara to absorb fully its humanist atmosphere.

Although he had an opportunity to meet Duchess Renée and "confirmed her in a sincere zeal for religion, to the utmost of his abilities . . .,"[37] she was no longer in a position to become his literary patron and plead the cause of the reformed religion before King Francis. In fact, she could not even provide for the safety of her protegés in Ferrara. The establishment of a missionary center for Italian Protestantism had to be postponed indefinitely.

Renée, only a few weeks after Calvin's departure, begged the French ambassador at Rome to seek an audience with the pope. The ambassador should ask the pope not to deal harshly with her countrymen accused of heresy. She pointed out that she was full of reverence and devotion toward the Holy Father, and that she, as her Most Christian ancestors, would always use her strength for the pope's benefit.[38] The sincerity of this sudden upsurge of loyalty to the Holy See can easily be questioned. But it does indicate that Renée found herself in a changed political and religious situation as a result of the Inquisition arrests and believed that such a protestation of fealty would be to her advantage.

The reformer's first biographer declared that Calvin did as well as possible in Ferrara "according to the existing state of affairs."[39] The recognizable obstacles to Calvin's effectiveness were the Jehannet incident and the duke's response to it. One suspects that Calvin was an innocent witness to a plot which Francis I or his diplomatic representatives arranged (or at least used) to exert pressure upon Duke Ercole to abandon his neutralist policy and adopt a pro-French policy. When Ercole had clashed with Madame de Soubise, French diplomats tried to conciliate the duke.[40] Now the tactic was to demand concessions from him.

On Easter Sunday, 16 April, a courier arrived at the Este court bearing a letter from the French ambassador in Venice. The ambassador demanded that the duke immediately release Jehannet, a French subject. The singer had been arrested only two days earlier. Ercole replied on 18 April that the ambassador must be ignorant of the reasons for the singer's detention, for he could hardly condone sacrilegious actions.[41]

What avenues were open to the duke? If he released the prisoners he would appear in the eyes of pope and emperor not only as a friend of the French but also someone who did not punish heretics. And if he permitted church authorities to wield extensive power in his duchy he would undermine the sovereignty of his own government. Ercole realized that if he chose the former policy he would alienate pope and emperor and be forced into the arms of the French.

The duke bided his time. In May the French obtained a papal brief removing the prisoners from the duke's jurisdiction to Bologna. They hoped that this move would embroil Ercole with their opponents; or at least it would give them more time to negotiate for the prisoners' release. Ercole's firmness in the face of French pressure paid off. He had eliminated the reformed circle surrounding the duchess and demonstrated to all that, despite traditional friendship with France, the house of Este could still follow an independent policy. The removal of the prisoners to Bologna removed them from the duke's concern.

Even if his mission to Italy seemed fruitless at the time, Calvin's fortune soon improved. By August, 1536, he had arrived in Geneva. His companion on the Italian sojourn, du Tillet, had preceded him to Geneva and informed the reformer Guilliame Farel of his presence. Farel persuaded Calvin to remain in Geneva and work among its people. The dream of a New Jerusalem that Calvin had hoped to realize in Ferrara came true in Geneva. What fate had not permitted in one city, it permitted in another.

But Calvin's Italian sojourn had definite long range results. Despite her outward adherence to Catholicism, Renée continued to hold Calvin in high regard.[42] The reformer reciprocated the admiration. In 1551 he wrote a friend a letter of introduction to Renée. He described her as "the hope and support of Reform in Italy."[43] Four years later, after Ercole had placed Renée under palace arrest for adhering to reformed doctrine and succoring at Ferrara almost every important Italian heretic, Calvin encouraged her to remain faithful to Scripture in adversity.[44] He signed this letter with the pseudoynm he had used in Italy: Charles d'Espeville.

But the friendship of reformer and duchess based on the encounter of 1536 blossomed forth only in the 1560s. She returned to France after Ercole's death in 1559 and openly espoused the Huguenot cause. Calvin wrote much to and about Renée in the last few years of his life. He wrote her three letters in 1564, the last dated 4 April, less than two months before his death.

A second result of Calvin's Italian sojourn was a continued interest in Italian Protestant affairs. Throughout the period Calvin welcomed reformed Italians to Geneva. Probably the most important of these refugees was the noted Capuchin, Bernardino Ochino, whom Renée sent to Calvin from Ferrara in 1542.[45] But equally important to him was the instilling of strong faith in Margaret, duchess of Savoy. This niece of Renée and sister of King Henry II of France followed in the footsteps of Marguerite of Angoulême and Renée: she leaned toward reformed doctrine.[46] The resurrected dream of a center for Italian Protestantism certainly enlivened Calvin's last years. In fact, part of his last letter to Renée dealt with the religious problems which Margaret faced.[47]

But the most important outcome of Calvin's Italian sojourn was the hardening of his attitude toward Catholicism and his harsh condemnation of Nicodemism (practicing Catholicism while holding Protestant beliefs). According to the French translation of his first biography, during his Italian sojourn he wrote two letters to friends in France: one to Nicholas Duchemin and the other to Gerard Roussel.[48] Both letters were published in early 1537.

Duchemin, whose hospitality Calvin had enjoyed as a student at Orleans, asked Calvin's opinion on whether a reformed person may attend Mass. In a preface to Calvin's works which appeared in 1552 (during his lifetime), the translator wrote that the reformer became aware of such a problem during his Italian journey.[49] Perhaps the question had become real as a result of the Jehannet incident. Calvin replied to Duchemin that man must obey God's commands in Scripture.

> This is specially forbidden you, that anyone should

see you sharing in the sacrilege of the mass, or uncovering any superstition whatever of a nature whereby the glory of God is dimmed, His religion profaned, His truth corrupted.[50]

Roussel, chaplain to Marguerite of Angoulême, had assisted in converting Calvin to reformed doctrine. In 1536 he was consecrated bishop of Oloron in Navarre. The reformer addressed his letter "to an old friend, now a prelate," whom he believed had sacrificed principle to comfort. Possibly contact with clergy in Ferrara and first-hand observation of religious conditions in Italy sharpened his opinion of the old church. He pointed out that the Catholic clergy were false teachers and inadequate shepherds to their flocks. They had obscured the meaning of Scripture and devised fables to corrupt the common people. Calvin denounced vicars (whom he himself had employed to operate the parishes which paid for his education) as "petty thieving and robbing rascals" who "committed infinite numbers of rapines, extortions, lootings, robberies, and brigandages" for parish priests and bishops. He summed up by telling Roussel:

I treat you again very sweetly, when I call you a murderer and a traitor. For there is a malodorous crime detestable above all others: your selling and crucifying the Son of God all your days . . .[51]

Unlike these two letters which make no direct allusions to his Italian sojourn, the third is specifically related to Calvin's experience at Ferrara. Calvin was told at Geneva that the reform-minded François Richardot, Duchess Renée's chaplain, had advised her to attend Mass to avoid giving scandal to others. Richardot contended that Mass attendance, even by the reformed, was considered admissable in German evangelical churches.

The reformer wrote Renée that Richardot, whom he had met in Ferrara, had impressed him as a man of ambition and greed who understood little of Scripture. He even was in error about the attitude of the German evangelical churches toward Mass attendance. Then Calvin reversed Richardot's argument by saying that attending Mass scandalized others by corrupting them to disobey God's commands through our bad example.[52]

Some historians contend that this letter was written in October, 1541,[53] not in 1537. But the letter begins, "I humbly beseech you that you would take in good part my boldness in writing . . ."[54] This appears to be an opening of a first letter to an important personage. That Calvin had not written Renée for five years after the trip he undertook to meet her would indeed be peculiar. From his reference to another author's book[55] (published in 1537) and his allusion to a letter he had recently written on the subject of Mass attendance[56] (probably the Duchemin letter) the preferred date of this letter is 1537. Since Richardot was already chaplain in 1537[57] and this letter contains no comment that he had changed his position on Mass attendance, Renée needed advice in 1537, not first in 1541.

One suspects that the reformer was disappointed that the duchess did not follow his advice. Renée kept Richardot as her chaplain until 1544, when he was arrested for plotting against the duke. Upon his release he returned to France. But Calvin's charge that Richardot was not strong in the reformed faith was vindicated when Richardot became bishop of Arras in 1561.

Within a few years after his leaving Italy, Calvin

acquired a reputation as a pastor of souls. The letter addressed to Duchess Renée and his work in Geneva illustrate this new side to his earlier interest in theology. The wide circulation of his textbook for theology students and manual for preachers, *Institutes of the Christian Religion,* characterized by rigidity of position and clarity of style, had in the same period of time earned for him the reputation of Protestantism's leading dogmatist. And the two letters written during the Italian sojourn gained him the respect due a leading polemicist.[58] This incident measures the growth of his reputation: when the citizens of Geneva in 1539 wanted a defense of their faith in reply to the letter of Cardinal Sadoleto, they requested Calvin to undertake the task —despite the fact that they had expelled him from their city in 1538!

The sojourn in Italy appears at the turning point in Calvin's life. Before 1536 the young Frenchman was a humanist with an interest in theology. After 1536 Calvin was a pastor who used theology to instruct his people on their relationship to God. How exactly his experiences in Italy transformed him is difficult to assess, for Calvin himself never speculated on the impact and significance of his Italian journey.

Why did Calvin, unlike Luther and Zwingli, not in over a quarter century recall his impressions of Renaissance Italy?

The answer seems to be that Calvin was of another generation and had an outlook different from that of the other two reformers. In their day ecclesiastical abuses and papal excesses were common knowledge and attacks on these problems were fashionable. Their prime years were noted for the bitter satires of Erasmus, Ulrich von Hutten, and the pamphleteers.

By the time of Calvin's Italian sojourn almost two decades had passed since Luther's posting of the Ninety-five Theses. What more could be said about clerical corruption after the appearance of Luther's three tracts of 1520 and Zwingli's pamphlet on papal avarice in 1519? These attacks were necessary to bring about a popular awareness of the need for a thoroughgoing and permanent reform. But by Calvin's prime Protestantism was a permanent part of life in vast sections of Europe. The goal then was not to fight for the survival of Protestantism; but, as shown from his correspondence with the English, Polish, and Danish kings in the 1550s, he sought to gain for it the aura of respectability which was necessary for its wider penetration.

Impressions of Italy usually included attacks on the papacy. Perhaps since Calvin did not visit Rome, he was not as shocked as the other two reformers. Also, unlike Luther, he concentrated on politics and culture as well as religion during his Italian sojourn. His major serious attack on the papacy came eight years after his Italian journey. He condemned Pope Paul III's letter of complaint to the emperor who proposed to call a reform council on his own authority. Even in the last edition of the *Institutes* (1559), only about twenty percent (Book IV, chaps. 4-11) of the book deals with the papacy and Catholic church structure. Only among second-generation Calvinists like the English Puritans did anti-papal vehemence revive. As in the days of Luther and Zwingli, anti-Roman sorties were again fashionable.

In Calvin's day the greatest challenge to the reformed religion did not come from Catholicism but from Lutheran and radical Protestantism. His major work on Catholic doctrine in this period was his antidote to the canons and decrees of the Council of Trent which appeared in 1547. But he wrote several lengthy tracts between 1554 and 1561 defending his doctrine on the Eucharist from Lutheran attacks. In 1542 Calvin published his anti-Anabaptist tract, *Psychopannychia,* and in 1553 he busied himself with the trial and execution of Servetus the Unitarian at Geneva. While Luther in the 1540s still heaped abuse upon the pope and Italians as recorded in the *Table Talk,* Calvin apparently felt that it was more beneficial to correct those who used their Christian liberty improperly.

One reason for the attacks of the other two reformers on Italy and Italians was political prejudice. Germany and Switzerland were decentralized states which foreigners could easily exploit. Luther held that the Germans were financially and administratively slaves to an ecclesiastical structure dominated by Italians. Zwingli condemned the use of Swiss mercenaries by Italian princes. But Calvin did not conceive of Italians as the enemy. In a centralized state like France, the monarch, not the pope, controlled the Church. Any suppression in France of what Calvin believed the Word of God was the work of native-born rulers and clergy, not of Italians. And at Geneva the enemy was not pope or bishop but the duke of Savoy, who was more French than Italian.

Calvin probably recognized that Renaissance Italy was in decline. Unlike in the two other reformers' prime years, its worldly atmosphere was no longer in sharp contrast with the religious atmosphere of northern Europe. The task now was to restore religion and morality in Geneva and elsewhere, not just lament that Italy was degenerate.

The reformer of Geneva might give some of these

reasons for not recording his reactions to Italy in 1536. All one can say with certitude is that the historian through research and conjecture can convert the blank page of Calvin's Italian sojourn into a hazy page.

NOTES

[1]Theodore Beza, *The Life of John Calvin* (Philadelphia: J. Whetham, 1836), p. 11.

[2]Williston Walker, *John Calvin* (New York: G. P. Putnam's Sons, 1906), p. 34.

[3]Beza in John Calvin, *Tracts and Treatises on the Reformation of the Church* (Grand Rapids: Wm. B. Eerdmans Publishing Co., 1958), I, 1x.

[4]Abel Lefranc, *La Jeunesse de Calvin* (Paris: Librairie Fischbacher, 1888), p. 80.

[5]Pierre, Abbé de Brantôme, *Book of the Ladies* (Boston: Hardy, Pratt and Co., 1902), p. 235. The author was a sixteenth century observer of French court affairs.

[6]Jules Bonnet (ed.), *Letters of John Calvin* (Edinburgh: Thomas Constable and Co., 1855), I, 36, n. 1.

[7]John Calvin, *Institutes of the Christian Religion,* trans. John Allen (Philadelphia: Presbyterian Board of Christian Education, 1933), I, 40.

[8]Guilielmus Baum *et al.* (eds.), *Corpus Reformatorum, Joannis Calvini Opera quae supersunt omnia: Institutio Religionis Christianae* (Brunswick: C. A. Schwetschke, 1869), XXIX, 26.

[9]Emile Doumergue, *Jean Calvin: les hommes et les choses de son temps* (Lausanne: Georges Bridel et Cie., 1899-1902), I, 513.

[10]Calvin, *Institutes,* I, 40.

[11]John T. McNeill, *The History and Character of Calvinism* (New York): Oxford University Press, 1954), p. 129.

[12]Doumergue, II, 6.

[13]Letter of Pope Paul III to Prof. Gaspare Insoni, dated 12 October 1537, reprinted in Bartolommeo Fontana, *Renata di Francia* (Rome: Forzani, 1889), I, 505.

[14]Calvin's reply to Sadoleto's letter to the people of Geneva in Calvin, *Tracts*, I, 47.

[15]Edmund G. Gardner, *Dukes and Poets in Ferrara* (New York: E. P. Dutton and Co., [1904]), p. 324.

[16]Fontana, I, 309.

[17]Francesco Guicciardini, *Storia d'Italia* (Paris: Presso Baudry Libraio, 1832), III, 135.

[18]Brantôme, p. 222.

[19]G. K. Brown, *Italy and the Reformation to 1550* (Oxford: Basil Blackwell, 1933), p. 99.

[20]Fontana, I, 333.

[21]Frederic C. Church, *The Italian Reformers 1534-64* (New York: Columbia University Press, 1932), p. 173.

[22]Fontana, I, 310-11.

[23]*Ibid.*, p. 311.

[24]Doumergue, II, 64.

[25]*Ibid.*, p. 52.

[26]Walker, pp. 151-52.

[27]Ludovico Antonio Muratori, *Annali d'Italia* (Naples: Giovanni Gravier, 1773), X, 249.

[28]Fontana, I, 501-503.

[29]*Ibid.*, p. 288.

[30]Lefranc, pp. 190-91.

[31]John Stoughton, *Footprints of Italian Reformers* (London: Religious Tract Society, [1881]), pp. 29-30.

[32]Doumergue, II, 86-87.

[33]McNeill, p. 131.

[34]Fontana, I, 329-30.

[35]*Ibid.*, pp. 304-305.

[36]Beza, pp. 11-12.

[37]*Ibid.*, p. 11.

[38]C. A. Cornelius, *Historische Arbeiten vornehmlich zur Reformationszeit* (Leipzig: Duncker und Humblot, 1899), p. 117.

[39]Beza, p. 11.

[40]Michel François, *Le Cardinal François de Tournon* (Paris: E. de Boccard, 1951), p. 128.

[41]Fontana, I, 314-15.

[42]Beza, p. 11.

[43]Doumergue, II, 68.

[44]Rudolf Schwarz (ed.), *Johannes Calvins Lebenswerk in seinen Briefen* (Neukirchen: Neukirchner Verlag, 1962), III, 745-46.

[45]Thomas M'Crie, *History of the Progress and Suppression of the Reformation in Italy* (2d ed.: Edinburgh: William Blackwood, 1833, pp. 221, 421.

[46]Giovanni Jalla, *Storia della Riforma in Piemonte fino alla Morte di Emanuele Filiberto 1517-1580* (Florence: Libreria Claudiana, 1914), p. 110.

[47]Schwarz, III, 1277-78.

[48]Doumergue, II, 22.

[49]*Ibid.*, II, 22, n. 1.

[50]Walker, p. 155; and Calvin, *Tracts,* III, 406.

[51]Dourmergue, II, 27.

[52]Cornelius, pp. 119-20.

[53]Bonnet, I, 281, n. 3.

[54]*Ibid.*, p. 271.

[55]*Ibid.*, p. 280.

[56]*Ibid.*, p. 281.

[57]Doumergue, II, 60.

[58]*Ibid.*, p. 28.

V

WHAT CALVIN LEARNED AT STRASSBURG

FRANKLIN H. LITTELL

We live in a time of rapid change. One of the marks of the age is a radical reshuffling of alignments and alliances among the churches. There was a time not long ago when any genuine traffic between Catholics and Protestants was strictly clandestine, regarded in both camps as a kind of ultimate disloyalty. Now most topics of concern are open-

---

Franklin H. Littell received the Ph.D. from Yale in 1946. He has served as minister of youth at Central Methodist Church in Detroit, dean of the Boston University chapel, president of Iowa Wesleyan University, and professor at Emory University, Perkins School of Theology, Chicago Theological Seminary, and Temple University. He has been a consultant to the National Conference on Christians and Jews, and president of Christians Concerned for Israel. He has contributed articles to Reformation Studies, *and has written several books, including* The Anabaptist View of the Church, The Free Church, The German Phoenix: A Tribute to Menno Simons, *and* Sermons for Intellectuals.

ly discussed, and Catholics and Protestants even celebrate communion together on occasion.

Similarly, among Protestant groups great change is evident. A man's worst adversaries are sometimes those of his own household, whereas in the congregations of erstwhile opponents he finds allies to go forth with him to cast out demons and heal the distressed. The relationship of those who stand in the tradition of Calvin's theocracy and those who claim spiritual descent from the Anabaptists is very much like that today.

A few years ago the two groups were still debating the "church type" and the "sect type" and arguing the measure of Christian responsibility in the conduct of government. Today there is a perception that the issues lie elsewhere. In the churches, they lie between a radical individualism and the renewal of Christian community. In the body politic, major areas of life—public education, social welfare, higher education, medical care—have been largely freed from church control or influence altogether. All Christians share a like restlessness, a feeling of being shoved to the margins of historical and national development. Whether this unease is firmly grounded or not, the descendants of both Calvin and the Anabaptists can surely agree that their chief problem is no longer with each other. A sketch of one period of the early and common history of the two groups, when encounter proved fruitful in spite of many obstacles, may indicate that both already owe each other much and that neither needs to feel any real embarrassment if the mutual indebtedness increases in the years ahead.

* * *

To take one example, the covenant theology of the Calvinist Reformers took firm shape in a lively exchange with the Anabaptists. It is a serious mistake, though an ancient one, to identify the *Täufer* as individualists or enthusiasts (*Schwärmer*). Such charges will no longer stand the best of historical evidence, as the distinguished scholar Leonard Verduin has made quite clear in *The Reformers and Their Stepchildren.* The Anabaptists were champions of religious liberty and the voluntary covenant, and they consciously separated from and condemned the revolutionaries and the spiritualizers.[1]

The first church covenant on record was adopted by an Anabaptist congregation in Frankfurt am Main. Michael Satteer's *Seven Articles* of 1527 were concluded in a covenant to do God's will, sealed by baptism of believers into the "body of Christ."[2] For the Anabaptists the "door into the sheep-stall" was adult baptism, and the covenant concept spread with the movement into Strassburg, Hesse, and the Netherlands. In a short time the writing of names in a book came to be practiced, referring to the angel's writing in the Book of Life.

One misses the real point of controversy if he erroneously assumes that the Anabaptists were individualists or defenders of private inspiration. On the contrary, they were critics of Christendom and defenders of the voluntary covenant. Even here it would be a mistake to accuse them of synergistic tendencies, much less Pelagian. This was the error of the famous Lutheran scholar Karl Holl, who assumed that because the Anabaptists advocated voluntary church affiliation *vis-à-vis* the government they must also be theological voluntarists. Holl used the term *Freiwilligkeitskirche* to elide the political and theological issues,[3] which tells us more about his view of church-state relations than it does of the actual Anabaptist position. It is perfectly possible to have a strong view of the independence of the church from political control (voluntary-ism) without having a theologically questionable stance (voluntarism). In point of fact, the general Anabaptist view anticipated that later articulated by Richard Baxter and John Wesley, although Pilgram Marpeck—for example—was a hardline Augustinian.

The distinguished Swiss Reformed scholar Gottlob Schrenk has shown how the idea of the covenant came to the fore in the debates of the sixteenth-century Reformed churchmen with the Anabaptists. The Anabaptists called themselves comrades of the covenant (*Bundesgenossen*) and referred to baptism as a covenant (*puntnus*). Schrenk summarized the results of the encounter between Anabaptists and Reformed leaders as follows:

> Zwingli is for Reformed theology the original renewer of the biblical view of the covenant, but the demand for it admittedly came to him from the Anabaptist side. . . . The battle with the Anabaptists and the determination to maintain the *Volkskirche* are the driving forces which stand behind this view.[4]

The conflict between Anabaptists and Reformed leaders was far more interesting than any ascribed conflict of individualists and churchmen. The Reformed churchmen, in line with their determination to effect a reformation of whole territories, accented the covenant of fathers and sons, the importance of continuity and tradition. The Anabaptists, in line with their radical break from the whole idea of "sacral" civilization ("Christendom"), accented the importance of the covenant of a good conscience toward God—among those present and accounted for.

Zwingli stressed the covenant with Adam, renewed in clearer terms with Noah and Abraham. There is only one covenant from the beginning to the end of the world: Abraham is saved in Christ, as we are. Thus infant baptism is like circumcision, and the children of Christians are secured in the covenant and the passover even as those of Israel of old.[5] For Heinrich Bullinger, the identity of the covenant is even plainer: the differences are in the "accidents," not the substance of the matter. For Calvin—especially as he expounded it in the 1559 edition of the *Institutes*—there is a single covenant of grace, different only in the *modus administrationis*. Others followed him:

Musculus, Ursinus, Olevianus. It was not until the time of the federal theologian and social reformer Johann the Elder (younger brother of William of Orange), of Herborn, that a quite different separation of covenants becomes normative—to be completed in the social and political philosophies of Althusius and Coccejus. With them, we can perceive the beginnings of an utterly voluntary church discipline on the one hand, and a political covenant pointing toward popular sovereignty and "secular" government on the other.

But before that happened there were conflicts and encounters of both negative and constitutive significance to both parties: the Anabaptists, pioneer free churchmen, and the Reformed churchmen, sometimes defenders of Calvinist state churches and the reluctant fathers of popular sovereignty and constitutional liberty.

* * *

For those who love religious liberty, the Landgrave Philipp of Hesse was—until his granddaughter's husband, William of Orange, became *Stadholder* in the Lowlands—the most winsome political figure of sixteenth-century Europe. It was Philipp whose troops, wearing the same colors as those of Duke John of Saxony at Speyer in 1526, stayed the emperor's intention forcibly to suppress the evangelical cause. It was Philipp who cooperated with the Archbishop of Mainz to defeat Franz von Sickingen and the revolt of the knights, and later pacified the peasants and joined with Bishop Franz von Waldeck to suppress the Münsterite revolt (1534-35). It was Philipp who cooperated with his friend Ulrich Zwingli to try to bring the evangelical parties together in a mighty alliance reaching from Zurich to Denmark[6]—a plan largely wrecked by Martin Luther following the Marburg Colloquy (1529). To Philipp alone is due the saving of Württemberg from the Habsburgs and for the Reformation.[7] Above all, it was

Philipp who, inspired by a vision of the New Testament and early church, encouraged his preachers to attempt to effect a genuinely apostolic reformation in *Land Hessen*.

Among the results of Philipp's churchly leadership was the founding of the first Protestant university in the world, at Marburg, as recommended by a church synod brought together at his instigation in 1526.[8] Another result was a policy of toleration, indeed reconciliation, which led him to embrace the truce of the Interim in spite of members of his own family, and to urge in his last will and testament that his sons work for a reunion of Protestantism and Roman Catholicism.

The measure by which he judged the matter of persecution or toleration was "not the Scripture, but the practice of the ancient church, which stood near the time of Christ and thereby best knew His opinion and that of the apostles."[9]

Another result of his churchmanship was that Hesse became, after the Ziegenhain Synod of 1539, the only *Landeskirche* with a formal structure of church discipline.[10] And, although even official *Kirchenpfleger* were unable to maintain a pattern of discipline within the established church of Hesse, the *Gemeinschaften* (fellowships modeled on the early church) gave a noteworthy quality of ethical and moral earnestness.[11] This whole policy of church discipline, which resulted from the 1538 Disputation of Butzer and the Anabaptist elders at Marburg, was fixed with Philipp's express encouragement. Although the consequences in Hesse were chiefly seen in the pacification of the Anabaptists, the ramifications for the liturgy and church order came to be felt as far away as England and Geneva. Both confirmation and church discipline, in Protestantism, derive to a large degree from the discussions and debates carried on by Martin Butzer with Philipp of Hesse's express encouragement, and the peculiar style of the reformation in Hesse was profoundly shaped by the

Landgrave's conviction that the true church is that which follows the model of Christ and the apostles.

* * *

The period of special reference is precisely the time of exile in Strassburg (1538-41), between Calvin's periods of leadership at Geneva.

There is no particular point here in discussing the general mutualities and conflicts between Calvin and the Wittenbergers, the Anabaptists (whom he never rightly knew), the followers of Zwingli and Bullinger (who were incorporated into the general Reformed camp with Calvinism in 1549), and Butzer and his associates. The question is whether presumptive evidence may be found for the conclusion that during his exile in Strassburg Calvin learned certain lessons of lasting significance for his thought and for the life of those churches he chiefly influenced.

The indebtedness of the Reformed churches to the Anabaptists in connection with the church covenant has been discussed. Let us now consider two other churchly practices that came to the fore during this period, both of considerable importance to the life of the Reformed churches: confirmation and church discipline.

During the Middle Ages there had been a churchly rite known as *Firmunge*, which occurred at approximately the time of transition from childhood to maturity—a kind of Christian puberty rite, as it were. Evangelical confirmation, with specific catechetical instruction and public profession of faith, was instituted as a result of public debates between the Strassburg Reformers and representatives of the "Left Wing of the Reformation." The South German Brethren, under the leadership of the lay theologian Pilgram Marpeck, were the wing of the Anabaptist movement most committed to covenant theology.[12] By them it was linked to believers' baptism. In the debate with Butzer that preceded his expulsion from the city, Marpeck charged that the city preachers had not

> preached freely under the Cross of Christ, but under the protection of the princes and cities. Therefore it is not to be wondered that the Word of God brought no fruit. To this day there is no Christian order in Strassburg.[13]

Those who came after him, including spiritualizers like Casper Schwenckfeld and Johannes Bünderlin, disagreed with Marpeck's strong insistence that the covenant of the Free Church was grounded in rigorous church discipline. But they too criticized the city preachers for accepting the baptized into full membership without training or personal decision.

In a public disputation of June 10-14, 1533, Schwenckfeld finally charged the city preachers that, if they would not desist from infant baptism, they should at least provide a "Ceremonie" at which young people, upon coming of age, could make public profession of the faith.[14] This proposal apparently took root, for the next year Martin Butzer advanced a plan for evangelical confirmation in his *Ad Monasterienses*. From there the rite spread to Zurich, Wittenberg, and other Protestant centers, and was written by Butzer into the 1551 *Book of Common Prayer*.

For Butzer, confirmation was related to the larger question of church discipline.[15] This too he learned in disputation with the Anabaptists.[16] Although the Strassburg city council refused to accept it, a plan of church discipline was incorporated into the church order of Hesse. The circumstances that led up to this action of the Ziegenhain Synod (1529) are remarkable.

In his confession of faith at Strassburg, Pilgram Marpeck had, like other Anabaptists, insisted that matters of faith ought to be governed solely by the Spirit of Christ in his church: no government had any authority over the *potestas Christi:*

> When the outward magistrate is allowed to rule in the Kingdom of Christ, then it is blasphemy against the Holy Spirit, the (true) Lord and ruler without human assistance.[17]

Philipp too felt that persecution was contrary to the standard of the early church, where differences had been handled by brotherly admonition, prayer, and dialogue. Rather than put the separatists (*Täufer*) to death, he pointed out the difference between them and the Münster revolutionaries, and insisted that none of his subjects be put to death for matters of faith. Only insurrectionists should be reduced by the sword. He called upon Butzer to engage Peter Tesch and other imprisoned Anabaptist elders in disputation, and himself attended many of the sessions. The result was that Hesse became the only land, Protestant or Catholic, in which the Anabaptists were reclaimed in considerable number to the established church.[18]

The Anabaptists claimed in the disputation that they had separated from the public services of the church of the land because no true apostolic discipline ("the Ban") was maintained; if there is a grievance, it must be taken to the church (Matthew 18:17). After considerable further exchange and the presentation of a confession of faith by the imprisoned, which was recognized to be orthodox, the Reformers of Hesse agreed to reinstitute church discipline, and the Anabaptists agreed to return to the public worship of God. Butzer informed Philipp that he felt the Anabaptists were right in criticizing the absence of church discipline, and Philipp ordered that the preachers be brought together in synod to institute such on the New Testament model. At Ziegenhain the responsibility for church discipline was separated from direct control by the civil power,[19] although the eldership was made an office of both congregation and town council.

The consequences of the settlement were far reaching, even though in Hesse the plan to use energetically both the *censura* and the ban was never carried out very effectively.

Butzer returned to Strassburg from his striking success at winning the Anabaptists back to the Protestant established order, and we may be sure that Calvin—his friend and sometime house guest—received the report at its most glowing.

*   *   *

Calvin was most reluctant to return to the misery of leading the faction-torn city of Geneva, and he did so only under strongest pressure from its representatives and his associates. Above all, he was compelled by his sense of the strategic importance of the gateway city to the cause of the gospel in France and Italy.

He agreed to go back only when the *Ordonnances ecclesiastiques* were provisionally agreed to, and these rules were presented to the first sitting of the city council (September 13, 1541) after his return. As is clearly indicated in the 1559 edition of the *Institutes*, Calvin was less concerned for the liberty of a Christian man than for the honor of God and the integrity of the true community of the faithful. Church discipline, expanded in detail and significance, came to be called the "third mark" (*tertior nota*) of the church—along with the word and sacramental life.

With Calvin's return, we have the beginning of the theocracy. Initially, the distinction between religious and socio-political concerns was recognized: the Venerable Company had charge of the preachers, and the consistory—made up of the preachers and twelve laymen—had charge of moral life and discipline. In effect, however, the often precarious political situation, the wars of religion and the threat of Roman Catholic power resurgent with the Council of Trent, and the attempted rebellion of the "libertines" erased the distinction in practical effect. In 1542-46, there were 58 hangings and 76 expulsions from the city (population about 20,000), and during a 1545 plague 34 women were burned or quartered as witches. Geneva, which functioned as a bastion of Protestant reform in dangerous territory, sacrificed religious liberty to international policy.

In Hesse church discipline remained a dead letter for the sake of a comprehensive church policy. In Geneva it was enforced by expelling dissenters. The Christianization of the city, and the use of the city as a base for international church politics—even as later in New England's standing order, erased for the time any religious liberty or practical distinction between the religious and the political covenant. As in the fortress of the high Middle Ages, "heresy" became treason and treason heresy.

Nevertheless, there was implicit in Calvin and Calvinism an awareness that discipline is, finally, a matter of the integrity of the church. In those other geographical areas where the logic of minority status worked itself out, for example, among the radical Puritans and in the religious pluralism of the Germanies, the double covenant was openly recognized. In a strictly voluntary situation such as the United States today, we may turn to the Calvin who learned from Butzer at Strassburg, rather than to the Calvin who was complicit in Servetus' burning, to find inspiration and style for the dialogue.

* * *

In the fulness of time, the priesthood of all believers that both Butzer and Calvin affirmed, which led them to accept the use of the ban as part of the essential equipment of the *ecclesia militans*, has produced a people in the churches who will not obey decisions they have had no part in making. Through loyally maintained covenants, however—thoroughly studied and "talked up"—they are in many places today resisting the blandishments of the new gnostic cults and mounting a new breakthrough in Christian mission and ministry.

In the process of resisting false ideologies and harnessing an effective witness, the spiritual descendants of Pilgram Marpeck, Martin Butzer, and John Calvin are again meeting in dialogue. This time, assigned a new task in a new situation, they find themselves more allies than adversaries. They have—to prejudge the terms of their coming cooperation—common enemies in totalitarianism and secularism, and a common Lord in him who is able to use the most unlikely instruments to effect his purposes and fulfil his promises to mankind. In the present battles, the Calvinists and the Anabaptists are not only learning to admit their mutual indebtedness: they are learning to call each other brother in Christ.

NOTES

1. Franklin H. Littell, *The Origins of Sectarian Protestantism* (New York, 1964), pp. 21f., 106.

2. Champlin Burrage, *The Church Covenant Idea* (Philadelphia, 1904), pp. 15f.

3. Karl Holl, *Gesammelte Aufsätze zur Kirchengeschichte* (Tübingen, 6th edition, 1932), I, 428-29.

4. Gottlob Schrenk, *Gottesreich und Bund im älteren Protestantismus* (Gütersloh, 1923), p. 36.

5. Schrenk, p. 39.

6. W. Lenz, "Zwingli und Landgraf Philipp," *Briegers Zeitschrift für Kirchengeschichte,* III (1879), 46-47.

7. Herbert Grundmann, *Landgraf Philipp von Hessen auf dem Augsburger Reichstag 1530* (Gütersloh, 1959).

8. Ernst Benz, "Die Gründung der Universität Marburg und die Reformation," 54 *Pastoralblatt für Kurhessen-Waldeck* (1952), 5:7-19.

9. Fritz Hermann, *Das Interim in Hessen* (Marburg, 1901), p. 213.

10. Heinrich Bornkamm, *Martin Bucers Bedeutung für die europäische Reformationsgeschichte* (Gütersloh, 1952), p. 15.

11. G. J. van de Poll, *Martin Bucer's Liturgical Ideas* (Assen, 1954), p. 65.

12. John C. Wenger, "The Theology of Pilgram Marpeck," *The Mennonite Quarterly Review*, XII (1938), 4:208.

13. J. Loserth, "Zwei biographische Skizzen aus der Zeit der Widertäufer in Tirol," *Zeitschrift des Ferdinandeums für Tirol und Vorarlberg,* XI (1895), III:39:282.

14. See "Konfirmation," in Christian Hege and Christian Neff (eds.), *Mennonitisches Lexikon* (Frankfurt, 1913–), II, 533-36.

15. Martin Butzer, *Résumé Sommaire de la Doctrine Chrétienne* (Paris, 1951), pp. 52, 62.

16. Franklin H. Littell, "New Light on Butzer's Significance," in *Reformation Studies* (Richmond, Virginia, 1962), pp. 144-67.

17. Pilgram Marpeck, "Confession of Faith Composed at Strassburg (December, 1531-January, 1532)," transcribed and edited by John C. Wenger, *The Mennonite Quarterly Review*, XII (1938), 3:197.

18. Franklin H. Littell, *Landgraf Philipp und die Toleranz* (Bad Nauheim, 1957), pp. 33f.

19. Jacques Courvoisier, *La Notion d'Église chez Bucer* (Paris, 1933), chapter IV.

John Calvin and Choral Music

by Edward Patte

The mysteries of the life of John Calvin have long interested musicologists. Many have thought Calvin's stern religious disciplines excluded musical participation. In search of first-hand information on Calvin's musical tastes, the author of "John Calvin and Choral Music" spent several weeks in Geneva in 1959 researching unedited manuscripts and Geneva City archives. The results are contained in the following article.

The author is a graduate of the University of Geneva, an ordained minister of music, and a member of *Choral Conductors Guild*. The fact that he is bilingual adds authority to his writings, and throws new light on the philosophy of John Calvin regarding church choral music.

• "Music is God's gift to re-create man . . ."

John Calvin and Choral Music

by EDWARD PATTE

CALVIN is not often associated with arts and music, while Luther, on the other hand, is frequently pictured enjoying a "sing song" with his commensals, happily ending a supper with a refrain or two.

Yet Calvin is not as dour and severe as he is depicted. It is an exaggeration to state that "the austere and almost ascetic sobriety of calvinism represses music as it condemns the painted or carved image." Obviously Calvin does not appreciate frolics. Arts, however, are to him a "benedictio Dei." He expresses himself plainly in those words: "God has especially granted Cain's kindred the invention of arts and sundry things that provide the ways and means of everyday life." So, arts are God's gifts. Granted. But then, what were arts in Calvin's time? Not fine arts, surely but 'liberal arts.' All liberal arts are of divine origin, medicine, jurisprudence, astronomy, dialectics, music, theology. They are of God. "In them all, we must see and acknowledge his goodness." "They all emanate from him, therefore must be considered divine inventions." One could not be more explicit. In other writings, Calvin will use those words which complete his thinking "Arts are rays of divine light" (divinae lucis radii) in all evidence "gifts of the Spirit" (praeclara spiritus dona), "abounding grace" (Excellentes gratiae).

Thus after all, the Reformer is not—indeed could not be—against those manifestations of the Spirit. And if, in Churches, he proscribes all "paintings and statues," and also "vain and light music" (levia et vana), it is in no way because of his antagonism against art, but because of his position against the Roman Catholic system.

Let us now sketch briefly the historical climate in which John Calvin's policy developed.

A) *Prescriptions of various Church Councils about singing prior to the Protestant Reformation.* Among many decisions on Church music, taken by the Councils, —all of them formative of the Roman policy in liturgical affairs—, we find a few that may have had, directly or indirectly, a bearing on Calvin's ideas. For instance, the Council of Auxerre, in 578, decided against the secular songs in Church services and also against the singing of young women in the sanctuary. In the latin quotation, the word 'canticum' should be noted. It does not refer at all to "psalms" or biblical renderings set to music, but probably to 'mood songs,' like hymns of joy, of sorrow, of Christian love, of exaltation, that seemed to the Fathers of the Church to be out of place in a priest-conducted formal service.

Also, just a few years later, in 589, the Council of Toledo decides against dancing and singing during the office, which throws a curious light on the liturgy of the 6th century. "Exterminanda est . . . consuetudo . . . ut populi . . . saltationibus ac turpibus invigilent canticis." Later, the priests are reminded by the Council to offer "their own singing with much care and dignity" (cum magna attentione compunctioneque) instead of chanting "in disorderly vociferation." This again shows that restrain was not then a mark of solo or choral singing.

As the Council's decisions had not resulted in noticeable changes, drastic measures are then taken. A set of rules is drafted by Rome wherein the modalities of ecclesiastical choral singing are defined. Among the rules we quote "The singers must refrain from making themselves too conspicuous." In other words, they will have to sing simply, without overdoing it. Calvin, seven centuries later will think along the same line. He will however express himself in his own inimitable way, and with Gallic flavor, about those "who bellow like beasts and bray like mules in Church services."

The same "Regulae canonicorum" quoted above contain the following recommendations for the 'cantores' or 'song leaders' of the Catholic office "They must be examples of humility, sobriety and chastity . . . Those persons who are of little musical talent should refrain from singing . . . The psalms must not be sung too fast, in a disordinate fashion, nor intoned too high. They must be rendered clearly, with poise (compunctio) to reflect the soul of the cantor and also to charm the congregation's ears. . . ."

St. Cyprian had declared, in the same vein, that the Christian should sing "cum modesta voce, quia Deus non vocis, sed cordis auditor est" (in a simple style, because God does not listen to the quality of the voice but to the state of the heart).

St. Jerome had gone even a little farther, showing that the quality or quantity of the voices had strictly no importance. And to make his point clearer,— to the dismay of the vocal artists and perhaps to the delight of the impenitent monotones — he had uttered this momentous sentence "Even the 'cacophonous' can be heard of God." What a relief to the good Church-goer who cannot carry a tune,' who sings out of pitch or with a raucous voice!

St. Augustine, on the other hand, aware of the poor quality of singing in Church exercises had encouraged the faithful in those words: "Sing to God, but do not sing poorly. God does not want men to offend his ears by poor singing." Calvin, in line with the tradition of the great Fathers of the Church and the Councils, and against the so-called 'church-style,' will emphasize the same ideas. Time and again he will write "We must sing to God with our heart rather than with our voice." God's worship in song cannot be likened to a theatrical performance. In Church Choral Music, polish and blending are among the nonessentials. "Therefore,"—he pointedly adds—, "let us not labor to soothen our throat and our vocal cords with drugs, as the tragedians do before a stage performance (he is apparently against throat discs and lozenges! . . .) just as if we had to sing couplets and frills, but let us sing to God in praise and fear. . . ."

B) *The Strasbourg community and psalm singing*. One remembers how Calvin, unable to obtain the support of the City Fathers for the policy he wanted to see established, left Geneva to find a home and a ministry at Strasbourg. The disagreement was not on trite things but on questions of principle. It had to do with the sovereignty of government over spiritual matters. Here is the sequence of events. Mass had been abolished in Summer 1535. Monks, nuns and priests had left the city. The "Conseils," under the guidance of Guillaume Farel, had accepted the Reformation.

Calvin, who perchance had just arrived in Geneva, on his way to Basle, is held up by Farel to help him organize the City and draft a project of Church laws based on the spiritual autonomy of the Church.

The City is divided: after all, which is the supreme authority, the local government or the Church government? When the Conseils decide finally for the doctrine of the sovereinty of the political power in spiritual affairs, Farel and Calvin, unwilling to compromise, leave Geneva for Strasbourg.

In that city, they find a group of French refugees under the leadership of a dynamic theologian, the Reformer Bucer. The core of the French Reformation is there. And yet Strasbourg is decidedly in the German sphere of influence. Most of the refugees, and Calvin himself, are from Picardy. "Plunged in Strasbourg in an atmosphere of German worship, they, the French, are bound together by Calvin by the powerful ties of the French liturgy he is going to publish."

And thus, the French group will remain a spiritual 'reformed' island in the midst of the German Lutheran Reformation. Calvin teaches them to sing eight psalms translated by Clement Marot. He himself translates 5 additional psalms, the Cantique de Simeon, the Decalogue, the Symbole des Apotres (Apostles' Creed). "The French Refuge is delighted. At home, in France, these men had not dared to sing at worship; here, in Strasbourg, they had learned to love the melodies of Alsace and Germany, but were unable to understand the foreign words of the chorales. Now, at last, they had, because of Calvin, the opportunity to sing God's praises in their own tongue. Calvin's genius had provided them, in Strasbourg, with their first Liturgy. And from then on the French Reformation will be a psalm-singing army of Christians. In Strasbourg was successfully effected the amazing conjunction of French literary clarity and German musical harmony. Perhaps nowhere else could it have happened so thoroughly. This is the feeling expressed by a young refugee, who in 1525, writes back home to Picardy "The singing of the women, in Church services, mixed with the male voices, makes delightful music, marvelous to hear."

In this climate of love for good melodies and delicate poetry 'Aulcuns Pseaulmes et Cantiques mys en Chant' is published in 1539. It is a great event in the History of the French Reformation and the Reformed Music.

C) *Popularity of the Psalms in the 16th century*. A curious phenomenon takes place early in the sixteenth century. The Psalms of David are suddenly 'discovered' and translated into French, sometimes into very refined French, with a charming literary turn and delightful rhymes. Some of those psalms are committed to memory and quoted in the conversation; others are sung as love songs and will be sung in other centuries and more gallant times.

The Psalms of David were good copy. They could easily be accommodated to the music of the day or adapted to popular tunes. Furthermore, when their first translation by Clement Marot was printed, the general enthusiasm knew no boundaries. Psalms began to be heard everywhere, at the Court, in the fields. on board the ships, even in prisons.

St. Jerome writes ". . . the farmer at his plow sings allelujahs; the harvester sweating under the sun, rests a while in the shade, singing a psalm; the winegrower, gathering the grapes intones the 'Odes of the Prophet David' (sic) . . ." Psalms are heard everywhere, in every place. It has become a frenzy. You can hear their melodies in town houses, on the market place, at dinner, in bedrooms, in the King's Palace and even in the 'outhouses,' since St. Gregory had been heard. . . "singing psalms while voiding his belly . . ." People were not much impressed by the spiritual messages involved in them. They simply liked poetry. They never felt that in singing them they were paving the way for the Protestant Reformation. As a matter of fact, many were good Catholics and remained so. They simply sang the psalms, because words and tunes were delightful. And so, "at King Francois Premier's court, every prince, every lady, every page had a favorite psalm that he was constantly humming." "No one delighted in the 'Sanctes chansonnettes' more passionately than the Dauphin, later Henry II . . . And so, very strangely, the recreation of a gay Catholic Court became the exclusive hall-mark of the severest form of Protestantism." The metrical psalms were sung by the common people for their private delectation in the same spirit as they were sung by the court for artistic recreation. Modern musicologists, like Sir Richard Terry, feel that the psalms were meant to be sung first and foremost in private homes, and not in church. The proof of it can be gathered from the fact that, "as late as 1599 Allison (the Englishman) in his psalter, provided accompaniments for the lute and the cittern, a presumable indication of singing the tunes as solos." Accompanied or not, the tunes were heard from one end of the Kingdom to the other end.

Of the King himself it is said that "he was singing all the time the stanzes of a psalm" (Rex ejus versiculos itemtidem cantabat). Encouraged by such a tremendous public demand, "the musicians of Charles V and the composers of the King of France put psalms into music, mix them with all types of love songs and publish them in numberless albums." Sometimes even "trivial airs are used to underline King David's verses, thus substituting in the memory of the public pious words for rather libertine couplets." This is, for instance, how 'Dearest lady, have mercy upon me, Open Thou Thy tender heart, . . . has been transformed into 'O Lord of hosts, Have mercy upon me, Open Thou Thy tender heart.' Or again, the Psalms are attached to a popular tune, as for instance the Psalm XXXVI, which is sung in 1532 on the tune of 'Au bois de deuil, a l'ombre de soucy,' or the Ps CXXIX, in 1540 sung on 'Des ma jeunesse ils m'ont fait mille maux . . .' (thousands of evils did I suffer from them . . .)

Singing is fashionable. The Psalms are the fad of the day. Clement Marot who gained fame with his literary translation of the Psalms, completes now his work at the King's urgent request and writes him

> 'Puisque voulez que je poursuive, o Sire
> L'oeuvre royal du Pseaultier commence
> Et que tout coeur aimant Dieu le desire,
> D'y travailler me tien pour dispense.'

The meaning is very simple: 'O King, since this is Thy will, of course, for God's sake, I'll comply.' Anyway he could hardly, in truth, have done otherwise or less . . . Who was this Clement Marot? A gay companion indeed, in the household of Marguerite de Navarre, then of Renee de France, duchess of Ferrare. In 1539 and 1540 he translates the Psalms of David. Immediate success. The poet becomes famous overnight. King Francois, more than delighted, finds him unexcelled. Less delighted is however the Sorbonne.

Wisely, Marot, sensing trouble ahead, takes the road and flees to Geneva, where he is welcomed by Calvin as a brother. Calvin had already used to great advantage, during the Strasbourg period of his ministry, eight of Marot's psalms. He would like, in his enthusiasm for such a masterly translation, to keep him in the City.

Unfortunately Marot has also produced in earlier years a few rondels, ballads and verses that were not exactly devout nor tame . . . The City Fathers raise their eyebrows. Then also this: The poet is a playboy . . . He spends much time at the Inn . . . He imbibes wine and hard cider . . . He pinches the maidens . . . He plays backgammon . . . In brief the happy topper is not of the Consistory's liking. The police are constantly after him.

And yet, Marot, who perhaps never became a Protestant, beautifully translated King David. To be sure, he had written the French translation purely for the enjoyment of the public and not for Church use. And this is why his poetry could be perfectly adapted to dozens of very secular melodies indeed. Florimond de Remond, who was a Conseiller at Bordeaux Parliament, and wrote in 1572 a 'Histoire de l' Heresie, mentions that everyone fitted Marot's psalms to 'any old tune,' particularly to gallant ballads.

Marot gone, there is need of a new translator. Calvin asks Theodore de Beze (Beza), a delicate humanist who will become a venerable Reformer, to undertake the task. He did his very best. But to this day, the rogue's verses remained more famous than the saint's.

Mention should also be made of another translator, the talented Eustorg de Beaulieu, who followed in Marot's and Beza's train. Minister of the Gospel, musician, composer, organist, writer and translator of the Psalms, he is probably the best 'chansonnier' of the French Reformation early history. If he wrote, in 1546, in addition to his psalms of David, a book of poetry entitled 'Chrestiennes Rejouissances' (Christian Joys), he unfortunately also published 'L' epinglier des Filles' (The Teaser of Girls) and 'le Blason du Corps Feminin' (the Display of the Female Body), that were hardly for Church consumption. . .

And the music? We suggested already two sources of melodies: First the tunes of German origin (Psalter of Strasbourg), and second, the popular songs of the day. But there were also able composers of original tunes, and arrangers like Loys Bourgeois, Pierre du Buisson, his pupil who wrote the music for sixty-two psalms of Beza in 1561, Claude Goudimel Philibert Jambe de Fer (1564), Richard Crassot (1564), H. Sureau (1565), Pierre Santerre (1567), Michel Ferrier (1568), Claude Le Jeune (1568), Estocart, Des Masures and many others. Among them all, however, is this XVIth century which saw at least 108 various editions of the Psalms of Marot or Beza, Loys Bourgeois is probably the most famous musician. His genius is made of inventiveness, imagination, good taste and technical mastery. He is a great melodist, and also a scholar who, in Geneva, really 'creates' a new type of music as a rival to plain-chant. For him, the music must "echo" the text.

Calvin, of course, is in full agreement. So much so that within six years after the Reformer's return to Geneva, from his Strasbourg exile, Bourgeois has become one of the most prominent persons in his *entourage*. He teaches psalms to the children, starts voice classes that are a sensation in the City. His school of music builds up an immense reputation. He has become, in 1545, the cantor of the Cathedral St. Pierre. He is given, in ceremony, the full rights of a citizen, "in recognition of his ministry as an educator and of his sterling character." Three months later, he is even relieved of all watch duty so that he might spend all his time developing music.

But times are hard, money is scarce. The Geneva weather is miserable and his poor little apartment is chilly. The Conseil gives him a 'stove' for his rooms. Then suddenly, of necessity, his salary is cut. He begs the 'syndics' to assure him a living wage. In vain, for a while. Finally, the Conseil, moved because of Bourgeois' poverty, and because of the advanced pregnancy of his wife, follows Calvin's suggestion and grants the poor Cantor "deux coupes de Ble" (wheat and flour). Bourgeois is not satisfied. How could he be?

Calvin intercedes again for his friend, but the Conseil feels that the musician begins to become rather overbearing. He produces "83 Pseaulmes de David, most suitable for instruments, to be sung as 4-, 5-, or 6-part songs, of which the tenor has the melody, so that unison, octave or harmony may be properly used." Quite a title page for a psalter! But it is a program as well as a title page. Touching the melody, "it seems better to make it moderate in scope, in order to convey peace and majesty according to the subject, and to render it appropriate for the Church."

So Bourgeois works, and works again, on each of his tunes until he is satisfied of his accomplishments. The Conseil does not always agree with him. Perhaps Bourgeois goes too far, and he changes things around. In 1551, he finally is imprisoned for having changed, without permission, the singing of the psalms in the regular church services. The 'Registres du Conseil' contain this entry: "RESOLVED that since the aforesaid Bourgeois has changed the song without due license, he be kept in jail. Be it further resolved that in the future only be used the old melodies as printed, and be left aside until further notice all the new songs."

So, innovations in the realm of psalmody or harmony are not of the Conseil's liking. Calvin interecedes again. After twenty four hours Bourgeois is freed, but the Cantor has learned his lesson and leaves the city, to Calvin's dismay and the Conseil's relief.

His psalm tunes, so beautiful that they have defied the times and are still favorite melodies of the twentieth century Reformed Church psalters, make him worthy of the title "Barde of French Psalmody." He leaves behind, in Geneva, the essential elements of the Psalter that will be, later on, harmonized by arrangers in numberless editions.

Before Bourgeois, Calvin had already welcomed Guillaume Franc, a refugee from Rouen, Normandy, who, like his successor, combined the skill of a teacher and a composer. He had created a School of Music in 1541, where children were taught the psalms and secular songs. He became the Cantor of the Cathedral, and may have composed 21 of the melodies of the 1543 psalter. Calvin honored him, helped him materially also, sending young pupils to his School. But the poor man could not live on his meager salary. He had to beg the Conseil for additional funds. Finally he was granted a shelter, 'a lodging in the Cantor's house, together with a little cellar under the steps of the church, and 100 florins a year.' But, unable to make a living on such a pittance, he left Geneva.

Other musicians come to the city, like Pierre Devantes, born in Bigorre in 1525, a refugee at 34 who, —hellenist, composer, printer, teacher—, renovates musical art by the invention of *'musicque chiffree.'* Calvin shows interest in his new system of notation. But of no avail. The 'new system' vanishes.

So, after having published a new edition of Clement Marot's and Beza's psalms, he abandons Geneva, disconsolate at his failure, and frozen stiff by the glacial 'bise' that blows from the North. Pierre du Buisson will write 62 new tunes for Beza's translation; but frankly, he does not show the marks of a genius, as did his master Bourgeois, and his psalms will soon pass into oblivion.

After the composers, the arrangers. Claude Goudimel worked on Bourgeois' melodies, and kept them absolutely as they were sung in the Church services, adding simply three parts to the lead. This he did, "not to have them sung in Church, but to rejoice in God within the family circle." The beautiful harmonization of his psalms is still in use in the French and German Reformed Church and remains perhaps more popular than the rendering by Claude Le Jeune, Le Bel, Champion, Queroult, Gindron and others of the same century.

The forewords to all these psalters—unison or in parts—adjure the Christians to sing them with the proper spirit, in their homes or at Church. Perhaps the following quotations will illustrate again that in the Calvinian tradition, simplicity and *retenue* were the mark of proper psalm rendering:

> 'Good musicans, lovers of the psalms,
> In the name of God, sing ye those new songs!
> Do not sing them, mooing like calves!. . .
> Remember that God wants first an humble
> And contrite heart. . . . Don't ever forget that.'

This passage, written under the very eyes of Reformer Guillaume Farel, in the same year, is just as indicative: "Read the fourth chapter of the first letter to the Corinthians, where St. Paul shows how the true Christian must preach, pray and sing alike: That all be done with clear voice, from the heart and the spirit, to bear fruit evident to all." So, the Reformation sings, both in French and in German, in Geneva and Wittenberg, in spite of the critics who also sarcastically write: "For her greatest joy Geneva psalmodizes the antique concerts of good old King David, trusting that God Himself takes His pleasure at miserable verses."

This is well said, lightly and witty. Perhaps not quite true to fact. But where else could psalms be heard in every home of the city?

II-Calvin's Choral Music . . .

After this description of the historical background and setting, we will now consider some of the Calvin's writings that refer to choral music. They are not numerous. Two reasons may be advanced for the paucity of references to music in the monumental work of the Reformer. First, Calvin was not a musician, much less a musicologist. Second, to him music is always an 'ancilla', a simple servant. We will find, therefore, just a few statements made here and there, —as a sort of a parte—, in Calvin Institutes, Commentaries or Sermons. Nowhere do we discover that 'religious music' is the object of a long, systematic, well ordered study. The search for comments on choral music is rather long and unrewarding.

In reading again his 'Commentaires sur les Pseaulmes,' we came across a passage of interest. This is a sort of practical exegesis of Psalm 81, verses 2-3 on those words: "Sing ye joyfully unto God our strength, sing loude to the God of Jacob Take the song, and bring forth the tabret, the merrie harpe with the viole." We are using here the English translation almost contemporary with Calvin, namely the famous Golding Translation of 1571 that we read in the original.

The Reformer's comments, in XVIth century English are as follows: 'The faythful should not stand deafe and dumbe at the Tabernacle, for God is not worshiped with idleness, nor with cold and empty ceremonies. . . . But by such exercises (as singing) they should cherish the unity of faith among themselves to true devotion. . . . As concerning tabret, harpe and viole, it was God's will so to trayne his people, which as yet were tender and chyldelike, until the coming of Christ . . . But now, when the brightness of the Gospel betaketh us in a playner sort, we should do but folly to counterfet that thing which the prophet appointed only for his tyme! Whereby it appeareth that "the Papists were right apes'." The main thought is here very simply: When the faithful worship together they should sing rather than remain passive in Church. The singing will give them consciousness of their spiritual unity. In the old days there was necessity of accompanying those hymns with drums and strings (i.e. rhythm and melody). Now, no longer. And the Catholics who still continue this type of accompaniment are simply 'aping' old ways! This was Calvin's view.

Another passage of the Psalms should also retain our attention, namely Psalm 47:8, in these words, "Sing unto God, sing yee, everyone of you that hathe understanding." Calvin's comments, again taken from the Golding translation read: . . . "The faythful should prayse God, by their mouth and with joyful heart. David exhorteth all that have skill of singing unto this exercyse . . . He requireth trewe understanding in singing of God' prayses that mennes tunges (tongues) should not only rose as wee knowe it done in the Papistrie. Therefore unto the lawful manner of singing there is required knowledge, that the name of God be not unhalowed with vayne yelling."

So, here do we find a new instruction in Calvin's exegesis of this psalm, namely that all singing 'must come from the heart.' In other words, sing your faith; sing what you believe to be true! Do not simply add your voice to the mumblings of a church assembly. This is done in the Roman church. Here, in our Churches, we must know and believe what we are singing about. Otherwise this would be vain shouting and shameful desecration of the name of the Lord! As a matter of fact, the French original is still more pungent and precise than the Golding translation of 1571. Calvin writes, 'Pour bien user de la chanterie, il faut science et connaissance de ce que l'on chante. Autrement, il n'y aurait que la voix qui s'escoule en l'air'. This could be translated in modern English, "To psalmodize properly, to be sure to grasp what you are singing, or your song will be but vibration of the air!'

An early Reformed Church theologian, commenting on Calvin's exegesis of this Psalm, writes in 1663 those illuminating remarks that we are quoting from the original, then in an abbreviated translation: "The words 'psalmodize with intelligence' do not simply mean 'sing with understanding,' but also 'sing in an intelligible fashion,' as the Hebrew words 'lammeron maskil' cover both understanding and knowledge. Those psalms are not meant to 'tickle your ears' but to 'enter into your soul and to fire your own faith!'

Here again, we notice the same fundamental idea: music is simply the servant of the spiritual message. This statement is also clearly enounced in Calvin's Twenty second sermon on Ps CXIX in those words: "When we want to magnify and praise God's name, our heart must be enclined to it and it will then produce a good melody" (Quand nous voulons magnifier le nom de Dieu . . . , que nostre coeur y soit dispose, et qu'il s'y accorde pour faire une bonne melodie. .).

Another passage of the Old Testament must now retain our attention, I Samuel XVIII:6. Here is the situation: According to the story, women and children are welcoming King David victorious over Israel's enemy. They sing hymns to the accompaniment of brass instruments, and dance in their exaltation. Calvin considers this dancing, this playing and this singing as perfectly proper under the circumstances. He says 'Those people were behaving like children, because they still were children in their faith. Nothing wrong there. They did not know any better' In the original words, we have: 'Musicam itaque illam instrumentalem teneamus tunc ratione temporis illius et populi fuisse toleratam, quod essent ut pueri' This is the only justification of their behaviour: they were like children, "ut pueri."

To honor God, since they were still "children," they did behave like children. Singing must be all to the glory of God. "Consensus omnium aetatum et sexum, ut senes cum juvenibus, viri cum mulieribus et virginibus uno omnes ore Deum laudent and praedicent." So, people of every age, men and women, must all sing to proclaim their faith and praise God. Always the same pre-eminence of the message, the 'praedicatio.' Then, "Caeterum, pro ut hominum ingenia sunt levia et vana, vix fieri potest ut divinae laudes adeo purae sint et sincerae quin aliqua laus hominibus tribuatue in iis carminbus, quibus facta ipsorum egregia decantantur." In brief, your song, far from being light and vain, must show the sincerity of your heart with which you can then, and then only, praise God.

Finally comes this timely warning: "Scimus autem ubi nulla est intelligentia, nullam etiam aedificationem esse . . . Quare fideles hortatur eo loco ut Deum precantes et ipsi psallentes, et precentur et psallent inteligentia, non lingua peregrina, sed vulgari et intelligibili, ut sit in ecclesia aedificatio." (Your singing needs to be intelligent . . . If you do not understand what you sing, how can you therein praise God? Do not use foreign tongues, but the vernacular! Then truly your worship will bear fruit.) ". . . sufficiat pura et simplex divinarum laudum modulatio, corde et ore nostro singuli idiomate . . ." (The simple melody is enough if it is the true voice coming from the heart). For the most important thing is to praise God and have him praised by others.

Such are the comments of Calvin on music in the Old Testament.

In the New Testament commentaries, Calvin completes his thinking, for instance, when he explains Ephesians V, 18-21: "To sing praises to God, it must be, of sort, as if the heart had to march forward first and intone a tune. Melody from the heart is indeed like the voice of angels in Paradise." There is nothing worldly about it. It has become heavenly! But "it is pure mockery when your mouth only sings! It is never enough to shout with an 'open gullet'."

Finally we have found in our perusal of several dozen manuscript sermons of Calvin, which are the property of the University of Geneva Public Library, and have never been printed nor edited, two passages that are directly related to the singing of psalms. The first one is a one-line comment on Psalm 148,1-2 "Praise God as the angels are doing," which is almost a repetition of the commentary on Ephesians V:18-21 quoted above. The second passage of significance, is a comment on Psalm 149:4-9, and refers to the singing of psalms not in church services but in private homes. Calvin writes there, 'There are many people who sing in the assemblies, with wide open mouth, to be seen of men' Then the Reformer adds this practical instruction, which is both touching and psychologically correct: 'Sing also in your own bedroom, because there you won't need to show off. In the privacy of one's home, one can indeed sing the praises of the Lord to one's heart's delight.'

So, here again the great calvinian principle is finding a new expression: "DEO SEMPER DEBITUM HONOREM REDDAMUS."

III-Calvin's Hymn Books . . .

And now, what are the important choral publications of this early Reformed Church? Let us speak first of the Strasbourg Psalter of 1539. This was indeed a "novum." Before it, we know of no other printed psalter with music for the use of the French Reformed communities. The title of this small work is *AULCUNS PSEALUMES ET CANTIQUES MYS EN CHANT, STRASBOURG 1539.* Lost during 350 years, this precious psalter was discovered by the Rev. David Deletra, and phototyped by Alexandre Jullien, publisher, in 1919, in Geneva, in an edition that, unfortunately, reproduces its many original mistakes.

A clearer edition was published in England by Sir Richard Terry, in 1932. It shows this first psalter in the obsolete notation of the

XVIth century, with clefs on various lines of the staff and no metronomic indication. The melodies are unharmonized and here and there remain subject to caution. The printers, evidently incompetent musicians, made serious typographical errors. Furthermore, verses written in old French with the use of Gothic letter press are rather difficult to decipher. The occasion for the 1539 printing in Strasbourg is not known. But we may infer that Calvin, who had seen and heard chorale singing firmly established among the Lutherans of Strasbourg, immediately grasped the importance of a psalter for public worship.

"AULCUNS PSEAULMES" contains 19 psalms and 3 hymns; its tunes show freedom and true variety of rhythms; the poetry varies in quality: 14 of the psalms were the work of Clement Marot, but John Calvin himself may have written the French verses of psalms 25, 36, 46, 91, and 138.

If Calvin, who was not a poet, took such pains to write the translation of the above psalms, it is because he was absolutely convinced of the value of singing in the common worship of the new church. Don't we have a proof of this assumption in the Archives of the City of Geneva, on the date of January 16, 1537, less than six months after the Reformer's arrival in Geneva?

In the "Memoire sur l'Organisation de l'Englise de Geneve" presented, together with Guillaume Farel to the Seigneurs Syndics, Calvin makes this capital statement, "Verily, the worship service of the faithful is so cold, that it puts us all to great shame and confusion. The Psalms will induce us to stir up our hearts and lift them up to God, to fill them with enthusiasm for invoking His name and exalting His glory!"

Unfortunately, the very next year, Calvin had been exiled and had found refuge in Strasbourg. And there, still convinced of the value of psalm singing "to lift our hearts up to God," he collects the materials for the first psalter. The tunes, some of them by Greiter, a former monk who had been the Cantor of Strasbourg Cathedral were perhaps in use already in Lutheran collections. Of them all only tune #8, for the psalm 36, has found its way into the English psalter, and remains to this day a part of this book.

The second psalter in the history of the Reformed Church, under the sponsorship of Calvin, was published in Geneva with an introductory note by the Reformer, dated June 10, 1543, as a part of the Liturgy to be used in church services. It is given the name *LA FORME DES PRIERES*. Calvin, recalled from Strasbourg in 1541, has brought with him *AULCUNS PSEAULMES*, probably with the idea of enlarging it for use at Saint Pierre. He had his new psalter published by the printer Jan Gerard at the end of 1542, completing and signing his introductory remarks on June 1543. There are significant additions to the earlier Strasbourg psalter, namely, 30 psalms of Clement Marot, instead of 13; also there are a few psalms that Calvin had translated while in exile. The music contains at least 21 totally new tunes, whose composers, to this day, remain unknown.

The mystery is complete. It is, for instance, impossible to link those songs with Loys Bourgeois, since he went to Geneva in 1545 only, i.e. 2 or 3 years after the first edition of *FORME DES PRIERES*. The present day musicologist Pierre Pidoux, a Professor at the Faculte de Theologie de Lausanne, in his 1959 re-edition of this psalter concludes his scholarly studies in those words: "None of the contemporary texts—documents, archives or private correspondence—, nor latter editions of the psalter give us the slightest indication as to authorship." The possibility that the composer might have been Guillaume Franc, the first Reformed cantor at the Cathedrale de St. Pierre, who already in 1541 had opened in Geneva his School of Music, should not be eliminated. But this is indeed pure speculation.

Perhaps as far as melodies are concerned "all was fish that came to the compiler's net." About them, at the end of his *Introductory Note to the Reader*, Calvin writes: "One must always watch that the song be not light and frivolous, but have weight and majesty," as says St. Augustine. "And thus one must take care that there be great difference between the music for entertainment at dinner table and in private homes, and the psalms which are sung in Church, in the presence of God and His angels. So, when you will judge unbiasedly the *FORME des PRIERES*, we hope that you will find it holy and pure, since its only purpose is to 'edify.' "

What Calvin means is that the melodies of the psalms are simple, genuine, worshipful and different from the secular tunes that men enjoy singing at home or around the dinner table. And, "they must be approached in a manner quite different from the enjoyment of music on other occasions or in other places."

The presentation of this second Psalter is not very different from the *AULCUNS PSEAULMES*. Perhaps the notes and the clefs are in clearer type. And, the words are no longer in Old Gothic, but in Roman letters, which render the reading much easier.

This famous psalter was re-edited several times, beginning with the year 1545. In the *Introduction*, the following words are particularly meaningful: "Music is God's gift to re-create man. It has, secret and almost incredible virtues."

We have to wait until 1562 to have a new and final evaluation of choral music. Calvin shows a penetrating understanding of it in his PREFACE to the 1562 edition of *LA FORME DES PRIERES*.

In this passage he claims that a melody anchors the words of a song into one's mind. If the words are perverse, they literally pierce one's heart. They "penetrate into one's soul as wine pouring through a funnel into a keg." Of course, this power of music to "funnel in" words can also be used for the good in congregational singing and in family singing to convey the spiritual truths emphasized by the Reformation. Calvin, educator, will encourage printers to publish psalters, and induce teachers and cantors to teach sacred songs to their pupils.

He writes, in his *Introduction* to the 1562 Psalter: "Christians, I caused this little book to be printed with the psalms I was able to collect, so that those 'honest songs' may teach you the love and the fear of God and take the place of those vulgar couplets so commonly heard, that are nothing but obscenity and vulgarity."

For the same reason, Calvin and Beza, in the regulations concerning the College and the Academy, will insert the following: "That all the College boys, winter and summer, return to their classes after lunch, at 11 A.M., and practice singing until noon." This was submitted to the Conseil and adopted on May 22 and 29, 1559.

For the same reason again, Calvin will support Loys Bourgeois, and other composers, whose little psalm books, so widely peddled through Switzerland and France, show how much the psalters were in the XVIth century "the symbol and the vehicle of the Protestants' personal communion with God." For use at home, —es maisons—, elaborate forms will be admitted and even encouraged. The singing of the psalter around the dinner table to keep the minds from worldly, futile thoughts, does not shun the charm that polyphonic art conveys to the audience as well as to performers themselves. . .

Thus encouraged, great masters like Goudimel or Le Jeune will set the psalms in a 4, 6, 8 or even 16-part form, using a syllabic melody, generally in the Tenor, and a chordal harmonization, or even an involved, contrapuntal score for experienced singers.

A splendid example of this harmonized psalter for several voices is found in *LES PSEAULMES MIS EN RIME FRANCOISE ET EN MUSIQUE A QUATRE PARTIES PAR CLAUDE GOUDIMEL.* Goudimel's strong, dignified harmonies are as fresh today as they were 400 years ago.

There were many other collections of harmonized psalms in the 16th century and the early 17th centuries. "But that was also the end. There and then they remain. There was no further development of them at the hands of later musicians as in the case of the Lutheran chorale. No Bach arose to do for the Geneva psalter tunes what had been done for the Lutheran chorales. The Geneva tune remains, in its primitive aloofness, like a noble marble statue frozen in its grandeur."

Granted. . . . But the Geneva tunes still became the battle songs of the Huguenots, the Cantiques des Camisards, the war cries of the Brave, the last notes heard above the crackling of the flames when the valiant and the faithful were burned at stake. Nobler songs no man will ever hear!

SUMMARY-"Let Man Sing With Heart and Intelligence" . . .

For Calvin, music is usetul to piety, provided it is devoid of "senseless and vain frills." No one can ever sing songs worthy of God, who did not receive them first from Him. Let man sing with his heart and his intelligence. Therein lies, indeed, the difference between man and bird: "a lark, a nightingale, a parrot, sing, but without any understanding, while man alone can sing, knowing what he says." A simple song, genuine and clear is God's gift. So let us all be humble in the use we are making of music, and let us avoid all 'disorderly, effeminate and lewd way of singing.' "I have always endeavored to be simple" wrote the Reformer. "I will sing with the spirit, and I will sing with the mind and the heart also."

So, SIMPLICITY is the first principle of Reformed music. UNISON is the second principle. But it pertains only to the Church services. Of course Calvin, while at Strasbourg may have heard chorale singing in the Lutheran liturgy. Was it not about such parts-singing that Gerard Roussell wrote from Strasbourg in 1525 "The song of women combined with the singing of men produces marvels.

Calvin may have attended such services, and like Roussell, may have been much impressed by the choral renderings. Yet, in spite of the fact that "it is very pleasant a thing when one hears the beautiful psalms of the Lord sung without a voice 'oversinging' another one" Calvin still felt that parts-singing was for group entertainment, rather than the common use of the Church.

Thus we must disagree with historians of the Church who, like Courtois or Douen draw a picture of a Calvin, enemy of all art, beauty of form or harmony. In fact, in his Sermon on Justification, Calvin speaks implicitly of the benefit of harmony, when he says: "One may sing with one voice only, but the song won't be perfect unless there is a perfect combination of several voices." This refers to harmony. Harmony is excellent, but not in a sanctuary. For Church use we need unison, because the clarity of the message will be then safeguarded. In unison singing, all the words can be heard and understood, while in polyphony or counterpoint or even parts-singing, it is often difficult to grasp the meaning of words. Harmony is not for Church use as "songs composed for the simple pleasure of the ears are not becoming to the majesty of the Church, and they displease God very greatly."

A last finding pertains to the psalmody of the Geneva church. Contrarily to a generally accepted opinion, Calvin did not endow the psalms with a sort of monopoly of choral music in the church services. The psalms are not the essential part of the Reformed worship. There never was any opposition of principles about other choral or musical pieces in worship services.

The proof of it is found first in the fact that in the first psalter, *AULCUNS PSEAULMES*, the Cantique de Simeon, as worded in Luke 2, is also included. Then a musical rendering of the Apostles' Creed is offered. Similarly, in the Geneva psalter, *LA FORME DES PRIERES*. Calvin keeps in this new psalter both the Cantique de Simeon and the Apostles' Creed, and he adds a musical score to accompany the Lord's Prayer.

Furthermore, in his Commentary on Colossians 3:16, the Reformer frankly admits that among the means of exhortation available to the Christian are found the Psalms, *and* the Hymns, *and* the 'spiritual odes.' Of course the Psalms seem to be put in evidence. And it is rather odd to discover that the essence of the gospel, namely justification by faith, by grace freely given, is not the main theme heard in the singing of the early Reformed Church. Accordingly, it would almost be true to say that in Calvin's time the sermon was Christian and the singing Jewish . . .

The reasons for such curious characteristics are very evident. Calvin capitalized on the century's infatuation for the poetry of the psalms, and singularly for the literary style of Clement Marot. "Nauseated by the unseemly and amorous songs that were corrupting the youth of his country," he relied heavily on the Psalms that were both fashionable and of great spiritual value.

So, Calvin could have made his the words of Archbishop Parker:

> "Depart, ye songs lascivious
> From lute, from harpe depart!
> Give place to Psalmes most vertuous
> And solace there your harte"

Calvin used a 'fad of the day' and made it a potent weapon for the Church.

Finally, the Reformer, very properly, saw in the Psalms the 'mirror of the soul,' expressing fully the struggles of man in his quest for a God who cares. Calvin could find "no songs better than the psalms of David, which the Holy Spirit dictated and gave to him."

The psalms, 'fully inspired' are used in preference over other passages of Scripture of a lesser literary quality. They were the logical choice in a period when they had become the most popular, and most often quoted piece of literature. Intelligence, convenience and availability, rather than dogmatics dictated the choice. There was no doctrine, nor monopoly, singling out the psalms for the Reformed Church services.

The dignity of the words, the profound humanity of the feelings, the SOLI DEO GLORIA found in every psalm, were making of the psalter the perfect vehicle of the Reformed faith.

Facsimile page of the 1st French Reformed Psalter of 1539
"Aulcuns Pseaulmes Et Cantiques Mys En Chant. A Strasbourg"

Facsimile page of the 1st Geneva Psalter of 1542
"La Forme Des Prieres"

BIBLIOGRAPHY OF BOOKS CONSULTED

Aulcuns Pseaulmes et Cantiques, Strasbourg, 1539
Bonifas, H. .... Chant et Culte Protestant, Geneve
Bovet, Felix .... Histoire du Psaultier des Eglises Reformees, Paris, 1872
Bourgeois, Loys .... Le droict chemin de musique, 1550
Bruguier, J. .... Discours sur le Cant des Psaumes, 1663
Calvin, John .... La forme des prieres et chants ecclesiastiques, Gen. 42
" " .... Comm. sur les Psaumes, Etienne, Geneve, 1563
" " .... Comm. on the Psalms, Arthur Golding, London, 1571
" " .... Sermons on Ephesians, Corpus Ref., LXXIX
" " .... Homelia on I Samuel, Geneva 1552
" " .... Sermons on the Psalms, Corpus Ref. LX
" " .... Recueil des Opuscules
" " .... Institutes, Livre III
" " .... Manuscript of Sermons (Ms fr 40a Bibl. Publ. Geneva)
Douen, O. .... Clement Marot et le Psautier Huguenot, Paris, 1878
Doumergue, E. .... Jean Calvin, Tome II
Estocart, Paschal .... 150 Psaumes de David
Gerold, Th. .... L'art du Chant en France au 17e siecle, Stbg, 1921
" " .... Les Peres de l'eglise et la Musique, Stbg, 1931
Goudimel, Claude .... Les psaumes mys en rime francoise, 1565
" " .... Les Psaumes de 1580, Henri Expert, Paris, 1895
Pannier, J. .... Histoire de la Reforme francaise
" " .... Calvin a Strasbourg (Rev. Hist et Philos. Rel.), 1925
Premier Livre des Pseaulmes de David, first edition, Gen., 1547
Psaumes et Cantiques, Gd papier, Bibli Univ. de Geneve
Terry, Rich. Sir .... Calvin's first Psalter, London
Sachs, Curt .... Our Musical Heritage, NY 1948
Labbe, J. .... S. S. Concillia
Schmidt, A. M. .... Jean Calvin et la tradition Calvinienne, Paris, 1956
Bordier, H. L. .... Chansonnier Huguenot du XVIe siecle, Paris, 1890
Archives de la City de Geneve, 1544, 1551
Benson, L. F. .... Hymnody of the Christian Church, NY, 1956
and VARIOUS ARTICLES by
Pierre Pidoux in Revue de Musicologie,
Henry Bruinsma in Choral & Organ Guide
Bernard Gagnebin in Bulletin de la Societe d' Histoire et Archeologie ets.

JOHN CALVIN AND THE BRETHREN OF THE COMMON LIFE: THE ROLE OF STRASSBURG

KENNETH A. STRAND
Andrews University

In an earlier issue of *AUSS*, I noted certain lines of influence by which ideals of the Brethren of the Common Life reached John Calvin early in his career in France, prior to his reform activities in Geneva.[1] This Brotherhood, a movement with whose schools both Desiderius Erasmus and Martin Luther had had direct contact, established no houses, schools, or dormitories in France. Nevertheless, Calvin there imbibed its influence in various ways, most notably during his stay at the College of Montaigu and through the Fabrisian circle of humanistic reformers.

But such contacts were neither the last nor the only means by which concepts and practices of this northern reform movement reached Calvin. In Strassburg, where the Geneva reformer made his home from 1538 to 1541 (for most of the duration between his First and Second Geneva periods) and where he pastored a group of French refugees and taught in the school system reorganized by Johann Sturm in 1538-39, he definitely felt the impact of ideals fostered by the Brotherhood. This was especially true with respect to matters of educational reform, and may have been true in other ways as well. It is the purpose of the present brief essay to outline some of the highlights of Strassburg's mediating role between the Brethren of the Common Life and Calvin.

1. *Sturm and Educational Reform*

Sturm's program of educational reform in Strassburg, instituted in the very year of Calvin's arrival, combined the various independent schools of the city into one system and utilized a "grade"

[1] See *AUSS* 13 (1975): 67-78.

or "class" structure in which students moved progressively to higher grades or classes according to their achievements. Sturm also introduced Greek into the curriculum and provided for specialization of subject matter at the two highest levels. His work along these lines has often been hailed as a pioneer achievement in the history of modern education, and the influence of that work on the system which Calvin introduced in establishing his famous Geneva Academy in 1558-59 is generally recognized.

What is often overlooked is that Sturm's educational "innovations" were really based on what he himself had learned by first-hand experience from the Brethren of the Common Life in Liège when he was exposed to their educational system during the years 1521 to 1524.[2] Indeed, he himself in a document dated February 24, 1538, makes this absolutely clear, for in outlining his plan for Strassburg education, he refers to the Liège pattern.[3] And Liège, in turn, followed antecedents fostered, or at least influenced, by the Brotherhood, such as the school system in Deventer and John Cele's work in Zwolle.[4]

And what, precisely, was the Liège pattern to which Sturm made reference? What was it that he discovered as he attended the Brethren's school?

By 1515 the Brethren of the Common Life in Liège had been

[2] See esp. R. R. Post, *The Modern Devotion* (Leiden, 1968), pp. 558-567, for a treatment of the Liège Brethren and their school. In some respects, Post's work must be taken with caution for reasons indicated in my review article in *AUSS* 8 (1970): 65-76.

[3] Post makes reference to this document in *The Modern Devotion*, p. 558. For the text and a more complete treatment see G. Bonet-Maury, *De opera scholastica fratrum vitae communnis in Neerlandia* (Paris, 1889), pp. 89-95. Also of interest is the document outlining curriculum as given in Karl Engel, *Das Gründungsjahr des Strassburger Gymnasiums 1538-1539* ("Festschrift I," n.p., n.d.), pp. 139-140. A photostatic copy of this curricular outline has been provided in "Appendix A: 1538 Program of Sturm in Strasbourg," in Julia S. Henkel, *An Historical Study of the Educational Contributions of the Brethren of the Common Life* (Ph.D. Dissertation; University of Pittsburgh, 1962), pp. 236-237.

[4] On the Deventer and Zwolle Brethren's educational interests and John Cele's activities, see esp. Albert Hyma, *The Brethren of the Common Life* (Grand Rapids, Mich., 1950), pp. 115-116.

given control of all education in that city.[5] This school had eight classes, and Sturm outlines the subjects taught in each. Reading, writing, and grammar were taught in the eighth, or lowest class. The ordinary university-preparatory or "gymnasium" type of instruction was given basically in classes 7 through 3. The top two classes furnished instruction similar to what might be found in university liberal arts courses, such as philosophy (Plato and Aristotle) and geometry (Euclid). Greek and rhetoric were additions to the curriculum beyond what was usual in the medieval schools. The latter two subjects were introduced at the "gymnasium" level, but continued to be taught through the 2d class. Theology was taught in the highest class.

It is not at all certain that the teaching of rhetoric at this level made its earliest appearance in Brethren-operated schools or in schools where the influence of the Brethren was significant; but it does seem that the addition of Greek to the curriculum was an innovation by the Brethren, at least in transalpine Europe. Instruction in Greek was in evidence, for example, under Alexander Hegius in Deventer before the end of the 15th century; and it seems also to have been taught in Zwolle by 1516 and in Gouda by 1521.[6]

The addition of theology as a subject at the highest level appears to be an innovation on the part of the Liège Brethren themselves. This is not to say that education generally was not religious. In that age it most certainly was, for the entire curriculum from first to last was pervaded by a basic religious concern; and particularly among the Brethren was such a religious concern in evidence. Moreover, the daily lives of students in Brethren schools or in Brethren dormitories were guided by a strong religious emphasis characterized by prayer and by the reading of Scripture and other religious literature.[7] Nevertheless, the introduction of

[5] For a succinct and good summary of the details (noted only very cursorily in the present essay), see Post, pp. 559-560.

[6] See ibid., p. 562.

[7] The spiritual emphasis in Brethren houses and schools has been noted by Albert Hyma in several of his major works, including *The Brethren of the*

theology as a specific subject taught in a pre-university educational setting seems to have been an innovation by the Brethren in Liège.

The upper two classes in the Liège school provided for instruction in philosophy, geometry, law, and theology; and it is interesting to note that these are precisely the same subjects which Sturm built into the curriculum of the top two grades of his system in Strassburg. Futhermore, both Liège and Strassburg had basically an eight-grade pattern, with Greek and rhetoric introduced into the curriculum. The Strassburg plan actually refers to nine classes (in this respect somewhat similar to the Brethren's nine-grade school in Amersfoort); but the first or lowest class seems to have been a preliminary year, with the gymnasium proper beginning with the second class.[8]

Shortly before establishing his Geneva Academy, Calvin paid a return visit in 1556 to Strassburg where once again he had opportunity for first-hand observation of Sturm's educational system. Calvin's own institution utilized a nine-grade plan, wherein the training in the lowest seven classes paralleled the training traditionally given in the gymnasia.[9] This lower division of the Academy was designated as the "schola privata." Each class in it was placed under a "regent"; but as a practical measure for actual instructional purposes, further subdivision into smaller

Common Life (see n. 4, above), and *The Christian Renaissance: A History of the "Devotio Moderna,"* 2d ed. (Hamden, Conn., 1965). In the latter publication the entire text of the original constitution of the Brethren of the Common Life at Deventer is given on pp. 441-474. This is an extremely valuable document which provides first-hand knowledge of the practices of the early Brethren.

[8] See esp. Henkel, pp. 212-213. (On Amersfoort, see ibid., pp. 68-69, 171-177; and W. van Rootselaar, *Amersfoort 777-1580* [Amersfoort, 1878], 2: 279, 354.) It seems that Sturm originally had in mind a 14-grade system, divided into nine lower classes and five upper classes; but this proposed 14-grade system he apparently never put into effect. What evidently is the main outline of its curricular content has been summarized by Hyma, *Christian Renaissance*, p. 296.

[9] Williston Walker, *John Calvin: The Organiser of Reformed Protestantism (1509-1564)* (New York, 1908; reprint ed. with introductory bibliographical essay by John T. McNeill, 1969), pp. 365-366, gives a most useful summary, a few highlights of which are indicated herein.

groups seems to have been made. Annually there was a promotion, a sort of "graduation" of students from one class to the next. Interestingly enough, Greek was made part of the curriculum, as was the case in Liège and Strassburg.

The top two classes in Calvin's Geneva Academy were termed the "schola publica," and they provided specialized training. For these highest classes there were "public professors" of Greek, Hebrew, and Philosophy, with Calvin and Theodore Beza serving as teachers of Theology.

In total perspective, the schools of the Liège Brethren, of Sturm, and of Calvin bear striking resemblance to one another in organizational scheme and in curricular content. The similarities, particularly in the context of Calvin's well-recognized dependence upon Sturm and of Sturm's personally acknowledged use of the Liège pattern, indicate that Strassburg played a significant mediating role in impressing the Geneva Reformer with the educational ideals and practices of the Brotherhood of the Common Life.

Although this particular line of educational influence from the Brethren to Calvin is the clearest and the easiest to document, it may not have been the only manner in which the Brethren's educational concepts reached him in Strassburg. In Schlettstadt, Louis Dringenberg had begun as early as 1441 to teach according to ideals fostered by the Brethren in Deventer, where he had studied; and among products of the Schlettstadt school system were the humanist Jacob Wimpheling, who in 1501 founded a gymnasium in Strassburg, and Jerome Gebweiler, who in 1507 went to Strassburg to supervise reform of the cathedral school in the city. Moreover, when Sturm arrived in Strassburg in 1537, the two Latin schools were taught by Otto Brunfels and John Sapidus, further educators of the Schlettstadt tradition. Thus, earlier than Sturm's arrival, education in Strassburg had already been touched indirectly by influences emanating from the Brotherhood, though certainly the impact was not as sweeping as when

Sturm introduced changes based on his first-hand experience with the Brethren's school in Liège.[10]

2. *Bucer and Theological Concepts*

Other influences from the Brethren of the Common Life also reached Strassburg. For one thing, the important Strassburg reformer Martin Bucer had been a Dringenberg student in Schlettstadt.[11] Moreover, Bucer was profoundly influenced by the writings of Wessel Gansfort, a humanist who had spent most of the last two decades of his life (d. 1489) in close association with the Brethren in Deventer; and Bucer had also been led to a significant change in thinking by a personal visit of Hinne Rode, rector of the school of the Brethren in Utrecht. Indeed, it was Rode who was chiefly responsible for Bucer's adoption of the latter's well-known views on the Eucharist. Of the visit from Rode, which took place in November of 1524, the Strassburg Reformer himself has given the following account:

> When the writings of Carlstadt appeared, I was forced to make an investigation. . . . I consulted Luther, who answered me in a friendly manner. . . . In the meantime there came to me a pious man, named John Rhodius. . . . Although he regards Luther as his teacher, he nevertheless owes at times more to Gansfort. I am amazed that we make so little of Gansfort.
>
> This man Rhodius was my guest. He, with the Bible in his hands, discussed consubstantiation with me at great length. I defended Luther's view with all the force at my command, but soon noticed that I could not meet his arguments, and that one cannot maintain the view I sought to uphold, if one adheres to the Bible as the final authority. So I had to relinquish my own view on Christ's physical presence, although I was still in doubt as to the meaning of the words ["This is my body"]. Carlstadt, for more than one reason, could not satisfy me.[12]

It may be of interest to note that Carlstadt had very likely been influenced toward his views on the Lord's Supper by a brief document on the Eucharist written by Cornelius Hoen, an

[10] On the role of Schlettstadt, and for information of the kind that is furnished in the present paragraph, see esp. Hyma, *Christian Renaissance*, pp. 284, 287-288.

[11] See ibid., p. 287.

[12] As given in English translation by Albert Hyma, *Martin Luther and the Luther Film of 1953* (Ann Arbor, Mich., 1957), pp. 186-187. For further details of the meeting between Hoen and Bucer, as well as for general background, see ibid., pp. 181-190, and Hyma, *Christian Renaissance*, pp. 285-286.

earlier product of the Utrecht Brethren's school, of which Rode was rector. Rode apparently carried this document with him as he made his contacts, not only with Bucer in 1524, but also with Oecolampadius in Basel and with Zwingli in Zurich in 1523.[13]

As for Calvin, it is well known that his theological focus and church administrative insights were significantly sharpened through association with Bucer in Strassburg during the years 1538-1541, even though the basic direction and content of the Geneva Reformer's religious and church-organizational concepts had been developed earlier. As for Calvin's already keen interest in the Eucharist, this was augmented at this time, if his expanded attention to the subject in his second edition of the *Institutes* as well as the production of his *Small Treatise on the Holy Supper* can be taken as evidence.[14] It has been suggested, as well, that Calvin's mature views on justification and on predestination were mediated to him through Bucer, who in turn had gained insights on these matters from northern reformers such as Gansfort and Rode.[15] Indeed, one expert in the field has even declared that "Hinne Rode was more of a 'Calvinist' in 1520 than Calvin was in 1535"![16]

3. *In Conclusion*

It may be well, in concluding, to reiterate a word of caution similar to that given in the previous essay; namely, that we

[13] See Hyma, *Martin Luther,* pp. 185-186.

[14] The *Petit Traicté de la Saincte Cene* was prepared in Strassburg, although it was not actually published until 1541, after Calvin's return to Geneva. Its place of publication was the latter city. Walker, p. 230, feels that in Calvin's attention to the Eucharist in his 2d edition of the *Institutes* (1539), as well as in the *Petit Traicté,* there is an irenic spirit; and the very language Walker uses in this regard cannot but make one conclude that somehow Calvin derived this conciliatory sort of attitude from Bucer. In a somewhat different vein, and in dealing with a broader sweep of religious practices and theological concepts, Hyma, *Christian Renaissance,* p. 287, indicates that in a number of particulars, Calvin took with him, when he left Strassburg in 1541, "the local [Strassburg] views." Among items which Hyma notes are such matters as church organization, the use of Psalms in the church service, church-state relations, justification by faith, the Eucharist, etc.

[15] See Hyma, *Christian Renaissance,* pp. 282-288.

[16] Ibid., p. 286.

must take care not to overemphasize the role which the Brotherhood of the Common Life may have had in molding Calvin's religious thought and practice.[17] Certainly Calvin absorbed numerous influences from many directions. Nevertheless, his stay at the Montaigu in Paris, his contact with the Fabrisian circle of reformers, and his association with Sturm and Bucer in Strassburg surely were among the more significant avenues through which ideals and concepts fostered by the Brethren of the Common Life did indeed reach him.

Perhaps the most striking, as well as the most clearly demonstrable, line of influence from this Brotherhood to him was that pertaining to educational reforms. Moreover, it was an area of activity that brought well-deserved recognition both to the Brethren themselves and to Calvin. The fame which the Brethren achieved as educators is quite aptly illustrated, for example, in a statement made by the Belgian Jesuit Miraeus about the middle of the 16th century: "Does not the Society of Jesus, following the example of the Brethren, open schools throughout the whole world?"[18] Calvin, on the other hand, did not personally, of course, "open schools throughout the whole world"; but his Geneva Academy soon became "world famous," and its influence reached truly afar. To it and from it streamed a multitude of reform leaders and educators of various European countries—reform leaders and educators who not only carried with them Calvin's Protestant theology of Geneva, but who also fostered and disseminated various spiritual and educational ideals which had, in reality, come to Calvin from that northern reform movement known as the Brotherhood of the Common Life.[19]

[17] See *AUSS* 13 (1975): 78.

[18] Quoted in Marcel Godet, *La congrégation de Montaigu (1490-1580)* (Paris, 1912), p. 107, n. (continuation of n. 1, p. 106).

[19] Walker, pp. 366-367, has a useful section on the impact which Calvin's Geneva Academy had from the very first. He points out that in its earliest three years, its students included Florent Chrestien, tutor of Henry IV of France; Thomas Bodley, founder of the Bodleian Library in Oxford; Francis Junius, of University of Leiden fame; and other individuals who have gained significant historical renown.

ADDITIONAL NOTE ON CALVIN AND THE INFLUENCE OF THE BRETHREN OF THE COMMON LIFE IN FRANCE

KENNETH A. STRAND

The foregoing article is the second (and concluding) one in my treatment of John Calvin in relationship to the Brethren of the Common Life. The earlier article, in *AUSS* 13 (Spring 1975): 67-78, dealt primarily with (1) the direct influence of the Brotherhood upon Calvin at the College of Montaigu, and (2) the Brotherhood's indirect influence on Calvin through the Fabrisian circle of humanists (including Lefèvre d' Étaples himself). Since the time when I prepared the manuscript for that first article, a valuable book dealing with Calvin's "spirituality" and the roots of that "spirituality" has appeared: Lucien Joseph Richard, *The Spirituality of John Calvin* (Atlanta, 1974). Because of the importance of this publication, brief attention to it will be given here, specifically in certain matters that relate to the theme of my own earlier article.

First of all, it should be noted that Richard's work takes basically the form of a theological analysis whereas my presentation was more historical in its emphasis. Richard not only deals with salient features of Calvin's thought, however, but also analyzes major thrusts of various forerunners, including the *Devotio Moderna* (of which the Brethren of the Common life formed a central component), Jean Gerson, Francesco Petrarch, Erasmus, and Lefèvre (pp. 12-77). His careful analysis does much toward uncovering—or at least toward pointing in the direction of—various strains of late medieval thought which informed Calvin's "spirituality."

With regard to the Devotio Moderna, Richard's summaries of the "inward" type of spirituality evidenced in works by early leaders and writers of the movement (see his pp. 13-39) are basically correct, and they provide a useful compendium for quick reference. Also, he properly acknowledges the influence of this movement in France (see pp. 32, 48-49).

His treatment of the Devotio is somewhat imbalanced, however, by his stress on the supposed "anti-intellectualism" and "asceticism" of that movement. His conclusions in this regard seem based largely on his analysis of a relatively few works of devotional type, with special emphasis on the Thomas à Kempis version of the *Imitation of Christ* (which admittedly reflects the attitude which Richard discerns).[1] But was the "inwardness" of the Devotio Moderna really as anti-intellectual and as ascetic as Richard has assumed? Constitutions of early Brother-houses, plus evidence regarding the Brethren's educational work and their book-copying and printing activities—these would seem to indicate otherwise.[2] One may wonder if Richard has not been unduly influenced by the monumental work of R. R. Post, *The Modern Devotion* (Leiden, 1968), which too tends to minimize the intellectual attitudes and activities of the Brethren.[3]

Richard seems to feel that an "Erasmian" humanistic influence in France brought theology and spirituality together there, whereas the Devotio Moderna had separated the two by its depreciation of the intellectual and theological.[4] In this regard two important questions must be asked: (1) Was the Erasmian influence as great in France as

[1] Even the *Imitation* itself had appeared in earlier versions that were less anti-intellectual, ascetic, and monastically inclined. For an excellent discussion of this matter, see Albert Hyma, *The Brethren of the Common Life* (Grand Rapids, Mich., 1950), pp. 145-194, and also Hyma's English translation of Book I of the *Imitation* as found in the Eutin manuscript: *The Imitation of Christ by Gerard Zerbolt of Zutphen* (Grand Rapids, Mich., 1950).

[2] Michael Schoengen has published the early Zwolle constitution in his *Jacobus Traiecti alias de Voecht narratio . . .* (Amsterdam, 1908), pp. 239-273. More readily accessible is the Deventer constitution edited by A. Hyma and included in his *The Christian Renaissance: A History of the "Devotio Moderna"* (Grand Rapids, Mich., 1924), pp. 440-474, and reprinted in K. A. Strand, ed., *The Dawn of Modern Civilization: Studies in Renaissance, Reformation and Other Topics Presented to Honor Albert Hyma* (Ann Arbor, Mich., 1962, 1964), pp. 361-395 (hereafter cited as *Dawn*), as well as in the 2d ed., enlarged, of *The Christian Renaissance* (Hamden, Conn., 1965), pp. 440-474. The basic treatment of the educational work of the Brethren of the Common Life is Julia S. Henkel, *An Historical Study of the Educational Contributions of the Brethren of the Common Life* (Ph.D. dissertation, University of Pittsburgh, 1962); and she has also provided important highlights of this educational work in "School Organizational Patterns of the Brethren of the Common Life," in *Dawn*, pp. 323-338 (reprinted in K. A. Strand, ed., *Essays on the Northern Renaissance* [Ann Arbor, Mich., 1968], pp. 35-50). For a brief but rather comprehensive survey of the printing interests and activities of the Brethren, see my chapter "The Brethren of the Common Life and Fifteenth-Century Printing: A Brief Survey," in *Dawn*, pp. 341-355 (reprinted in *Essays on the Northern Renaissance*, pp. 51-64), and also cf. works cited therein.

[3] See my review of Post in *AUSS* 8 (1970): 65-76.

[4] Two striking quotations from Richard will suffice to illustrate the point: "It is in this new vision of theology that Erasmus' original contribution was made. It is here also that he differed most from the *Devotio Moderna*. Instead of abandoning theology as being a distraction to the spiritual life,

Richard assumes? (2) Was this influence so diametrically opposite to that of the Devotio?

Though admitting that Erasmus himself surely did make an important impact on French humanism, we may wonder whether that impact has not been overestimated by Richard—at least with respect to the earliest French humanists. First of all, the various early transalpine humanists tended to draw on *common sources,* such as Italian humanism, and *both* Erasmus and Lefèvre imbibed of influences from the Devotio Moderna as well (historical realities recognized by Richard). Second, there was interaction also among early Northern humanists themselves, whether Dutch, French, German, or English—but the process generally was indeed one of *interaction* rather than one-way borrowing (a matter evidently not so readily discerned by Richard). In any event, the following statement by Richard is quite jolting: "A majority of the French Humanists born around 1490 were Erasmians, men like Lefèvre d' Etaples, Guillaume Budé and others" (p. 57). Lefèvre was born about 1455 (if not earlier), and he had studied classics and had also visited Italy a number of years before Erasmus first began manifesting humanistic interests! And even Budé, born in 1467, was a young adult by 1490, as well as probably being slightly senior in age to Erasmus (if Erasmus was born in 1469, his more likely birth year than the alternatively suggested 1466).

The crucial question that needs attention here, however, is whether or not Richard is correct in his concept that Lefèvre, through Erasmus's influence, worked to "breach the separation between theology and spirituality" (p. 70) *in contrast to* a separation which presumably the Devotio Moderna had made in this respect. Richard recognizes that Lefèvre was "deeply influenced by the *Devotio Moderna*" too, and he properly states that this fact has been "conclusively demonstrated by L. Salley [actually, C. Louise Salley]" (p. 69). But Salley's work, called to attention in my earlier article, reveals that the Devotio Moderna nourished Lefèvre's religious thought in *very much the same way* in which Richard declares that Erasmus did! It is unfortunate that Richard apparently had access only to the abstract of Salley's Ph.D. dissertation, not to the dissertation itself, nor even to Salley's extensive chapter in the Albert Hyma Festschrift

Erasmus integrated theology into it" (p. 67). "But although in continuity with the *Devotio Moderna* in many of its tenets, the spirituality of the French humanists differed from the *Devotio Moderna* in its most original contribution: its integration of the intellectual and spiritual life. This integration of theology and spirituality began under the influence of Erasmus and resulted in the elaboration of a *docta pietas*" (p. 73).

volume *The Dawn of Modern Civilization.*[5] Moreover, if Richard had dealt more broadly with both Erasmus and the Devotio, the distinction which he has made between the influence of Erasmus and that of the Devotio would certainly be blurred, if not obliterated.[6]

The Northern humanists generally (including Erasmus) and the Devotio *both* looked back to ancient sources for religious thought as well as for practice, a fact rightly stressed by Richard for Erasmus but apparently not given due consideration by him for the Devotio. However, as far as purely *theological* interests are concerned, we may go a step further: Although both the humanists and the Brethren of the Common Life tended to decry finespun scholastic argumentation, the latter appear to have been more open toward scholastic theology than were the humanists, if the kinds of books used and disseminated by the Brethren may be used as any sort of criterion in this regard.[7] And in the same connection, one may ponder also the fact that a staunch and conservative theologian Noel Beda, who attacked the Fabrisian reformers, could quite readily be the successor of his mentor Jean Standonck (a disciple of the Brethren of the Common Life) as head of the College of Montaigu. Would such a facile transition have been possible if Beda's predecessor had been a humanist of the

[5] Her extensive chapter, "Jacques Lefèvre d' Étaples: Heir of the Dutch Reformers of the Fifteenth Century," appears in *Dawn*, pp. 75-124.

[6] Richard's analysis of Erasmus's thought, careful as this analysis is (see his pp. 57-69), rests too heavily on a rather limited range of that humanist's works, especially the *Enchiridion Militis Christiani* (important as that work certainly was in France); certain other major productions of Erasmus, such as the *Praise of Folly* and *Familiar Colloquies,* have been more or less bypassed. As for Richard's treatment of the Devotio Moderna, materials of the kind mentioned earlier in this "Additional Note" (see the references in n. 2, above) would have provided a more adequate and accurate perspective than was obtainable from his attention so exclusively to a limited number of works of devotional type.

Even his treatment of certain pioneer leaders of the Devotio who were responsible for some of these devotional works seems, however, to suffer somewhat too. For instance, Gerard Zerbolt of Zutphen (d. 1398), whose *De Reformatione Virium Animae* and *De Spiritualibus Ascensionibus* Richard summarizes quite fairly, surely deserves more recognition for scholarship than what Richard grants him. (Thomas à Kempis, e.g., wrote of Zerbolt in Vita Ger. Sutph., par. 6, that the "scholars and great writers gave him high praise for his learning.")

[7] See my chapter in *Dawn*, referred to in n. 2, above, and the sources called to attention in that chapter. Works by scholastic theologians, such as Anselm of Canterbury and Bonaventura, were among the kinds of books in which the Brethren of the Common Life took an interest.

"Erasmian" or "Fabrisian" sort? (Then too, there is the case of nominalist theologian Gabriel Biel, who was actually a leader of the Brethren in Upper-Rhenish Germany.[8])

Finally, a word must be said about Richard's concluding remarks. He states that Calvin's spirituality "differed radically from the *Devotio Moderna* on three essential points: it was a spirituality of service within the world; it was accompanied by a new religious epistemology which made possible a reinterpretation of ecclesiological models and laid sound foundations for individualism in spirituality; and it asserted the inner unity of Christian life and theology" (p. 174). On all three counts, Calvin's spirituality was more similar to, than different from, the emphases of the Devotio Moderna. Especially in connection with the first of Richard's three "essential points" of difference, it may be pertinent to add here a fact aptly called to attention by Albert Hyma:

> Unlike many of the monks, the Brethren of the Common Life, with rare exception, preferred a busy life of "good works" in the cities to peaceful meditation in the country. "We have decided," wrote the brethren at Zwolle in 1415, "to live in cities, in order that we may be able to give advice and instruction to clerics and other persons who wish to serve the Lord."[9]

The foregoing analysis of Richard's publication is not intended to be a comprehensive review, nor should the questions I have raised be allowed to detract from the real worth of this book. I have dealt specifically with issues relating to the topic treated in my own article on the Brethren's possible impact on Calvin in France; and in this matter, Richard's work has failed to take into account several important matters. However, it is well to repeat here two cautions set forth in my original article: (1) the need to take care, in harmony with Salley's suggestion, not to consider Lefèvre as a "Protestant before the Reformation"; and (2) the necessity to remember, as I emphasized (reiterated also in my second article), that both "Lefèvre and Calvin were certainly influenced by factors from more than one direction," the latter's religious development being "especially complex."[10]

Richard's work is valuable in that it cuts new ground in the per-

[8] William M. Landeen has treated Gabriel Biel in a number of publications. For a brief summary of pertinent information, see Landeen's article "Biel, Gabriel" in *Twentieth Century Encyclopedia of Religious Knowledge,* 1: 161-162.

[9] A. Hyma, *Renaissance to Reformation* (Grand Rapids, Mich., 1951), p. 131.

[10] *AUSS* 13 (1975): 77-78.

spective from which it presents and analyzes various important aspects of Calvin's theology. But it is important too, as indicated earlier, in pointing toward some of the varied medieval backgrounds which informed and nurtured Calvin's "spirituality."[11] (A more general review of Richard's *The Spirituality of John Calvin* will appear in the "Book Reviews" section of a forthcoming issue of *AUSS*. This will take note particularly of several pertinent matters not dealt with in the foregoing discussion.)

[11] On p. 51, above, I have indicated the main "forerunners" mentioned by Richard. His analysis could probably well have been expanded to include Nicholas of Cusa (1401-64), whose work influenced Lefèvre; and in my own article too, perhaps at least a passing reference to this important cleric would have been appropriate.

Indeed, as early as 1490 Lefèvre was acquainted with Nicholas of Cusa's writings. The latter, in turn, had been influenced by the Brethren of the Common Life, having attended school in Deventer and also having had later contacts with the Devotio Moderna. Shortly before his death, he provided funds for the establishment of a dormitory in Deventer, where the pupils were to dress like the Brethren. See Hyma, *Christian Renaissance*, p. 262, for these and other details.

HISTORY AS RHETORICAL WEAPON: CHRISTIAN HUMANISM IN CALVIN'S REPLY TO SADOLETO, 1539

James R. Payton, Jr.

Preliminary Considerations

The title of this paper assumes answers to two important and related questions of 16th-century historiography. Time does not permit a detailed defense of these answers but it may be worthwhile to mention those questions and articulate the answers to them--answers which reflect the growing consensus of historiographical scholarship.

The first question is that of the relationship of the Renaissance to the Reformation, or, put more precisely, of the relationship of Christian Humanism to the Reformation. The second question pertains to John Calvin's relation to Christian Humanism. With regard to the first question, the hoary postulate of an unmitigated antithesis between a man-centred Renaissance and a God-centred Reformation, of a man-glorifying humanism (such that "Christian" Humanism is virtually a contradiction in terms) and a God-glorifying Reformation, has not stood the test of careful historical inquiry. Jacob Burckhardt's assertion of nascent individualism as the philosophical core of the Italian Renaissance[1] still has its defenders,[2] to be sure; nevertheless, the preponderance of recent Renaissance scholarship moves in quite a different direction, one which leads the attentive traveller to a destination far removed from that irreconcilable antithesis.[3] Through the studies of Paul Oskar Kristeller and a host of scholars indebted to him, the unifying core of the Renaissance has come to be recognized, not in a philosophical orientation, but in a pedagogical one.[4] According to this growing consensus, Italian Renaissance humanism was, as is presupposed in the term, concerned with the humaniora, those humane studies which cultivate responsible manhood and citizenship. The distinctive element of that pedagogy, however, was the shared opinion that this could be best attained by the study of and intense involvement with antiquity--Greek, Roman and, especially for Northern Europe, Christian.[5] Unquestionably, such a pedagogical perspective could be put to the service of attitudes toward humankind, the world, God and the Church, inimical to those espoused in the Protestant Reformation. However, it is just as unquestionable that such perspectives could well be used in the service of the Evangelical movement. Recent scholarship has shown that the majority of those who joined Luther's cause in the early years of the Reformation were steeped in the Christian Humanism of Northern Europe.[6] Further, scholarly assessments of the subsequent careers of these allegedly erstwhile Christian humanists serving in leadership roles in the Protestant Reformation, in general, and of their curricular innovations and instructional objectives, in particular, demonstrate an unmistakable and continuing adherence on their part to the enthusiasms of the Christian humanist movement.[7] Clearly, these 16th-century leaders discerned no radical antithesis between their Christian Humanism and their Protestantism; leading scholars of the 20th century have shown that we should agree with them. Whatever questions about the relationship between the movements still remain, it has become historiographically irresponsible to assert a radical antithesis between the Renaissance and the Reformation, or between Christian Humanism and Protestantism.[8]

In regard to the second question, and tying in to the assessment just given, this essay assumes the viability of recognizing a strong Christian humanist vein in Calvin's thought and writing.[9] While no careful historical monograph has yet appeared to update the study of Quirinus Breen[10] in light of the more penetrating evaluations of Christian Humanism which have appeared in the last two generations,[11] these evaluations offer much that could corroborate, sharpen, and improve on Breen's assessment of Calvin's humanism. Drawing upon some of these evaluations, the author hopes that his essay will contribute to a better appreciation and understanding of Calvin's Christian humanism by elucidating his rhetorical use of history in the 1539 Reply to Sadoleto.

With regard to the point of concentration in this paper, converging on Calvin's rhetorical use of history is neither a gratuitous focus nor a fortuitous discovery of elements in the text of Calvin's reply. Historical scholarship of the last generation has cogently shown that the humanism of both Italy and Northern Europe diligently pursued rhetorical expertise.[12] The ideal of the orator as personified by Cicero and Cato in ancient Rome, as set forth in the instruction offered in Cicero's De Oratore and Quintilian's Institutio oratoria, and as literarily embodied preeminently in the writing of Cicero, was so compelling to the humanists that one scholar of the era has categorized the Renaissance as "the pursuit of eloquence".[13] This eloquence, however, carried for the humanists none of the negative connotations sometimes associated with the term rhetoric in the present day. Rather, in concert with their pedagogical goal, the study of rhetoric purposed after the development of a winsome, refined, articulate, clear-thinking and consequently effectual spokesman for the wisdom with which men should conduct all their affairs.[14]

Rhetoric provided a compelling and attractive form for the presentation of wisdom. That wisdom, however, was for the humanists bound up with the material of a budding historical awareness unknown to the medieval chronicler but fundamental in shaping humanism's outlooks. The sense of historical distance that dawned with Petrarch and Boccacio[15] enlightened the humanists who followed them with a sensitivity for historical anachronism.[16] That is to say, the humanist movement was endowed from the beginning with a perspective on history which no only legitimized their rejection of the medieval period and espousal of antiquity, but which also invited curricular renewal.[17] Recent Renaissance scholarship has affirmed the significance of this new sense of history for the whole humanist movement. Within that movement, some humanists were more alert to the implications of that sense and the possibilities it offered for their rhetorical pursuits than were others, of course,[18] and the very sense of history itself demanded much further development than could be expected at that point in its nonage.[19] Nevertheless, humanism found in this budding historical sensitivity both a new way of looking at the world and a potent weapon for the assault on things medieval.

Given these scholarly assessments of the fundamental humanist enthusiasms, if it can be demonstrated that Calvin deliberately manifested rhetorical finesse while developing an historical argument in the defense he offered of the Evangelical movement in his Reply to Sadoleto, then the conclusion will seem incontrovertible that Calvin embodied the ideals of Christian Humanism as he sought the welfare of the Protestant Reformation. If that can be shown, then a suggestive inference regarding the thrust of Calvin's reply arises.

Introduction to the Reply

Jacopo Cardinal Sadoleto was well-known among learned men in his day: he was one of the leading humanists in Italy, an accomplished Ciceronian Latinist, a respected scholar and author, a would-be reformer of the Church from within the College of Cardinals, and a biblical commentator/theologian of some note.[20] Recognizing all these qualities, the Council of Geneva sought someone of stature to answer him. It was a daunting task but offered Calvin an inviting opportunity, to which he responded with a restrained but unmistakable élan. Calvin never intended his 1539 Reply to Sadoleto to be a piece of private correspondence. He saw to it that his work was published along with the cardinal's letter as a public defense of his and Farel's labours in Geneva and, by extension, of the whole Protestant movement.[21]

The text of the reply indicates that Calvin had a particular reading public especially in mind. The opening words refer to the contemporary society doctorum hominum, "of learned men," and are quickly followed by Calvin's recognition that he was addressing Sadoleto publice inter eruditos, "publicly among the well-informed." The third sentence already expresses a certainty that this work will become well known apud omnes literatos, "among all the liberally educated."[22] Throughout the reply, Calvin addresses that audience, writing always in the style of contemporary learned discourse--namely, a refined and elegant Ciceronian Latinity.[23] In his presentation, he adopts the posture of an adroit lawyer, whose skillful defense ends up indicting the prosecution as well.[24] When one recalls that Calvin's formal humanist training lay in the study of civil law at Orleans, when one keeps in mind that the emulation of Cicero's Latin style was a goal of the humanist movement, and when one recognizes that, at least in the minds of the humanists of the period, the society of Christian Humanism, the conclusion seems abundantly warranted that Calvin directed his 1539 Reply to Sadoleto to a Christian humanist audience, whoever else may have ended up reading it as well. By publishing his reply along with the text of Sadoleto's letter, Calvin gave a Christian humanist readership, which was at the time divided in its loyalties between the Romanist and Protestant obediences,[25] much to consider.

Rhetorical Finesse

Calvin was much less well-known in the scholarly world of his day than his opponent. Calvin's 1536 Institutio had, of course, occasioned considerable interest in the religious world. His more technical study of Seneca's De Clementia had not, however, captured the interest of the scholars.[26] Consequently, in the matter of esteem among his intended readership, Calvin was at a considerable disadvantage. He respectfully acknowledged Sadoleto's outstanding reputation numerous times in his reply. The first sentence of the work speaks of the cardinal's "excellent learning and distinguished eloquence" which served to distinguish him among the "great abundance of learned men whom our age has produced," such that Sadoleto was "among the few whom all, who want to be considered studious of liberal arts, honour and respect."[27] Shortly thereafter, Calvin described the Italian humanist as a man qui de bonis disciplinis sit optime meritis, a man "who deserves the highest respect for his excellent learning."[28] This deferential acknowledgment of Sadoleto's eminence showed considerable respect for the Italian humanist, to be sure; it also indicated that Calvin shared with Sadoleto and with his intended readership a concern for the eloquence and the liberal arts which were the enthusiasms of the humanist movement.

In regard to the matter of eloquence, Sadoleto's letter to the Genevans actually fell considerably short of his reputation, however. Acknowledged by many in his own day as a master of Latin style, the Italian humanist's previous letters to Melanchthon and Johann Sturm had been elegant treatises. Neither had produced the positive effect intended by Sadoleto. His letter to the Genevans, the third of his forays into Evangelical circles, lacked the stylistic polish for which he was otherwise renowned.[29] It has often been observed that Calvin's reply, in contrast, was one of the most eloquent literary masterpieces of a man who has been widely recognized by subsequent scholarship as one of the best Latinists of the 16th century.[30] Was this literary difference lost on the man who saw to it that the two pieces were published together? This can hardly have been the case; rather, writing as he was for a learned public, Calvin made full use of his literary abilities and contrasted his composition with the feebler effort of the renowned Italian humanist, as a subtle but significant element in Calvin's defense of the Evangelical movement. For those who prized eloquence--as the Christian humanists of his day unquestionably did--, Calvin produced a work of literary artistry to be appreciated and which, consequently, already in its elegant style served as a defense of the Protestant movement for the intended readership.

In the course of his reply, Calvin frequently referred to the liberales artes which the Christian humanists prized and to the effects such a course of study would have on those who mastered it: the opening sentence already mentioned many in that day who were bonarum artium studiosi and was soon supplemented by a reference to the humanist goal, hominem liberalibus omnibus doctrinis expolitum, "a man refined by all kinds of liberal learning."[31] Calvin contrasted such training with that of the scholastics, styling them "sophists,"[32] referring with disgust to the "kind of doctrine being taught in the schools to candidates for ecclesiastical ministry, "instruction which as "mere sophistry, [so] contorted, involved, tortuous and perplexing that scholastic theology deserved to be called a species of secret magic."[33] With such criticism of scholastic learning and, especially, scholastic theology, Calvin joined in the common Christian humanist disdain for the intellectual training proffered in scholasticism, of course. He also thereby clearly identified both himself and the Protestant movement he was defending with the humanist program of liberal arts which would enhance genuine doctrinae, prudentiae, gravitatis.[34] This gave Calvin the opportunity for an oblique but devastating attack on Sadoleto's humanism and afforded a subtly powerful appeal to the humanist movement. By affirming the liberal arts and their expected benefits, and by tarring the Italian humanist with the brush of the scholastic theology which the cardinal never criticized in his call to the Genevans to return to the Roman obedience (where such theology was still taught), Calvin gave the learned world of his day to understand that Christian Humanism's rejection of scholasticism found a more welcome home in Protestantism than it could even with renowned Christian humanists as leaders in the Roman obedience. As a subtle rhetor, Calvin did not need to draw out that implication explicitly; no Christian humanist could possibly miss it.

Calvin did explicitly draw out another criticism of Sadoleto which raised further questions about the cardinal's faithful adherence to humanist emphases--namely, to the canons of humanist discourse. As over against the disputation mentality of scholastic training, with its openness toward invective and misrepresentation for the purpose of winning a disputation, humanism placed the winsomeness of the orator who, dealing fairly with his opponent, won him to agreement rather than vanquishing him in battle.[35] Consequently, Calvin's protest against misrepresentation and against unseemly invective on the cardinal's part was not merely the vigorous defense of a wounded opponent but more importantly an appeal to the genteel audience of Christian Humanism. Calvin eschewed the ill will, harshness, and hostility[36] with which Sadoleto had assailed Farel and him. He further accused the cardinal of "calumnious accusation," of failing to maintain "mildness and restraint" but instead engaging in "intemperance, violent passion, and harshness," of "the bitterest expressions," of "many other violent reproaches," and of "pouring out the venom of your bitterness."[37] In addition to the spirit and tone of the cardinal's letter, Calvin objected to Sadoleto's "futile slander," his failure to deal "truly and candidly," his seeking to generate "extreme and malicious ill-will," and his attempt "to prejudice our cause."[38]

By such conduct, Calvin averred, the Italian humanist had ad illiberalem usque calumniandi licentiam descendas ("descended to an indulgence in false accusation unbecoming to one trained in the liberal arts").[39] Sadoleto's presentation had been indecorum, ne dicam illiberale ("unseemly, not to say illiberal") and was cadere non videtur in hominem liberalibus omnibus doctrinis expolitum ("unworthy of one who has been refined by all kinds of liberal learning").[40] It was Sadoletum, ista doctrinae, prudentiae, gravitatis existimatione, vehementer dedecet ("exceptionally unbecoming to Sadoleto, considering his reputation for learning, prudence, and gravity").[41] Altogether apart from his response to it, Calvin asserted, the cardinal's letter was existimationem tuam apud probos et graves viros, nobis quoque tacentibus, vehementer laesura est ("extremely injurious to your [Sadoleto's] reputation with honorable and serious men").[42] Calvin's repetition of this assessment made unmistakably clear for his readers what the self-inflicted injury of Sadoleto was: the Roman cardinal had failed his humanism and had conducted himself like a medieval scholastic.

By way of contrast, Calvin declared,

> "I will conduct myself so that all may perceive that I have the great advantage over you, not only in the goodness and justice of the cause, in conscientious rectitude, sincerity of heart, and candour of speech, but have also been considerably more successful in maintaining mildness and restraint."[43]

Gentleness and moderation, indeed, did not keep Calvin from making the numerous objections to Sadoleto's presentation cited above, but he declared that he would not dwell on these points as much as might have been warranted.[44] Calvin basically lived up to his declaration in his often sharp responses to the cardinal, avoiding the humanist litany of rhetorical sins just cited.

Of the two men, it had to be consequently clear to the Christian humanist reader of Calvin's reply that the young Protestant had been much more faithful to the humanist orientation of how men in disagreement should interact. Again the esteemed Italian humanist had appeared in the unwelcome role of the scholastic in whom Christian Humanism found its foil, and in the young Evangelical leader seemed embodied the refined humanist rhetorical attitude and procedure.

Finally in this regard, it should be noted that the argument as Sadoleto had developed it in his letter to the Genevans fell considerably short of the ideal of carefully and winsomely reasoned assertion which the humanist movement prized in an orator. It has been noted that Sadoleto's was not a terribly logical or consequential mind; in contrast, Calvin is known for his logical mind.[45] In regard to the argument as presented in the two documents, where Sadoleto's presentation was loose, verbose and meandering, Calvin's was taut, measured and deliberate in direction.[46] This was a difference which any humanist would readily observe as he read the two pieces which had been published together. Even so, Calvin took the opportunity to expose Sadoleto's failure. He expressed disappointment in Sadoleto's unskillful argument, rhetorically addressing the cardinal in astonishment, "O, Sadoleto, who could ever have expected such a statement from you?"[47] The pointedness of Calvin in this regard was clear when he asserted that the cardinal's argument was utterly implausible.[48] As the skilled young humanist lawyer, Calvin could hardly have been more suggestively critical than when he declared to the Italian humanist, iactum est abs te defensionis meae fundamentum ("the foundation of my defense was laid by you").[49]

Sadoleto had again failed his reputation as a humanist. His argument had been inept and had provided his opponent with the weapons for defense. Calvin, on the other hand, manifested in his argument--to which this study shall turn more explicitly below--the measured, careful, articulate, elegant, and cogent argument prized by the practitioners of ancient rhetoric in the 16th century, the Christian humanists.

In summary, it can be seen that Calvin's presentation in his 1539 Reply to Sadoleto appealed to the rhetorical enthusiasms of the Christian humanist movement. His literary style was the Ciceronian elegance they prized; his anti-scholastic educational orientation and his concomitant preference for the humanist curriculum of liberal arts which culminated in the development of an effective orator were hallmarks of Northern Christian Humanism; his treatment of his opponent in debate manifested the expected attitude of a faithful Christian humanist engaged in this rhetorical pursuit; and, finally, his opposition to poor argument alongside his own presentation of a careful legal defense were aspects of the rhetorical tradition as it had developed among Northern Christian Humanists, especially among the lawyers. In all of this, by way of contrast, Jacopo Cardinal Sadoleto, the Italian humanist of some renown, came in for considerable implicit and explicit criticism. Calvin came forth as a polished and accomplished rhetorician in the name and for the sake of Protestantism.

Historical Argument

This examination of Calvin's Reply to Sadoleto must now turn from the rhetorical form in which the author cast his defense to the historical argument he incorporated in it. This is not, of course, turning from mere packaging unessential to the defense to the truly substantial in the argument, if one appreciates the orientation of the Christian humanist movement. For its practitioners, rhetorical finesse was an essential aspect of convincing argument,[50] and Calvin manifested considerable expertise in this fine art as he wrote for them, as has been seen. Even so, in order fully to appreciate the embodiment of Christian humanism's ideals in Calvin's 1539 defense of the Evangelical movement, consideration must now be given to the use he made of history in this reply.[51]

In examining Calvin's defense, it is hardly surprising to find the Protestant leader taking his stand first of all on the Scriptures. He criticized Sadoleto's urging the people of Geneva simply to follow the Church's tradition when confronted with a question as to which way to go; instead, the people of God were to follow the instruction of the Word of God, by which the Spirit of God would guide the Church. That is what Sadoleto should have advised the Genevans to do, urged

Calvin[52] in the manner to be expected of a Protestant spokesman.

However, Calvin pressed this basic Evangelical point with a subtle twist: when he returned to it a few pages later, he used the language of tradition to describe the responsibility of pastors to be guided by the Word of God in all that they do and teach. He said that their office non quae a se ipsis placita temere excuderint, confidenter ingerere, sed quae ex ore Domini oracula acceperint, religiose ac bona fide proferre, "is not boldly to set forth teachings devised on their own, but religiously and in good faith to deliver the oracles which they have received at the mouth of the Lord" (emphasis added).[53] Calvin was quite unwilling to relinquish the cherished conception of tradition: it simply had to be the proper tradition, that of faithfulness toward the Word of God. This was for him no ahistorical and unattainable ideal; rather, it had demarked the Church, in the main, during the course of her history and found its contemporary embodiment among the Protestants. He argued that the church is, properly, only that societatem ... per omnes aetates dispersa, una tamen Christi doctrina et uno spiritu colligata, "the society which ... existing in all ages, nevertheless [is] bound together by the one doctrine and the one Spirit of Christ."[54] In thus describing the way of the Church through history, Calvin focused the understanding of tradition in a manner allowing both for historical and theological criticism of the Church in any particular era, on the one hand, and for an historical and theological continuity of the Church, on the other. He went on to declare, Cum hac esse nobis quidquam dissidii negamus, "with this [Church] we deny that we are in disagreement."[55] More specifically, in the two particulars Sadoleto had addressed in his letter to Geneva--the question of pure worship and of true doctrine--, Calvin stated that Protestant worship entailed no departure ab ea colendi Dei ratione, quam semper observavit ecclesia catholica, "from that method of worshipping God which the Catholic Church always observed,"[56] and that dogma ... nostrum ... in ecclesia semper habitum pro confesso fuerit, "our doctrine ... has always been confessed in the Church as an acknowledged point."[57]

For all their criticism of the medieval period and their preference for Christian antiquity, the Christian humanists nonetheless believed as Christians that the Church had never ceased to exist, even in the darkest medieval night. In some fashion still undefined in relationship to their sense of historical distance, there had to be an essential continuity, a true tradition. According to Calvin--and the same could be said of Philip Melanchthon and Martin Bucer--, that tradition had been preserved and then existed among the Protestants, and not in the Roman obedience.[58]

Calvin not only reclaimed the prized conception of tradition, however; as has already been seen, he affirmed the place of preeminence held by Scripture within it. For a Christian humanist readership, sensitive to the claims of tradition but especially enthused for Christian antiquity, this would occasion no particular difficulty, for, if nothing else, the Scriptures were, indeed, a monument from antiquity. However, Christian humanism also looked upon the writings of the ancient Church Fathers and the decisions of the ancient ecumenical councils with special reverence as sharing in the authority inhering in Christian antiquity. Calvin identified with that enthusiasm when he declaimed against the Roman church's persecution of omnes religionis nostrae sanctionis, et quae Dei oraculis sunt proditae, et quae sanctorum quoque patrum libris sunt consignatae, et quae priscis conciliis approbatae, of "everything sanctioned by our religion, both as delivered by the oracles of God, and vouched for in the books of the holy fathers, and established by ancient councils" (emphasis added).[59] By way of contrast, the Protestant opposition to Roman teaching and practice was non divini verbi modo virtute, sed sanctorum etiam patrum praesidio armati sumus, "armed not only with the power of the divine Word, but with the support of the holy fathers also" (emphasis added).[60] More will be noted about Calvin's appeal to Christian antiquity below, but it is essential here to notice that his Protestant stance upon the Word of God was not of such a nature as to require him to posit a huge disjunction between the ancient Word of God and other written monuments of Christian antiquity. He recognized and forthrightly presented a distinction, indeed, declaring, Tametsi enim solum Dei verbum extra omnem iudicii aleam constituimus, conciliis vero et patribus ita certam demum autoritatem constare voluimus, si ad eius normam respondeant: eo tamen honore locoque concilia et patres dignamur, quem obtinere sub Christo par est, ("although we hold that the Word of God alone lies beyond all judgement, we genuinely maintain that councils and fathers certainly have an indubitable authority if they accord with its rule; we still deem councils and fathers worthy of the honour and rank which it is appropriate for them to hold under Christ").[61] Their authority operated, for Protestantism, on different levels, with Scripture the ultimate and only unquestioned authority, to be sure.[62] For all the distinction, however, Calvin gave a place to the ancient fathers and councils which he accorded to no other claimant to religious authority, and that place was so close that he could readily connect the ancient Scriptures, on the one hand, and the ancient fathers and councils, on the other, simply with a coordinating conjunction.[63] Here was a possibly modified, but nevertheless unmistakably recognizable, Christian humanist orientation on religious authority. According to Calvin, that perspective had been abandoned within the Roman communion but was held by the Protestant movement.

Calvin fleshed out his claim to antiquity with citations from Cyprian, Ambrose, Basil the Great,

Chrysostom, Augustine, and by a general reference to "the testimonies of the Fathers."[64] Calvin could have marshalled a host of other citations, had he chosen to do so: his 1539 Institutio was distinguished from the 1536 edition by, among other things, extensive patristic references.[65] Although the citations he offered were not plentiful, given the audience he was addressing, they were more than adequate, in the circumstance, to carry the point, for Sadoleto's letter--a letter from a humanist enthusiast for Christian antiquity--had offered no explicit citation of any Church Father![66]

Furthermore, extensive references to the fathers proved unnecessary, inasmuch as Calvin went on to cite the authority of the ancient Church numerous times as he continued his defense of the Protestant movement. Speaking to the heart of humanist desires for the rebirth of classical antiquity, Calvin declared that the Evangelicals' efforts had been endeavors ut instauretur aliquando vetusta illa ecclesiae facies, "to restore at last that ancient form of the Church" which had been defaced by later developments in the Roman communion under the papacy.[67] Protestants had been antiquae pietatis ac sanctimoniae studio, "zealous for ancient piety and holiness," leading them to attempts restituere in pristinum nitorem," "to restore it [the Church] to pristine splendour."[68] Nequē vero in doctrinae dubitamus ad veterem ecclesiam provocare, urged Calvin: "Neither in regard to our doctrine do we hesitate to appeal to the ancient church."[69] Although he admitted that the Evangelicals still had some way to go before they could claim to embody faithfully the wise discipline of the Church in antiquity, he could state that more veteris ecclesiae ("the practice of the ancient church") was the pattern they sought to emulate and which they urged locum hodie ... diligenter ac bona fide custodiatur, "should be in place in the present day and be carefully and faithfully observed."[70]

To be sure, Calvin did not allow that the ancient church was "without spot or wrinkle or any such thing," as St. Paul had stated the church would ultimately be (Ephesians 5:27). Calvin pointed out, "we admit that in times past seeds of superstition [semina ... superstitionum] were sown, which detracted somewhat from the purity of the Gospel."[71] He noted that the ancient church included nonnullam in precibus mortuorum mentionem ("some mention of the dead in their prayers"), but he urged that it was infrequent, soberly done, included only a few words, and was meant as an expression of affection for those who had departed this life.[72] Further, the church in antiquity had some requirements of penitential satisfactions, through which unfeigned repentance was demonstrated.[73] These were the only two semina superstitionum Calvin mentioned, and it is significant to notice that he offered mitigating explanations for their presence in Christian antiquity. Neither of them was, in itself, objectionable, in Calvin's estimation.

According to him, the actual corruptions had only

developed later on: what was objectionable was the misuse subsequently made of them within the Roman communion to elaborate the doctrines of purgatory and of the expiation of sins by the offering of penances and satisfactions, respectively.[74] In a striking architectural image incorporating the humanist sense of historical anachronism, Calvin said to the cardinal, At nondum nati erant architecti, a quibus purgatorium istud vestrum construeretur: qui postea in tantam amplitudinem illud dilaturunt, in tantam extulerunt altitudinem, ut potissima regni vestri portio ipso fulciatur ("But the architects were yet unborn by whom your purgatory was constructed: who subsequently extended it to such a breadth and raised it to such a height, that it secures the principal section of your kingdom").[75] This all took place after the close of Christian antiquity quum mundus ignorantia et hebetudine, velut alto sopore, oppressus esset ("when the world was overcome with ignorance and dullness, as in a very deep sleep")[76] and the Church was led by hominibus indoctis ("unlearned men"). These medieval developments found their source in pontifice romano et eius factione, "the Roman pontiff and his party," who had achieved and now protected the ruin of the ancient form of the Church[77]: contemptuous disregard of ancient ecclesiastical discipline, destruction of the ancient understanding of ministerial service, and a host of errors medieval in origin all had to be credited to them.[78] In a stinging judgement of the medieval papacy and the subsequent occupants of the papal throne, Calvin declared, prostratum denique fuisse Christi regnum, quum erectus fuisset hic principatus, (the kingdom of Christ was prostrated when this primacy [of the pope] was erected.)[79]

Roman expostulations such as Sadoleto had made against supposed Protestant departures from antiquity in all this were consequently vacuous, since Rome practiced none of it herself.[80] With regard to the areas of controversy in that day, Calvin wrote to the cardinal, in istis omnibus non obscurare a nobis stare veterem ecclesiam: vobisque nihilo minus, quam nos ipsos, adversare, (in all these points, the ancient Church clearly stands by us and not at all with you, to oppose you as we ourselves do).[81] He claimed that Sadoleto knew this but had disguised the fact that longe meliorem nobis cum antiquitate consensionem esse quam vobis, (our agreement with antiquity is far closer than yours).[82] Calvin summed up this repeatedly and powerfully made point clearly when he declared non fecimus, nisi suffragante nobis veteris ecclesiae consensu: cuius umbra frustra conaris ... obtegere, (we have not acted without the unanimous support of the ancient Church, under whose shadow you endeavour in vain to hide ...)[83]

In writing for a Christian humanist readership, Calvin could hardly have coordinated a more telling indictment than the one he offered, for two reasons. First, Calvin's criticisms of Christian antiquity were limited, actually, not to the ancient practices themselves, but to their subsequent medieval abuse under the aegis of the papacy. His adherence to the ancient Church and, by implication, that of the Protestant movement he was defending, could hardly have been suggested any more broadly. Secondly, in thus criticizing developments within the Roman Church, Calvin affirmed the sense of historical distance foundational to humanism's perspectives and, in so doing, artfully situated the distinctives of the Roman obedience firmly within the medieval period to which humanism professed such unmitigated opposition. In thus assessing these historical developments, the judgments of Christian humanism upon the medieval period issued unchanged from the lips of a leader of the Protestant movement as he criticized the Roman Church. By thus expressing the case, Calvin gave the scholarly world of his day to understand that the Protestant objection to Rome was the Christian humanist objection to the medieval period.

In summary of this point, it can be seen that Calvin developed a significant historical argument in the defense he offered of Protestantism. There are four main aspects to that historical argument.

First, while he stressed the preeminence of Scripture as a religious authority for the Evangelical movement, he did so in a twofold historical context. On the one hand, in speaking of Scripture he utilized the language of tradition, thereby appropriating for the Protestant movement a fundamental concern for the Church's continuity. On the other, he treated Scripture as a part--preeminent to be sure, but nevertheless a part--of Christian antiquity. His presentation of religious authority was such that he could connect a reference to Scripture with that to the Church Fathers or the ancient Church with a coordinating conjunction (or the converse, with a neither/nor connection of Scripture and elements of Christian antiquity). Had he learned this from Martin Bucer? Living in Strasbourg and in close contact with Bucer, he had already been influenced in various ways by their collaboration. By this time, the use of a coordinating conjunction to connect Scripture with various elements of Christian antiquity was virtually a mark of Bucer's theological style.[84] Whatever be the case in this regard, Calvin's view of Scripture as presented in this reply, and as representing that of Protestantism, tied Scripture to Christian antiquity.

In the second place, Calvin dealt substantively with the question of tradition. The answer to that question was still undefined for the Northern Christian Humanists. Obviously, it posed a significant problem for them. They could, on the one hand, criticize the medieval period cogently; on the other, as Christians, they held to an historical continuity of the Church. For his part, Calvin tried to define that tradition in terms that were at once Protestant and Christian humanist. Thus Calvin addressed the question of continuity, and was one of the first Christian humanists to do so in a significant and compelling fashion.[85]

Thirdly, with regard to that antiquity which Christian Humanism so highly prized, Calvin made a wholehearted and virtually undifferentiated claim of it as support for the Protestant movement. With regard to the Church Fathers, Calvin offered citations in his reply, whereas Sadoleto had offered none in his letter. With regard to the ancient Church, more generally, Calvin urged that the Protestants were zealous for the repristination of Christian antiquity in the present day. By way of glaring contrast, Calvin affirmed, Sadoleto sought to conceal Rome's multifarious violations of Christian antiquity. Thereby Calvin indicated that Rome could stake no legitimate claim to the prized heritage of Christian Humanism.

Fourthly, while Calvin recognized the failures still within Protestantism, he urged that the problems within the contemporary Church were medieval in origin and Roman in provenance. Thereby Calvin appealed to the opposition to things medieval, on the one hand, and to the sense of historical distance, of discontinuity, essential to Christian Humanism's outlooks, on the other, in defending Protestantism and accusing Rome.

From the above, it can be seen that Calvin certainly propounded a powerful historical argument for his Christian humanist readership in his Reply to Sadoleto, 1539.

Conclusion

I have demonstrated that Calvin, as he sought the welfare of the Protestant Reformation in the document examined, embodied the ideals of Christian Humanism, as those ideals have been articulated by recent scholarship. He deliberately manifested a rhetorical finesse as he offered a significant historical argument in the Reply to Sadoleto, 1539. In so doing he offered a defense of the Evangelical movement which became a powerful indictment of the Roman obedience, and that along specific lines which suggest a further inference regarding the thrust of Calvin's response.

Calvin's treatment both explicitly and implicitly brought wide-ranging criticism of Sadoleto as a humanist and of the Roman Church he represented as medieval. In contrast, his defense of Protestantism represented the Evangelical movement as holding to and being the contemporary embodiment of Christian Humanism's deepest interests. Bound together as the two aspects of the defense were (and as the two writings in publication were), Calvin's presentation suggested that Sadoleto had failed his humanism as a Roman churchman and that Calvin had embodied Christian Humanism as a Protestant. Written to a Christian humanist audience, still divided in its loyalties between the Roman and the Protestant obediences, is it too much to deduce that Calvin intended that inference to be drawn by the readers? Given the concern for persuasive subtlety in the rhetorical tradition, is it too much to infer that Calvin wanted the Christian humanists to understand that they would either entirely lose or else irreparably modify their Christian Humanism if they stayed with

Rome, and that if they wanted to find that Christian Humanism fulfilled they should identify with Protestantism? More pointedly--and this in utter contradiction to the old conception of an irreconcilable antithesis between Christian Humanism and Protestantism-- is not Calvin implying to his readers that if they wanted to stay Christian humanists, they should become Protestants?

This type of pregnant insinuation on Calvin's part would fit well with the rhetorical tradition of seeking to persuade by allowing one's audience themselves to come to a conclusion broadly indicated but not explicitly stated. With the clear evidence of Calvin's rhetorical expertise everywhere evident in this 1539 reply, this inference seems warranted.

Whether this suggestion moves entirely in the right direction or not, however, it has been seen that in his Reply to Sadoleto, Calvin embodied what recent scholarship has shown to be the ideals of Christian Humanism as a leader and a defender of the Protestant movement.

Notes

[1] Burckhardt urged this in his influential Die Cultur der Renaissance in Italien: Ein Versuch (Basel, 1860).

[2] Steven Ozment has recently pointed out that proponents of Burckhardt's approach still constitute one of the schools of Renaissance research in his "Humanism,

Scholasticism, and the Intellectual Origins of the Reformation," in F. Forrester Church and Timothy George, eds., Continuity and Discontinuity in Church History: Essays Presented to George Huntston Williams on the Occasion of his 65th Birthday, Studies in the History of Christian Thought, vol. 19 (Leiden, 1979), p. 136.

[3]Heiko A. Oberman, "Quoscunque Tulit Foecunda Vetustas," in Itinerarium Italicum: The Profile of the Italian Renaissance in the Mirror of its European Transformations, eds. Heiko A. Oberman and Thomas A. Brady, Jr., Studies in Medieval and Reformation Thought, vol. 14 (Leiden, 1975), pp. xviii-xxviii.

[4]Kristeller encapsulated his perspective when he wrote, "Renaissance humanism as such was not Christian or pagan, Catholic or Protestant, scientific or antiscientific, civic or despotic, Platonist or Aristotelian, Stoic or Epicurean, optimistic or pessimistic, active or contemplative, although it is easy to find for any of these attitudes, and for many others, a certain number of humanists who favored them. What they all have in common is something else: a scholarly, literary and educational ideal based on the study of classical antiquity" in his "Studies on Renaissance Humanism during the last Twenty Years," Studies in the Renaissance 9 (1962):22. A more expanded treatment can be found in his Renaissance Thought: The Classic, Scholastic, and Humanist Strains (New York, 1961). For the widespread influence of Kristeller's position among Renaissance scholars, cf. Oberman, pp. xviii-xx,xxviii, and William J. Bouwsma, The Interpretation of Renaissance Humanism (Washington, D.C., 1959), pp. 12-13.

[5]Kristeller, Renaissance Thought, p. 10; Myron P. Gilmore, The World of Humanism 1453-1517 (New York, 1962), pp. 204-206.

[6]Bernd Moeller, "The German Humanists and the Reformation," in Imperial Cities and the Reformation: Three Essays, trans. H.C. Erik Midelfort and Mark U. Edwards, Jr. (Philadelphia, 1972), pp. 25-26, 35-36; see

also Lewis W. Spitz, "The Third Generation of German Humanists," in The Reformation: Basic Interpretations, 2d ed., ed. Lewis W. Spitz, (Toronto, 1972), pp. 46-47. Spitz notes, "Of the two dozen leaders (of the Reformation movement) at the time of the Diet of Augsburg in 1530 all except Luther and Nicholas von Amsdorf (1483-1565) had come to the Reformation from humanism.... The leadership of the Reformation was in the hands of the young men with a humanist experience...."(p. 57).

[7] Among these are, for Martin Bucer, the study by Friedhelm Krüger, Bucer und Erasmus: Eine Untersuchung zum Einfluss des Erasmus auf die Theologie Martin Bucers (bis zum Evangelien-Kommentar von 1530), Veröffentlichungen des Instituts für Europäische Geschichte, vol. 57 (Wiesbaden, 1970): cf. Ernst-Wilhelm Kohls, Die Schule bei Martin Bucer in ihrem Verhältnis zu Kirche und Obrigkeit, Pädagogische Forschungen: Veröffentlichungen des Comenius-Instituts, vol. 22 (Heidelberg, 1963); for Philip Melanchthon, in his Melanchthon zwischen Humanismus und Reformation (Forschungen zur Geschichte und Lehre des Protestantismus, vol. 15 [Munich, 1959]), Adolf Sperl notes that the study of Melanchthon in the twentieth century has been dominated by the attempt to understand the influence of humanism upon Melanchthon's teaching and practice as a reformer and an educator (p. 9); a further helpful tool for Melanchthon research in this regard is the survey by Peter Fraenkel and Martin Greschat, Zwanzig Jahre Melanchthonstudium: Sechs Literaturberichte (1945-1964) (Geneva, 1967); studies of other reform leaders, such as Johann Sturm, Johann Bugenhagen, and Joachim Camerarius, while not as numerous as those on Bucer and Melanchthon, nonetheless move in the same direction; for the general educational pattern among the Protestant leaders, cf. Ozment, pp. 136,141.

Consequently, when Bernd Moeller describes these reformers as "former humanists" (p. 35), he exposes a predilection on the nature of humanism by which his otherwise stimulating study of the German humanists is nonetheless historiographically vitiated--namely, to treat it as rooted, not in a pedogogical orientation, but in a philosophical one. He nevertheless recognizes that these men all "came to differ with Luther on certain theological questions and ... unconsciously formed a common front against him" (p. 37), but without noting that these other men sensed neither incongruity nor unfaithfulness in doing so. The humanistic background they shared led them to perspectives and practices which reflected their continuing humanistic orientation.

[8]Heinz Liebing has pointed out that a wide variety of nuanced interrelationships between Christian Humanism and Protestantism can be discerned in the sixteenth century in his "Die Ausgänge des Europäischen Humanismus," in Geist und Geschichte der Reformation, eds. Heinz Liebing and Klaus Scholder (Berlin, 1966), p. 360. After reviewing recent developments in the understanding of both the Renaissance and the Reformation, Lewis W. Spitz vigorously excoriates the notion that there was irreconcilable opposition between the two movements in his "The Course of German Humanism," in Itinerarium Italicum (p. 379); a recent example of the dated perspective opposed by Spitz is offered by the forthright declaration of W.F. Dankbaar in his Hervormers en Humanisten (Amsterdam, 1978), "Er loopt een principiële sceiding tussen het anthropocentrische Humanisme en het theocentrisch bijbels-reformatorisch geloof" (p. 18).

[9]François Wendel has argued that Calvin's humanism is evident throughout the course of his life in his method of thought and of writing (Calvin: The Origins and Development of his Religious Thought, trans. P. Mairet [London, 1969], pp. 31-34).

[10]Quirinus Breen, John Calvin: A Study in French Humanism (Grand Rapids, 1931).

[11]The studies of Kristeller (and, of course, those who have learned from or advanced beyond him) have all appeared in the approximately two generations since the

publication of Breen's work.

[12]The outstanding presentation of this is by Hanna H. Gray, "Renaissance Humanism: The Pursuit of Eloquence," in Renaissance Essays, eds. Paul Oskar Kristeller and Philip P. Wiener (New York, 1968), pp. 199-216.

[13]Hanna H. Gray (n. 12 above).

[14]Gray, pp. 200-201.

[15]Denys Hay, Annalists and Historians: Western Historiography from the Eighth to the Eighteenth Centuries (London, 1977), p. 90.

[16]E. Harris Harbison, The Christian Scholar in the Age of the Reformation (New York, 1956), p. 35; Hay, p. 91.

[17]Myron P. Gilmore, Humanists and Jurists (Cambridge, Mass., 1963), p. 20; cf. also his The World of Humanism p. 202.

[18]Hay, p. 92.

[19]William Harrison Woodward, Studies in Education during the Age of the Renaissance 1400-1600 (Cambridge, 1906), p. 17; cf. Hay, p. 110.

[20]Richard M. Douglas offers a biography of Sadoleto in his Jacopo Sadoleto, 1477-1547: Humanist and Reformer (Cambridge, Mass., 1959). In his Studies in Education, Woodward states, "Sadoleto himself was amongst the greater scholars of his time" (p. 168) and that he was "the most learned and most respected member of the Sacred College" (p. 169).

[21]T.H.L. Parker, John Calvin: A Biography (Philadelphia, 1975), pp. 78-79; R.J. Mooi, Het Kerk- en Dogmahistorisch Element in de Werken van Johannes Calvijn (Wageningen, 1965), p. 60.

[22]Corpus Reformatorum, vol. 33, eds. William Baum, Edward Cunitz, and Edward Reuss (Braunschweig, 1866),

column 385. (Hereafter in this essay, references to this work will be rendered as CR, followed immediately by the volume number and the column number where the citation is to be found.) Calvin's Reply to Sadoleto is found at CR 33:385-416.

The English translation done by Henry Beveridge and published in John Calvin, Tracts and Treatises on the Reformation of the Church, vol. 1 (Edinburgh, 1844; subsequently reprinted in 1958 and 1983), is badly in need of revision, in view of the many advances in understanding the thought and terminology of the sixteenth century. The author of this essay has noted several places where the full force of Calvin's usage is lost in the Beveridge translation. Consequently, where English translations appear in the text of the essay, they are the responsibility of the present author (who freely acknowledges his debt to the preliminary labours of Beveridge).

[23]Parker, pp. 78-79; Wendel. p. 35.

[24]Parker, p. 79.

[25]Moeller, pp. 30-31; cf. Spitz, "Third Generation," p. 58.

[26]Parker, pp. 25-28.

[27]The relevant section of Calvin's lengthy first sentence is, Quum in magno doctorum hominum proventu, quos tulit nostra haec aetas, id sis, quum excellentis doctrinae tuae, tum vero insignis facundiae merito assequutus, ut te inter paucos colant ac suspiciant quicunque videri volunt bonarum artium studiosi.... (CR 33:385).

[28]CR 33:385.

[29]E.T. Campagnac, in his "Introduction" to Sadoleto on Education: A Translation of the De Pueris Recte Instituendis, (trans. E.T. Campagnac and K. Forbes [Oxford, 1916]), points out Sadoleto's distinguished

reputation as a genuine follower of Cicero in the matter of Latin style (p. xxiii). Douglas deals with the cardinal's letters to Melanchthon (pp. 117-124), to Johann Sturm (pp. 131-135), and, most extensively of the three, to the people of Geneva and Calvin's reply (pp. 143-150). In describing the cardinal's letter, Douglas says that it "shows signs of fatigue and was clearly less substantial than that of his thirty-year-old antagonist" (p. 147).

[30]Parker, pp. 78-79.

[31]CR 33:385,388.

[32]CR 33:415.

[33]CR 33:396.

[34]CR 33:390.

[35]Gray, pp. 202-203.

[36]... invidiae et acerbitatis ... hostiliter (CR 33:385).

[37]... calumniosas tuas criminationis (CR 33:387); lenitate et modestia (CR 33:387); intemperiem ... impotentiam ... asperitas (CR 33:387); acerbissima ... verborum (CR 33:388); plurima alia ... convicia (CR33:390); virus tuae acerbitatis (CR 33:414).

[38]... futili maledicto (CR 33:389); vere ac candide (CR 33:394); At tu perquam maligne hic invidiam nobis facies (CR 33:397); ad gravandam causam nostram (CR 33:416).

[39]CR 33:394.

[40]CR 33:391,388.

[41]CR 33:390.

[42]CR 33:394.

[43]Calvin stated, Faciam enim ut omnes intelligant, non causae modo bonitate et aequitate, conscientiae rectitudine, cordis sinceritate, sermonis candore me esse multo superiorem: sed etiam in retinenda lenitate et modestia aliquanto constantiorem, (CR 33:387).

[44]Nolo tamen in singularis immorari (CR 33:391).

[45]Douglas, p. 79; Parker, pp. 78-79.

[46]Douglas, p. 147.

[47]....vide quam imperite ratiocineris....O Sadoleto, quis abs te unquam talem vocem exspectasset? (CR 33:399).

[48]CR 33:416.

[49]CR 33:392.

[50]Gray, pp. 199-200.

[51]It should be noted at this point that the argument being developed in this essay does not require that history was necessarily the only or even the main rhetorical weapon wielded by Calvin.

[52]CR 33:392-394.

[53]CR 33:404.

[54]CR 33:394.

[55]CR 33:394.

[56]CR 33:392.

[57]CR 33:400.

[58]James R. Payton, Jr., "Sola Scriptura and Church History: The Views of Bucer and Melanchthon on Religious Authority in 1539," (Ph.D. dissertation, University of Waterloo, 1982), pp. 103,178-180.

[59]CR 33:395.

[60]CR 33:402.

[61]CR 33:415.

[62]Cf. Payton, pp. 176,188.

[63]Calvin can argue the converse, as well: neque Christi mandat, nec veteris ecclesiae instituto fuisse traditam (CR 33:400).

[64]References to Cyprian, Ambrose, Basil the Great, Chrysostom, and Augustine occur at CR 33:394, with an additional reference to Chrysostom at CR 33:393 and one to Augustine at CR 33:400, the patrum ... testimonia citation occurs at CR 33:401.

[65]Mooi, p. 347; Wendel, p. 115.

[66]Sadoleto's letter has been reproduced in CR 33:369-384; it is remarkable that no citation of any of the Church Fathers occurs in the letter.

[67]CR 33:394; Calvin repeated this claim when he had the Protestants affirm before the judgment seat of God that the Evangelical movement had brought the Church ad suum fontem reduceret, et velut a faecibus repurgatam suae puritati restitueret (CR 33:412).

[68]CR 33:394.

[69]CR 33:395.

[70]CR 33:395,390,406.

[71]CR 33:402.

[72]CR 33:401.

[73]CR 33:399.

132

[74]CR 33:401-402,399.

[75]CR 33:401.

[76]CR 33:412.

[77]CR 33:394.

[78]CR 33:395,406-407, 402.

[79]CR 33:413.

[80]CR 33:406-407, 402,395.

[81]CR 33:402.

[82]CR 33:394.

[83]CR 33:400.

[84]Cf. Payton, pp. 157-158.

INTRODUCTION

Ford Lewis Battles

I. THE ROAD TOWARD THE INSTITUTES OF 1536 (1532-35)

A. The Prelude to the First Edition of the Institutes

1. The Dilemma of the French Evangelicals. Behind the writing of the *Institutes of the Christian Religion* as well as overshadowing the development of the Gospel faith in France in the 1520's and 1530's stands the enigmatic figure of Francis I, Most Christian King of the French, Most Mighty and Most Illustrious Monarch—to quote the high-sounding titles with which the apologies of Calvin and other religionists introduce their appeal.

John Calvin's first direct contact with the anger of Francis I came after All Saints' Day (1 November) 1533, marked in the city of Paris by the address of Nicolas Cop upon assuming the rectorship of the University of Paris, actually a sermon expounding the lectionary Gospel text of the day, Matthew 5:1-12. Whether Calvin wrote that discourse or at least had a hand in its composition is still a matter of scholarly debate; that he was presumed by the authorities to have had a part in it may be assumed by his sudden flight from the city. In my opinion, enough parallels can be adduced to Calvin's later works to substantiate what Theodore Beza has written about his authorship of it.[1]

Near the close of Cop's Address, we read the following call to the Gospel cause:

> "Blessed will you be," he says, "when men hurl insults at you and reproach you, and say all evil against you falsely, for my sake." [Matt. 5:11]. Why, then, do we conceal the truth rather than speak it out boldly? Is it right to please men rather than God; to fear those who can destroy the body, but not the soul? O the ingratitude of mankind which will not

1. ". . . Calvin furnished him [Nicholas Cop] with one in which religion was treated more purely and clearly than it was previously wont to be." Beza's "Life of Calvin," in *John Calvin's Tracts and Treatises*; H. Beveridge, translator (Grand Rapids: 1983 [Edinburgh: 1844]), Vol. I, p. lxiii.

> bear the slightest affliction in the name of him who died for the sins of all, him whose blood has freed us from eternal death and the shackles of Satan! The world and the wicked are wont to label as heretics, imposters, seducers and evilspeakers those who strive purely and sincerely to penetrate the minds of believers with the Gospel; (in such evildoing) "they think they are offering service to God." [John 16:2] But happy and blessed are they who endure all this with composure, giving thanks to God in the midst of affliction and bravely bearing calamities. "Rejoice," he says, "for great is your reward in heaven."[2]

The response to these fighting words was not long in coming. Cop and Calvin fled from the city. The Sorbonne did its work well. On the tenth of December, Francis sent instructions to the Parlement of Paris on how to ferret out and dispose of the heretical sect responsible for this seditious message. Francis makes specific reference to the Cop incident:

> Dear faithful friends! . . . We are very troubled and displeased at what has taken place in our beloved city of Paris, chief and capital of our kingdom, and where at the principal university of Christendom that accursed heretical Lutheran sect swarms. Its further spread we wish with our might and power to prevent. And to that end we wish and understand that such grievous punishment should be meted out that it would be a correction to the accursed heretics and an example to all others.[3]

The letter just quoted, and the letter of the same date from Francis I to Jean du Bellay, Archbishop of Paris, provide for two counsellors of the Parlement of Paris to be assigned to the Archbishop to investigate the clergy and prepare a trial of those who are espousing heretical opinions. The letter also calls for an investigation "of the Doctor who has preached certain propositions . . . and his Rector . . ."; apparently, the king did not realize that "doctor" and "rector" were the same person, Nicolas Cop, who had by this time taken refuge in Basel.

It would be impossible within the compass of this brief introduction to review the complex history of church-state relations and political events leading to the writing of Calvin's appeal to Francis I. We can only sketch in a few broad strokes the character of that background and of its chief political actor.

Throughout his reign, Francis I was a beleaguered monarch, fighting in his vacillating and inconstant way for the integrity of his realm. The growth in the heart of his kingdom of a movement of protest against the ecclesiastical establishment, one of the few bulwarks of his regime, could only be looked at by him and by his chief religious advisers as seditious. Frustrated in being passed over for election as Emperor, frustrated three times in Italian campaigns (one of which led to a savage sack of the city of Rome), imprisoned for a time in Madrid by his archrival the Emperor Charles, repeatedly threatened by in-

2. For the full text see Appendix III.

3. A.-L. Herminjard, *Correspondance des Réformateurs. . . .* (Genève et Paris: 1870), Vol. III, No. 440, pp. 114-115.

vasion, shorn of some of his territories, Francis I was indeed desperate for support. That is why he went to such lengths as concluding a treaty of peace with the Protestant princes of Germany in January 1534, while at the same time actively persecuting the "Lutherans" in his own kingdom. That is why he entered into an ill-conceived concordat with Leo X in 1515 and conferred with Clement VII in October-November 1533 at Marseilles. That is why he even proposed at one time settling the conflict with the Empire by a duel between him and Charles; and went so far as to enter into an abortive alliance with the Sultan against his Christian foes. The whole reign of Francis I is one of vacillation and uncertainty. How, then, could his religious policy not reflect the character of this monarch?

It was this unstable monarch, "whose opinion was often that of the last man with whom he had talked," with whom the French Evangelicals had to deal. The intense diplomatic activity of the French king reached its height in 1534; between May and August there were consultations with the German and Swiss theologians on Church reunion after a secret treaty had been signed the preceding January between Francis and the German Protestant princes. Of all the foreign Protestants with whom Francis' envoy, Guillaume du Bellay, negotiated, the Swiss Protestants were least taken in by the false peace moves of the French king. The Reformation had already spread through the Swiss cities, beginning in Zürich, then passing to Berne, Basel and other cities in German Switzerland, and ultimately to the French-speaking territories in the west, although not yet to Geneva. Many French Protestants had sought refuge in Switzerland from the threat of death at home. The city of Neuchâtel, which had declared for the Reform in 1530, was the haven to which two Frenchmen from Lyons had fled: Antoine Marcourt and Pierre de Vingle, minister and printer respectively. With the help of Pierre Viret and at the behest of Guillaume Husson de Blois, a pungent critique was prepared from a tract of Viret's colleague, Antoine Marcourt. This critique in the form of placards done at de Vingle's press was smuggled into France to be affixed in public places so that the "poor ignorant" ones could be told the truth about the abomination of the Mass.

These posters mysteriously appeared in Paris and other places on the night of 17 October 1534. One was even tacked, it is claimed, to the door of the King's bedchamber in Blois! They provoked a bloody persecution and had fateful effects on all subsequent European religious history. Thanks to the chance discovery of strips of the original placards, used in the binding of other books, it is now possible to read for the first time in over four hundred years the authentic original text of this important pronouncement. Let us pause to quote from it and to discuss its significance.

Four simple trenchant points are made:

(1) that the once-for-all character of Christ's high-priestly self-sacrifice as described in the Letter to the Hebrews is set aside by the oft-repeated sacrifice of Christ in the Roman Mass;

(2) the Mass is an act of idolatry, localizing in countless earthly places for adoration a glorified human body which is really in heaven;

(3) the so-called priestly miracle of transubstantiation is an utter denial of Scriptural teaching about the Supper and about examination of self before communicating, for which auricular confession to a priest is substituted;

(4) the benefits of the Mass are clean contrary to those taught in Scripture as coming from the Supper.[4]

Let us sketch in a few words now the development of transubstantiation. Transubstantiation is in actuality a philosophical effort to explain a real presence of Christ in the Supper, physically perceived. Transubstantiation first took a canonical status at the Fourth Lateran Council of 1215. It was placed among those canons to counter the anti-clerical, anti-sacramental teachings of the Albigensians that were imperilling the medieval church, especially in France. The theological outworking of this canon took more than two generations, reaching its formulation at the hands of Thomas Aquinas in his two *Summae*, and also its liturgical fruition in the establishment of the feast of Corpus Christi for which he also wrote the service and its hymns.

Rapidly the Mass and its attendant priestly miracle became the kingpin of the whole medieval ecclesiastical system in the west. With the related withholding of the cup from the laity by the doctrine of concomitance, it had to stand unchallenged if the delicately poised system of Church and State was to survive. Hence, any questioning of its scriptural validity, any hesitation about its attendant features—the remainder of the seven-fold sacramental system, indulgences, treasury of merits, invocation of saints and all the rest was fought fiercely by Church and State equally.

Wyclif's determined campaign against transubstantiation at the end of the fourteenth century, despite the weakened and divided condition of the papacy at that time, was firmly suppressed. Even Hus' milder efforts to reform the Supper met with conciliar condemnation and a martyr's death at Constance in 1415.

When Luther's theses of 1517 entered these sacred precincts questioningly, and when in 1520 he unmistakably dealt a body blow to the medieval ecclesiastical system in his *Babylonian Captivity of the Church*, the long-suppressed criticism of this central dogma of a repressive and unscriptural church could flow freely. Luther was, however, mild in his critique alongside his Swiss counterpart, Huldreich Zwingli, whose views are in part reflected in the statement of the placards.

The point we would make here is that the most necessary and most dangerous critical act the Reform party could perform was to question the Mass. In the slashing strokes of this popular document, the authors first aroused the reactionary theologians of the Sorbonne (e.g. Robert Ceneau) who had unsuc-

4. The full text is given in Appendix I.

cessfully been trying to suppress "Lutheranism" ever since it appeared in France; secondly, highly placed "Catholic" humanists like Guillaume Budé and Jacopo Sadoleto who raised the flag of warning with the King; thirdly, the King himself who saw grave danger to his political designs, the threat to religious and civil order, and to his plans (however hollow) for religious peace; and finally, the common folk whether of superstitious traditional belief or moderately interested in the reform of the Church.

2. Calvin's Seneca Commentary (1532): A First Apology to Francis I? It is into this troubled chapter of France's history that Calvin was reborn an evangelical Christian. To these first steps of his we now turn. In April 1532, he published his first book, the *Commentary on Seneca's De Clementia*. Here we shall view it as a first step on his religious journey. Much has been written about the relationship of this humanist commentary to Calvin the Christian. Some have confidently tied it to his faith; others have noted that it is virtually devoid of religious reference, if not religious interest.

A problem in dealing with the question is the long-held notion that Calvin's theological views never really changed and that what he wrote in the final edition of 1559 of the *Institutes of the Christian Religion* applies more or less indiscriminately to his whole Christian life. This is simply not true: great consistency there is throughout his literary expression of the faith, but also much movement, reconsideration and recasting of his thought. Even a brief comparative glance at the five chief editions of the *Institutes* will show this.

Hence, most scholars have either directly or instinctively compared the mature Christian with the pre-conversion author of the Seneca. If, however, we concentrate our vision on the 1536 *Institutes* and view the Seneca in the light of it, a different picture begins to emerge. The *Institutes* opens with the famous letter to Francis I, an eloquent appeal to that monarch on behalf of Calvin's Reformed compatriots in France in the troubled year of 1535. Taken as a whole, this letter and the theological essay that follows, especially the final chapter, are a literary whole and hold up to Francis a model of the Christian monarch.

This search for "mirrors for magistrates," "instructions for a Christian prince," and the like constituted one of the most prolific literary genres of the sixteenth century. Few indeed were the Renaissance humanists who did not try to show their scholarly excellence and their political sagacity to the monarchs they wished to shape to more humane dimensions. Francis I had his Guillaume Budé; Philip II had his Erasmus. The threat on the one hand of political chaos due to internal revolutionary tendencies and external wars, and of oppressive tyranny by frightened rulers on the other, led sensitive and moderate men to scour antiquity for models of political behavior.

No worse tyrant appeared in Roman imperial history than Nero, yet no monarch ever had better political and moral instruction at the outset of his imperial career. Is it not possible that Calvin took up Nero's old Stoic teacher's advice not only to carve out a place for himself among the humanists, but also to bring, somehow, to the attention of Francis I, the right way to rule: between perilous laxity on the one hand and overbearing severity on the other? As a nominal Christian at least already of great ethical sensitivity, Calvin perhaps felt his modest learned little commentary might come to the attention of the King who had just assured Renaissance humanism a central place in French culture by the establishment of the Royal Lectureships, of which Calvin was then at least briefly availing himself. Perhaps Calvin knew Budé's as yet unpublished *L'Institution du Prince* in which that architect of the Royal Lectureships had already provided a classic treatise of guidance for his King.

That Calvin had his eye on Francis I when he chose the *De Clementia* of Seneca to test his newly acquired linguistic and historical skills, is a view that had been advanced before: J. Bohatec, among others, suggests that ". . . his Seneca *Commentary* signifies an open struggle of the young humanist against the absolutist claims of his native country."[5] Nowhere does Calvin explicitly say this, but looked at in the light of the 1536 *Institutes* and the use the latter book makes of material from the former, the theory becomes more plausible. It suggests a forensic dimension to Calvin's conversion explicitly prepared for in the *Seneca Commentary.* Let us for the moment suppose that the *Seneca Commentary* was Calvin's first apology to Francis I.

3. Theological First Steps of Calvin. We have already noted the comparative absence of explicitly religious teaching from the *Seneca Commentary.* It therefore would seem quite difficult to bring this early work into a discussion of Calvin's conversion. We hestitate to launch out on this topic, which has tantalized the minds of many greater scholars with as yet no clear answer in sight. Calvin's personal reticence on this point, the slenderness of the direct sources in his own writings, and the mysterious gaps in our information as to his whereabouts at this crucial time in his career make any precise dating of the conversion impossible. John T. McNeill's summary of past guesses, that it probably took place between 5 April 1534 (when he visited LeFèvre d'Étaples at Marguerite's court at the castle of Nérac) and 4 May 1534 when he returned to his native city of Noyon in Picardy to resign his benefice, seems as plausible as any, although Ganoczy more recently pleads for an even later date. Fortunately for our purpose, dating is not important; the content and structure of his conversion are. On this latter we are, I think, on firmer ground.

Before we examine formally the sources for our knowledge of his conversion, let us look at whatever religious content can be found in the *Seneca Commentary.* Basically, three religious questions seem to concern this young man on the eve of his conversion: (1) the contrast between paganism and Christianity or, more broadly stated, between superstition and true religion; (2) the origin and nature of the human soul; (3) the question of governance, divine and human, or in other words, the place of human authority within the divine prov-

5. J. Bohatec, *Calvins Lehre von Staat und Kirche* (Breslau: 1937), p. 43.

idential frame. Let us take a moment to look at these three points in a little more detail.

A constantly reiterated Calvinian criticism of Roman Catholicism concerns the "humanly devised" character of its liturgical practices. Always strongly questioned, such things are frequently the subject of Calvin's most biting satire: one thinks of the *Treatise on Relics* as the chief example of this. One sees this predilection already in Calvin's remarks in the *Seneca Commentary* on public recognition of the ruler among the Romans:

> Clemency kept Augustus secure during his lifetime; after his death, it has kept his reputation alive. Decrees of the senate made in praise of living princes can seem to be either forced out by fear, or precipitated by rashness. Servile rites which are performed by the people, acclamations also . . . serve the presence of a ruler. The praises given to a dead man are spontaneous and thus to be preferred. So the Roman people believed Augustus a god, not because they were bidden to do so, but because they knew by experience that he was a good prince. It was a solemn custom of the Romans to place their Caesars amongst the gods through apotheosis. . . . Herodian sets forth the rites and ceremonies for the consecration of emperors. As often as I reread that passage, I cannot keep from laughing, so silly was that religion of the Romans. [*Comm. Sen. de Clem.* p. 187][6]

Such rites are the product of superstition rather than of true religion. In another place Calvin sums up the difference between the two: "Superstition bears the same relationship to religion as pity does to clemency; just as cruelty stands in the same relationship to clemency as impiety does to religion" [*Comm. Sen. de Clem.* p. 363]. It is true that Calvin at this point quotes the obvious philosophical authorities on the meaning of these terms. But when we look at the clear Christian use to which this material is later put in the *Institutes* (1.12.1) we must admit that the fundamental issue of true versus false religion was already on Calvin's mind in early 1532.

A second fundamental theological question which was later to shape Calvin's faith is that of the soul, its nature and origin. Again, to turn to the *Seneca Commentary*, Calvin says:

> In passing he lightly touches upon the contradictory notions of the philosophers, who have not yet settled upon a sure and definite location for the soul. Herophilus has located it in the ventricle of the brain; for Plato and Democritus it seems more likely to rest in the entire head, Erasistratus considers it to be around the membrane of the brain, Strato in the space between the eyebrows; Parmenides and Epicurus in the whole breast; Diogenes in the arterial ventricle of the heart; the Stoics assign it to the whole heart or spirit; others the whole cervix of the heart; others

6. *Calvin's Commentary on Seneca's De Clementia*, edited and translated by Ford Lewis Battles and André Malan Hugo (Leiden: 1969). All page references are to this edition.

the diaphragm; Empedocles the concretion of the blood. [*Comm. Sen. de Clem*. p. 93]

Here he is quoting Plutarch in Budé's Latin translation and citing Cicero's *Tusculan Disputations*. This with other passages in the *Seneca Commentary* mark the topic as one of importance for Calvin, later crucial for his whole theology.

A third theological concern is the divine governance of the world and its relation to human political rule, barely hinted at in this early document:

> This statement, moreover, derives from the opinion of the Stoics, who attribute the superintendence of human affairs to the gods, assert providence, and leave nothing to mere chance. The Epicureans, although they do not deny the existence of the gods, do the closest thing to it: they imagine the gods to be pleasure-loving, idle, not caring for mortals, lest anything detract from their pleasures: they deride Stoic providence as a prophesying old woman. They think everything happens by mere chance. But he who professes himself vicar of the gods, surely confesses that the gods look after human needs. [*Comm. Sen. de Clem*. pp. 29-30]

There follows a significant string of classical proof-texts for the vicegerent character of earthly monarchs. After quoting Plutarch, "Princes are God's ministers, for the welfare and care of men; as God bestows upon them, they distribute part; keep part," he adds (following Romans, ch. 13) "Our religion, too, has such a confession: 'Power comes from God alone, and those that exist have been ordained by God.' " [*Comm. Sen. de Clem*. p. 31]

These three small points, expressed as they are in what seems to be a humanistic if not outright pagan tone, may not say much by themselves about the later champion of the faith. But less than two years after these lines were published, they began to take a new and unmistakably Christian turn in Calvin's first theological writings.

In Calvin's first explicitly "Evangelical" writing, his French preface to his cousin's translation of the New Testament probably penned in late 1534 or early 1535, we find emerging what may have already been in his mind when he compared, by implication, the silly rites of the pagan Romans with Christian worship. Here he succinctly rehearses the whole salvation history in a few pages "for those who love Christ and his Gospel."

> It is true enough that the Gentiles, astonished and convinced by so many goods and benefits which they saw with their own eyes, have been forced to recognize the hidden Benefactor from whom came so much goodness. But instead of giving the true God the glory which they owed him, they forged a god to their own liking, one dreamt up by their foolish fantasy in its vanity and deceit; and not one god only, but as many as their temerity and conceit enabled them to forge and cast; so that there was not a people or place which did not make new gods as seemed good to them. Thus it is that idolatry, that perfidious panderer, was able to exercise

> dominion to turn men away from God, and to amuse them with a whole crowd of phantoms they themselves had given shape, name and being itself.[7]

From this fairly conventional Scriptural treatment of idolatry it is a short step to the identification of the current Roman Catholic cultus with idolatry.

Calvin's learned parrotting of various classical views on the location of the soul just quoted from the *Seneca Commentary* rather quickly gives way in the *Psychopannychia* written perhaps two years later (1534/5) to the following:

> Here let human wisdom give place; for though it thinks much about the soul it perceives no certainty with regard to it. Here, too, let Philosophers give place, since on almost all subjects their regular practice is to put neither end nor measure to their dissensions, while on this subject in particular they quarrel, so that you will scarcely find two of them agreed on any single point! Plato in some passages, talks nobly of the faculties of the soul and Aristotle, in discoursing of it, has surpassed all in acuteness. But what the soul is, and whence it is, it is vain to ask them, or indeed the whole body of Sages, though they certainly thought more purely and wisely on the subject than some amongst ourselves, who boast that they are disciples of Christ.[8]

In the previously cited *Preface to Pierre Robert's New Testament,* Calvin begins his discussion with Genesis 1:27, the making of man in the image of God. More precisely, the *Psychopannychia* identifies this image with the spirit or soul of man: "Whatever philosophers or these dreamers [the Anabaptists] may pretend, we hold that nothing can bear the image of God but spirit, since God is a spirit."[9] Later this identification of the divine image *par excellence* with man's rational faculty will be more fully developed. We see here, beginning in the *Seneca Commentary,* the early stages of that development in Calvin.

Our third theological concern noted in the *Seneca Commentary,* that of divine and human sovereignty, is marked in the very structure of the first edition of the *Institutes of the Christian Religion*, penned in 1535. Read the letter to Francis I; then skip over to the final chapter, or even the very last section. You will then observe that the *Institutes* is set in a political frame. At the heart of Calvin's thought was the relation between the King and the King of Kings, between the providential rule of our Heavenly Father and the sometimes capricious and cruel rule of him who should be the father of his country. Having

7. *Calvin's Commentaries*, edited and translated by Joseph Haroutunian and Louise Pettibone Smith, The Library of Christian Classics, Vol. XXIII (Philadelphia: n.d.), pp. 60-61. The original text may be found in the *Corpus Reformatorum* edition of Calvin's works: *Opera Calvini* [OC], Vol. IX, p. 797. The preface to the entire French Bible of Pierre Robert Olivetan, in Latin, may be found in OC, IX, 787-8.

8. *Psychopannychia*, in *John Calvin's Tracts and Treatises*, Vol. III, p. 420. The original text may be found in OC, V, 178.

9. *Psychopannychia*, op. cit., Vol. III, p. 424. The original text may be found in OC, V, 181.

looked at what may have been Calvin's first theological steps—or at least his paramount religious interests immediately before and after his conversion—let us turn to the conversion itself.

B. Some Speculations on the Shape and Content of Calvin's Conversion

1. The Conversion Viewed from the Sources. In the present essay we propose to lay aside the vexed question of the dating of Calvin's *conversio subita* as he calls it; this will free us to speculate on the theologically more interesting features of that obscurely documented event in his life. Perhaps we should rehearse first the sources themselves. Here we are on oft-trodden ground.[10] Where does Calvin in his own words speak of his conversion? Very briefly but directly in the preface to his *Commentary on the Psalms* a late writing (1555) but one of prime importance. Obliquely, Calvin in 1539 refers to his conversion in his account of the Evangelical layman before the judgment seat of God. This is in his eloquent response to Cardinal Sadolet's appeal to the city of Geneva (now that Calvin is exiled therefrom) to return to the bosom of the true Church. Cardinal Sadolet in his appeal to the people of Geneva had penned a dramatic scene before the judgment seat of God where a loyal Catholic made his last confession, and contrastingly a protestant (Calvin, thinly disguised) also made his final fruitless appeal. Calvin skillfully turns this around: in place of the schismatic pictured by Sadolet, he presents essentially a sketch of himself as churchman struggling against error after his conversion. These are the two usually cited sources for the conversion. To them I should like to add what I call "the kernel of Calvin's faith" contained in the first few pages of Chapter I of the 1536 *Institutes*; to it might be appended also, possibly, the *Preface to Pierre Robert's New Testament* as a whole. This is not a very impressive list, but it is what we have.

In many of the great conversions recorded in Christian history there is a particular verse of Scripture which is reputed to have "triggered" the experience. Without making a long list of such potent texts we shall be satisfied with recalling that Romans 1:17 so functioned for Luther; "The just shall live by faith." Now we have no such clear record for Calvin. It is probably foolish to speculate whether a particular verse so moved Calvin. For him as for Luther, Paul's Letter to the Romans was the prime book of Scripture in his grasp and formation of the Christian faith. Yet one is tempted to single out one verse or at least a larger context as determinative of his faith. Unquestionably, the first chapter of Romans can be so marked; I think one can be even more precise in noting Romans 1:18-25. If one verse is to be selected I would suggest Romans 1:21: "For

10. The voluminous literature on Calvin's conversion has been thoroughly surveyed and the question reconsidered by Alexandre Ganoczy, *Le Jeune Calvin* (Wiesbaden: 1966), pp. 6-15 and 271-303.

although they knew God they did not honor him as God or give thanks to him, but they became futile in their thinking and their senseless minds were darkened." Why? The central feature of Calvin's piety is the two knowledges, of God, of man. Initially mentioned in the edition of 1536, they became by 1559 almost an organizing principle of his thought. In summing up the knowledge of God, Calvin lists the "*virtutes Dei*," excellences or powers of God—too dynamic to be called attributes. The list of these given at the head of Chapter I of the 1536 *Institutes* is almost identical with those given in the *Romans Commentary* (1540) at 1:21. The same passage in Romans is alluded to in Calvin's *Reply to Cardinal Sadolet* (1539), when he sets forth his true confession of faith before God's judgment seat, to replace the false one Sadolet had in his letter put into Calvin's mouth. Calvin, speaking of the false faith against which he had reacted, wrote in the form of a prayer; "They [the people], indeed, called thee the only God, but it was while transferring to otbers the glory which thou hast claimed for thy Majesty. They figured and had for themselves as many gods as they had saints, whom they chose to worship."[11] To sum up, the emphasis on honoring God and being thankful to him are central themes in Calvin's piety.

To look at this probable Scriptural base of Calvin's conversion more broadly we see that as with Luther so with Calvin, it is *the constellation of Psalms and Romans* that holds the secret of their faith. Luther's first commentary was on Psalms; his second on Romans, years before the 1517 experience, but leading to it. Calvin's first commentary was on Romans; in fact the *Institutes* itself may be thought of as an extended commentary on Romans. While his *Psalms Commentary* came much later, it is his most explicitly personal commentary (with sometimes veiled references to his own spiritual states under those attributed to David), and as we have seen contains in its preface the one explicit testimony to Calvin's conversion.[12] Also, statistically, whatever mere quantities mean in religious scholarship!—Romans and Psalms are far and away the chiefly used Scriptural books in the *Institutes*. In the final Latin (1559) edition Romans is cited or quoted at least 598 times; Psalms, 580. The third most-used book is Matthew with 542 references. Thus, when Calvin characterizes Psalms as "An Anatomy of All the Parts of the Soul," we see what a high place he gives it; and add to this the fact that he makes the Psalter the hymnbook of the Reformed Church.

Louis Goumaz, whose pioneer work, *La Doctrine du Salut d'après les Commentaires de Jean Calvin sur le Nouveau Testament* (Lausanne: 1917) set the pattern of correlating the theology of the *Institutes* with the exegesis of his commentaries, sums up the crucial place of the Scriptures in Calvin's conversion:

11. "Calvin's Reply to Sadoleto," in *Tracts and Treatises*, Vol. I, p. 57.

12. See J. Walchenbach, *The Influence of David and the Psalms on the Life and Thought of John Calvin* [unpublished Th.M. thesis, Pittsburgh Theological Seminary, 1969].

> Scripture was the instrument for Calvin's conversion . . . he found in it the food which fed his religious nature and the document consonant with his humanistic and legal spirit.[13]

Let us now construct, out of the pieces given in the above-mentioned documents, a coherent picture of Calvin's conversion. There are five "moments" to the conversion experience: (1) the preparation, (2) the travail of conscience, (3) the call of the Gospel, (4) the conversion, (5) first steps in the Christian life. Here in a strophic translation are Calvin's own words, with the bracketed lines taken from the Psalms commentary.

I The Preparation

O Lord, as I had from childhood been so brought up,
I have always professed the Christian faith.
From the beginning I had no other sort of faith
Than what everywhere prevailed at that time.
Thy word which like a lamp ought
To have shined upon thy whole people,
Had been taken away or at least had been suppressed among us.
And lest anyone might desire a greater light
This notion had been planted
In the souls of all, that the search
For that heavenly and secret philosophy
Were better delegated to a few
From whom oracles were to be sought:
No higher intelligence befitted lowly minds
Than for them to yield themselves
In obedience to his Church.
Now the rudiments to which I had been introduced
Were of such sort as would not instruct me
To the lawful worship of thy presence.
Nor would they open the way for me
To a sure hope of salvation.
I indeed had learned to worship thee as my God:
But since the true way to worship thee
Utterly eluded me,
I was stumbling at the very threshold
As I had been taught, I believed
Myself redeemed by the death of thy Son,
From the claim of eternal death;
But I was imagining that redemption
As powerless to reach me.
The coming day of resurrection I awaited
But its memory as a luckless thing
I loathed.

13. Goumaz, p. 429.

And this sense had not come to me
Privately at home,
But from the very teaching which at that time
Conceived by the ministers of the Christian people
Was passed on to the people.
These persons were then preaching thy mercy
Toward me, but only toward those
Who had shown themselves worthy of it.
Worth they were lodging in works-righteousness
So that at last only he would be received
By thee into grace
Who reconciled himself toward thee with works.
Yet in the meanwhile they were now deceiving us
That we are miserable sinners,
Who would often slip because of the weakness
Of the flesh,
And that accordingly thy mercy ought to be
The gate of salvation for all:
But the way to obtain it, they showed,
Was to make satisfaction to thee
For our offenses.
Then they enjoined satisfaction upon us;
First, having confessed all our sins to a priest
We should humbly seek pardon and absolution;
Then by good works blot out
From thy remembrance our bad deeds;
Lastly, to make up for what we lacked,
We should add sacrifices and public expiations.
They now showed thou wert a stern judge,
A strict avenger of iniquity,
And thus, how dreadful
Thy presence must be.
Therefore they urged us to flee to the saints
That by their intercession
We might render thee open to our plea
And more favorable to us.
[From my early childhood
My father had destined me
For theology:
But after a time,
Having considered that the knowledge of the law
Commonly enriches those who follow it,
This hope suddenly made him change his mind.
That was the reason
I was withdrawn
From the study of philosophy
And put into the study of law,
To which, although, in obedience to my father,

I tried to apply myself faithfully,
God nevertheless by his secret providence
Finally made me turn
In another direction.]

II The Travail of Conscience

Though I performed all these rites
And they afforded me intervals of repose,
Still I was far away indeed
From real peace of conscience.
As often as I descended into myself
Or raised my mind to thee,
I was struck with utter horror
That no expiations,
No satisfactions could cure.
The more closely I looked at myself,
The keener the darts that pricked my conscience,
Leaving me no other solace
Than to delude myself in oblivion.
Yet nothing better offered itself,
So I kept to the road on which
I had already set out.

III The Call of the Gospel

At this point a far different sort of teaching arose,
Not one to lead us away
From the profession of Christianity
But to lead us back
To its very source,
And, purging it of the dregs,
To restore it to its purity.
Still, I was offended by novelty
And lent a reluctant ear,
Even at first, I confess,
Stoutly and vigorously resisted.
Such is the persistence of stubbornness
With which men cling to a course once undertaken,
That only with the greatest reluctance
Was I led to confess
My whole past life had been steeped
In ignorance and error.
One thing especially averted my mind
From these things:
Reverence for the Church.
[For I was so obstinately devoted
To the superstitions of the Papacy
That it was difficult to pull me

Out of that very deep morass.]
But when I let my ears be opened
And myself be taught,
I understood that fear of departing
From the Church's majesty
Was groundless.
For they reminded me what a big difference
There was between leaving the Church
And trying to correct the faults
Corrupting it.
Eloquently they spoke of the Church
Showing the highest zeal
To cultivate its unity.
Lest they seemed to quibble
Over the name "Church,"
They showed it nothing new
That anti-Christs preside over it
In place of pastors.
They set forth plenty of examples
Which showed their sole concern
To be the upbuilding of the Church.
In this they were making common cause
With many servants of Christ
We had counted among the number
Of the saints.
They inveighed rather freely
Against the Roman pontiff
Revered as Christ's vicar,
Peter's successor,
And prince of the Church:
This they excused on the grounds
That such titles are empty bugbears
Which should not so seal
The eyes of the godly
As to frighten them from looking into
And investigating the matter.
When the world was oppressed by dull ignorance
As by a deep slumber,
Then it was that the pope
Rose up to such a peak.
Surely it was not by God's Word
He was established,
Not by the lawful calling of the Church
Was he ordained prince of the Church,
But self-elected by his own will.
If we would have Christ's kingdom
Safe amongst us,
Such tyranny preying upon God's people

Is not to be borne.
And these preachers had the strongest arguments
To confirm all their charges.
First, they clearly disposed of everything
Then commonly adduced
To establish the papal primacy.
After they had withdrawn all its supports,
By God's word they also tumbled it
From its lofty eminence.
They made it abundantly clear,
As far as they could,
Both to the learned and the unlearned,
That the true order of the Church had perished;
The keys holding the Church's discipline
Had been dreadfully perverted;
Christian liberty had collapsed—
In short, Christ's kingdom lay prostrate
After this primacy had been set up.
To prick my conscience
Lest I should nonchalantly wink
At these matters as having nothing to do with me—
This is why they talked to me.
Far, far art thou from supporting
Any voluntary error
That not even one may err with impunity
Who is seduced from the path
By mere ignorance.
This they proved by the Son's testimony:
"If a blind man leads a blind man,
Both fall into the ditch." [Matt. 15:14]

IV The Conversion

[My mind which, despite my youth,
Had been too hardened in such matters,]
Now was readied for serious attention.
[By a sudden conversion
God turned and brought it
To docility.]
I realized as light broke upon me
In what a dunghill of errors
I had been wallowing,
How infected I had been
With filth and spots.
Thunderstruck at the misery
In which I had slipped,
And even more at the misery
Which threatened me
With awareness of eternal death,

I made it my first concern
To condemn, not without groaning and tears,
My previous life
And to betake myself into thy life.
And now, O Lord,
What remains for a wretch like me
But to offer thee my prayer of pardon
In place of trying to defend myself,
Lest thou hold to strick account
My dreadful desertion of thy Word,
Desertion from which
Thou once for all didst
By thy marvellous kindness
Vindicate me?

V First Steps in the Christian Life

[Having therefore received
Some taste and knowledge
Of true piety,
I was suddenly fired
With such a great desire to advance
That, even though I had not forsaken
The other studies entirely,
I nonetheless worked at them
More slackly.
But I was utterly amazed
That before a year had passed
All those who yearned
For pure doctrine
Were coming again and again to me
To learn it.
Even though I had scarcely commenced
To study it myself.
For my part, being of a nature
Somewhat unpolished and retiring,
I always longed for repose and quiet.
Hence I began to seek
Some hiding place
And way to withdraw from people.
But, far from attaining my heart's desire,
All retreats and places of escape
Became for me like public schools.
In short, although I always cherished
The goal of living in private, incognito,
God so led me and caused me to turn
By various changes
That he never left me at peace in any place
Until, in spite of my natural disposition

He brought me into the limelight.
Leaving my native France,
I departed into Germany
With the express purpose
Of being able to live,
At peace in some unknown corner,
As I had always longed.]

These are Calvin's own words drawn mainly from the Reply to Sadoleto of 1539, and the Commentary on Psalms of 1555. In them is reviewed the whole conversion, its preparation and its immediate aftermath. His was a conversion which cannot be confined to a merely personal, inward change. The inner change that took place was truly brought about within the larger context of stirring events in the history of the Church; in turn the new-born Calvin left his own impress on that history. We may therefore be pardoned if we call his conversion *forensic* for it involves a total reorientation to history and to the institutions—political, social and ecclesiastical—of Calvin's own time. This is one reason why his theology defies ultimate systematization: it is a salvation-history faith. It must be told as the story of Israel, narrowly begun in the Old Testament, but in Christ embracing all nations.

That is why we cannot leave our discussion of his conversion without examining what may be called the "first" and "second" drafts of his theological restatement of the conversion experience.

2. *The Conversion Theologically Restated: the History of Salvation.* Encouraged by Bucer and Farel, Calvin's cousin Pierre Robert completed on 12 February 1535 his French translation of the New Testament, published at Neuchâtel by the printer Pierre de Vingle on 4 June 1535. Calvin was asked to provide two prefaces for the book, one in Latin,[14] and one in French. It is the latter that we would like to call his "first draft" of the theological restatement of his conversion experience. Since Calvin was in Basel by January 1535, at the latest the Preface must be dated early in that year when his full energies were being given to writing or completing his first edition of the *Institutes of the Christian Religion* (finished 23 August 1535; published by March 1536).

The Preface to the New Testament expressed in a succinct fashion the familiar Pauline-Augustinian summary of human history: man's creation in the image of God . . . continuing mercy of God through conscience (Gentiles) and law (Israel) . . . further apostasy . . . coming of the Savior . . . call of the Gospel. The preface ends with an appeal to kings and magistrates and to bishops and pastors to support the right preaching of the Gospel and the health of the church. From our point of view, the center of this brief essay, as a theological restatement of Calvin's conversion, is the section we have labeled "The Call of the Gospel." There is no question that the fundamental shift in Calvin's outlook, the insight that led him, inwardly, to abandon the search for wisdom among the

14. For a translation of the Latin see Appendix IV.

philosophers, was the crucial place of the fall of man. The fall, not understood by the philosophers in their glorification of human wisdom and their speculation upon the soul [cf. *Inst.* 1.15.8], is the point at which weak human wisdom is to be differentiated from the divine wisdom of Christ, what Calvin has elsewhere called the *philosophia Christi*. It is the pursuit of this higher wisdom that imparts joy to Christians joyously serving their Lord even in the midst of persecution. In Jesus Christ all Old Testament types of great men converge. "All that we think or desire, all that we express, is to be found in Jesus Christ, whom to know the whole of Scripture calls us."

From this reading of the Gospel Calvin moves out from personal experience to reflect upon the whole history of salvation. It is all in this brief preface, Calvin's first theological reflection upon his conversion. Here is the reason why Calvin abandoned the literary career of a humanist, or to put it in his own words:

> Having therefore received
> Some taste and knowledge
> Of true piety,
> I was suddenly fired
> With such a great desire to advance
> That, even though I had not forsaken
> The other studies entirely,
> I nonetheless worked at them
> More slackly [see Strophic translation above].

The "second draft" as well call it, of this theological restatement of the conversion experience followed the first by a few weeks or months during the first half of the year 1535. We have already alluded to it as "the Kernel of Calvin's faith." It occupies the initial nine pages of Chapter I of the 1536 *Institutes*. It covers the same ground as the *Preface to the New Testament* but more explicitly theologically than the earlier document, which is more narrowly Scriptural in its emphasis. It commences with the "two knowledges," of God and of man, passes to the law—unwritten and written—and concludes with "another way," i.e., Christ.

In the summary of Calvin's conversion there is an important phrase for all later Calvinism:

> As often as I descended into myself
> Or raised my mind to thee. . . .

These two movements of the human mind lead to the antithetical knowledge of God and knowledge of ourselves, the gulf between the all-holy God and the fallen sinner which only the incarnate Son of God can bridge. Calvin felt this deeply in his conversion and sought to express it in concentrated form in these first few pages of his critical chapter on the law. Successive editions of the *Institutes* were to see these thoughts dispersed through the growing bulk of the work, ultimately offering for it a kind of organizing principle. But, here, and here alone, they stand in a coherent brief theological summary of Calvin's religious experience.

What is the knowledge of God? God is infinite wisdom, righteousness, goodness, mercy, truth, power and life; all things have been created for his glory; he is a just judge; he is merciful and gentle.

What is the knowledge of ourselves? Adam, our common parent, was created in God's image with all the virtues; by his fall into sin this image was effaced and canceled; he was stripped of the virtues, which were replaced by the corresponding vices; all of us born of Adam are ignorant and bereft of God, powerless to do his will, deserving of eternal death.

Into this impasse in his creation, the merciful Father brings the law: the unwritten law upon the conscience; and then the written law. To keep us from ignorance of our true condition, God stamped upon our hearts a witness of what we owe him: conscience, the law within. Still blinded by self-love, we have been provided by God with a written law to teach us how to keep perfect righteousness; since, however, we do not perform the law's requirements, we still deserve the curse of eternal death.

To this second impasse of man, God in his infinite mercy offers another way. In our despair we must seek help from another quarter, in deepest humility: in Christ God gives us all the gifts we cannot earn for ourselves; but we must grasp Christ with a true and living faith in order to avail ourselves of his benefits; through him is the only way to reach eternal blessedness in the Father.

Stamped upon this summary is not only Calvin's fresh study of the Scriptures but the memory of his crisis of faith so recently experienced. Here are the deep currents of faith which issued in a life of dedication to Christ and his church. Here are the sources of Calvin's *Institutes of the Christian Religion*, of his exegesis, his preaching, and of all his other multifarious activities in behalf of the Reform.

II. THE FIRST EDITION OF THE INSTITUTES OF THE CHRISTIAN RELIGION (1536)

A. Catechism or Apology?[15]

1. The Original Catechetical Intent. One of the results of Calvin's conversion was the demand placed upon him, almost as soon as he began his new

15. Luchesius Smits, *Saint Augustin dans l'Oeuvre de Jean Calvin.* 2 vol. (Assen: 1957). In Vol. I, p. 28 Smits notes the lack of "homogeneity" in the 1536 edition due to the combined catechetical and apologetic purposes of the work. He suggests that this double purpose has an example in Seneca's *De Clementia.* Smits quotes Calvin's Seneca Commentary [p. 337] to this effect: "It seems, moreover, that Seneca's plan in this book was different from his plan in the first. While in the first Seneca accommodated himself to the popular understanding, the second he sprinkled with Stoic paradoxes and scholastic subtleties." Frankly, I think this "parallel" falls short of the mark.

Scriptural studies, as a teacher of those hungry for the true faith. His new popularity has already been set forth in the words of the Preface to the *Commentary on the Psalms*. Despite his own comparative inexperience, seekers flocked to him for true doctrine. He concludes with the characteristic phrase: "God never left me at peace in any place. . . ."

There are scattered references to Calvin's early preaching in France but these are fragmentary and impossible to date in a coherent way. They do suggest, however, that what Calvin says of his unsought popularity as a preacher and teacher is true. Unquestionably, his mind was drawn to the need for a good catechism which might answer the demands of his acquaintances. It was in the brief leisure of Basel, where the unknown French exile who knew no German lived in 1535 and early 1536, that he found time to write down the first fruits of his theological studies. The long title tells the story: "Institutes of the Christian Religion, Embracing almost the Whole Sum of Piety, and Whatever is Necessary to Know of the Doctrine of Salvation: A Work most Worthy to be Read by All Persons Zealous for Piety. . . ." How much of his projected catechism he brought already written or in notes from France one cannot say. Some older authorities thought that the Dedicatory Letter to the French King and possibly chapters 5-6 were written at Basel, the first four chapters coming from his earlier intervals of leisure, especially in the library of his friend Louis du Tillet at Claix in Angoulême. Ganoczy, the most recent writer on this period of Calvin's life, credits the whole book (although not necessarily the entire preparatory study for it) to the first seven months of Calvin's Basel sojourn, pointing out the incredible speed with which the reformer worked. We will not try to settle this question here.

In the French Reformed tradition, Calvin did not have many predecessors as catechism-writers. Besides translations of Luther, there had appeared in the French language, Guillaume Farel's *Sommaire et briefve declaration dauscuns lieux fort necessaires a ung chascun chrestien pour mettre sa confiance en dieu et ayder son prochain*, first published at Basel in 1525 at the urging of the Basel Reformer Oecolampadius.[16] An English translation of the long title would read: "Summary and brief declaration of some passages very necessary for each and every Christian to put his confidence in God and help his neighbor." The *Sommaire* went through numerous editions. A second French summary of the Reformed faith was written in 1529 by Francis Lambert of Avignon, entitled *Somme Chrestienne*. It was to this rather meager store that Calvin proposed to add his own "short" work.

Farel's *Sommaire*, Piaget tells us, was "the first work in French to expound the principal points of Reformed Christian doctrine, in a simple and popular fashion for the use of those 'who knew no Latin.' " It was written "in order that

16. N. Weiss identifies a 1523 imprint, *La Summe de l'Escripture Saincte*, as likely of Farel's authorship. See *Bulletin de l'Histoire du Protestantisme Français* 68 (1919) 63-79.

all those of the French language could have a more correct understanding and knowledge of Jesus, who by so few is purely known and served." Based on Holy Scripture, "which contains God's plan and will," it is addressed to all those who "love truth."[17] While there may be some echoes of Farel's tone and general position, Calvin's work seems to owe nothing to it in style, structure, or even content, although two such works, covering as they do the same field from the same general theological vantage point, would necessarily overlap.

Calvin very clearly describes his literary intention on the first page of the Letter to Francis I:

> When I first set my hand to this work, nothing was farther from m mind, most glorious King, than to write something that might be offerec to your Majesty. My purpose was solely to transmit certain rudiments by which those who are touched with any zeal for religion might be shaped to true godliness. And I undertook this labor especially for our French countrymen, very many of whom I saw to be hungering and thirsting for Christ; very few who had been imbued with even a slight knowledge of him. The book itself witnesses that this was my intention, adapted as it is to a simple and, you may say, elementary form of teaching.

This, then, was Calvin's catechetical intent. If we take his words at face value, he must have planned a French version to follow soon after, for a Latin work, however simply conceived, would be a closed book for most of his "French countrymen . . . thirsting for Christ." That he put it first in Latin may in part be due to the fact that he wanted it as an apology to reach foreign nations that they "might at least be touched with some compassion and concern" for the persecuted French Protestants. Latin was the lingua franca of the time, the logical medium to bring his case before the world. A lively debate among scholars of a generation ago discussed whether in fact such a French work was ever published. The first extant French edition of the *Institutes* is dated 1541, a translation of the second Latin edition of 1539. However, Calvin adapted from the 1536 Latin the Geneva *Catechism* of 1537. Obviously, he found the 1536 *Institutes* too long and complicated for a mere catechism; in fact, even the 1537 Catechism proved too learned for this popular use and was replaced, as Calvin gained pastoral experience at Geneva and Strasbourg, by the familiar Genevan question-and-answer type of catechism.[18]

2. *The Institutes becomes an Apology.* But Calvin's plan for a simple catechism was not to be. History dictated otherwise, and at the heart of the bloody events which changed the book was Francis I, Most Christian King of the French.

The stirring of religious reform in the early Sixteenth Century brought a

17. A. Piaget, ed., *Guillaume Farel. Sommaire et Briefue Declaration* (Paris: 1935) pp. 7-8.

18. For the relationship between the 1536 *Institutes*, the 1537 (French) and 1538 (Latin) *Catechism*, and the 1539 *Institutes*, see *John Calvin: Catechism 1538*, tr. ann. F.L. Battles (Pittsburgh: 1972).

wide variety of movements, from a most conservative effort to cleanse the existing church to radical attacks on the entire social fabric. George H. Williams has well shown the almost hopeless complexity of the varied personages who put forward their plans for the amelioration of humanity during the first half of the century.[19] In church history it had long been characteristic of the supporters of the establishment not to differentiate too precisely between moderate and radical critics. To offer but one example of many, the medieval church lumped the simple Bible faith of the early Waldensians with the Manichaean dualism of the Cathari of the Thirteenth Century. And in actuality it has always been difficult to differentiate movements of religious reform: there are shades and combinations of all kinds. The defenders of the establishment, too, have reasons of their own for perpetuating such confusion. The most reasonable demand for reform of corrupt or outmoded institutional forms and practices can be blunted and discredited if it can be attached to more exaggerated and dangerous demands for change. Perhaps this failure to discriminate is only partly conscious and deliberate: the beleaguered supporters of the *status quo* may in fact see the threatening forces as a single entity.

In both Luther and Zwingli we see a certain effort to prove their essential orthodoxy to Rome, especially in their forcible repudiation of radical movements which seemed to threaten their own recently constructed establishment. Luther against the Peasants' Revolt, Zwingli against the nascent Anabaptist movement in Zürich, in fact Luther over against Zwingli's more radical handling of the Lord's Supper—all may serve to illustrate our point.

When Lutheran ideas reached France in the 1520's, moderate reform was already represented by Jacques Lefèvre d'Étaples, Bishop Guillaume Briçonnet,[20] and the so-called Cercle de Meaux. But travelers brought more radical views from the Low Countries, from Germany and Switzerland. There was already a ferment at work in France; medieval sectarian ideas had been kept alive underneath the surface. Thus, there was ample evidence of revolutionary tendencies which might prove subversive to church and state. The spreading of French translations of the Bible through printing encouraged even uneducated persons to reflect on the meaning of Scripture. The Sorbonne saw all these tendencies as one threat to the ecclesiastical establishment and labeled them all as heretical. The impressive machinery for the suppression of heresy inherited from the Thirteen-Fourteenth Century fight to extirpate the Cathari was brought into action to cope with "Lutheranism," the name under which all dissident movements were now lumped.

Francis I, who in his humanist sympathies had earlier resisted Sorbonne

19. George H. Williams, *The Radical Reformation*. (Philadelphia: 1962).

20. On Bishop Briçonnet's tragic recantation of the Evangelical cause, see Herminjard, I, Nos. 77, 78. He officially decreed against Luther and his doctrines on 15 October 1523. On the work of Lefèvre d'Étaples see now: P.E. Hughes, *Lefèvre: Pioneer of Ecclesiastical Renewal in France* (Grand Rapids: 1984).

attempts to suppress Erasmus and other advocates of Christian humanism, went along with the Sorbonne's demands to purge France of heresy. This internal campaign of persecution, particularly as it threatened Germans resident in France, became an embarrassment to Francis' negotiations with the German Protestant princes and their theological advisers. The diplomatic accomplishments of 1534 were dashed by the affair of the Placards in October of that year, as we have seen. So, in the continued negotiations with the Lutherans of early 1535, in the midst of persecutions at home, it became expedient to picture the whole matter as an affair of national security and to isolate the French Evangelical party from the respectable Protestants outside France. Three groups of supporters of this reading of French Reform emerged: Catholic theologians like Cochlaeus and Ceneau wrote that Calvin was to call "lying pamphlets, tarring all French evangelicals with the same dire Anabaptist brush; otherwise respectable humanists like Budé and Sadolet snobbishly treated the whole movement as that of an ignorant rabble; finally, Francis' memorandum to the German Protestant princes on 1 February 1535 (drafted by his diplomatic envoy Guillaume du Bellay) presented this view of the whole movement toward Reform in France. To summarize the memorandum: the sovereign attempted to justify to his Protestant allies the persecutions undertaken in France following the affair of the Placards, an act of anarchy and revolt against the internal order of the kingdom. The government not only had the right but the duty to take vigorous steps. The French Evangelicals, the memorandum asserted, unlike the German Protestants, were seditious persons in no respect different from the Anabaptists. Were not such persons quite justly put to death even in Protestant Germany?

So went the reasoning of the royal memorandum. It did not serve its purpose of allaying the fears and misgivings of the Germans, but it did convince the more conservative spokesmen of the French Evangelical party of the need to dissociate themselves, theologically and politically, from more radical forces of reform, and to make their distinction very clear not only in the minds of their fellow Protestants outside France but to their own monarch and his advisers. The immediacy of this was borne out by the tragic events of Münster now approaching their apocalyptic climax: the polygamous Kingdom of Münster was to fall on 25 June 1535.

Calvin's response to this question: how can the true Evangelicals be proved of a different stamp from their more radical brethren? took two forms. He first set out to deal with what he considered the most damning theological aspect of the question in his *Psychopannychia*, written in 1534/5, published finally in 1542. He then mounted a more comprehensive literary campaign in the 1536 *Institutes*. Let us look at each of these documents in turn.

The *Psychopannychia* poses considerable critical problems. Against what groups or group was it originally intended? How much of the 1542 published version represents, actually, what Calvin originally wrote in 1534/5? Fortunately for us, these questions are not central to our present task, so they can be laid aside. We are concerned with only the message of the book.

Why did Calvin choose for his first theological essay obscure questions of what happened to soul and body at the time of physical death? If the book is directed against the Anabaptists, the doctrine of soul-sleep or soul-death was not one widely held in that movement.[21] By whatever groups it was held, unquestionably the doctrine was accepted more in France than in other lands that had been touched by Reform. Calvin must have felt the need to refute it in the interests both of protecting his fellow religionists from it and in assuring the Catholics that this heretical notion was not held by the authentic Evangelicals of France.

Among the Catholic doctrines rejected by the Protestants was that of purgatory and of prayers for the dead, and of the intercession of the saints. The Catholics who supported these doctrines thought their opponents must of necessity be rejecting the continued existence of the soul after the death of the body, a doctrine dictated to Pope John XXII by the University of Paris in the Fourteenth Century, and reiterated recently at the Fifth Lateran Council, against dangerous Aristotelian tendencies of Averroist origin stemming from the University of Padua. Did the Evangelicals in fact, by rejecting prayers for the dead, assume the death of the soul?

This question was posed to Calvin by Cardinal Sadolet in 1539:

> Nor would I say anything either of the prayers of the saints of God for us, or of ours for the dead, though I would fain know what these same men would be at when they despise and deride them. Can they possibly imagine that the soul perishes along with the body? This they certainly seem to insinuate, and they do it still more openly when they strive to procure for themselves a liberty of conduct set loose from all ecclesiastical laws, and of a license for their lusts. For, if the soul is mortal, Let us eat and drink, says the Apostle, for tomorrow we die; but if it is immortal, as it certainly is, how, I ask, has the death of the body made so great and so sudden a disruption, that the souls of the dead have no congruity, in any respect, no communion with those of the living, and have forgotten all their relationship to us and common human society? And this, especially, while charity, which is the principal gift of the Holy Spirit to a Christian soul, which is ever kind and fruitful, and which, in him who has it, never exists to no purpose, must always remain safe and operative in both lives.[22]

Just as the rejection of prayers for the dead, invocation of the saints, etc., was the key to overcoming the whole oppressive Catholic system of indulgences against which Luther had already taken his stand, so the continued assertion of the life of the soul, independent of the body, was requisite to dissociate the Evangelicals from fantastic and subversive tendencies which could, theologi-

21. On this question now see: Willem Balke, *Calvin and the Anabaptist Radicals* (Grand Rapids: 1981), pp. 25-33.

22. Op. cit. in Note 11 above, p. 15.

cally, be tied to a doctrine of soul-death and soul-sleep. We shall later take up the sacramental and political consequences of this.

And so, in his first theological essay, Calvin had set out, through painstaking word studies of "soul," "spirit," and other scriptural terms to assert the immortality of the soul against those who claimed either that it died or went to sleep until tbe general resurrection. The theological presupposition upon which Calvin's view rests is that the soul, pre-eminently, is to be identified with the image of God. If this be so, to assert that that image is destroyed for a time or even for a period sleeps, is unthinkable. As God never dies, never sleeps, so the image of him in man must be ever watchful until the blessed reunion of soul with body at the general resurrection. To this essentially Christian doctrine, however, Calvin was to add the Protestant insistence that communication between the souls in living bodies on earth and the disembodied souls of the dead awaiting the day of resurrection was impossible. To postulate such would be to detract from Christ's sole mediatorship.

The *Psychopannychia* itself went through several literary stages with the first of which we are primarily concerned at this point. Writing on 3 September 1535 to his friend Christopher Libertet, he speaks of his first draft in these terms:

> As for that essay . . . it contained my first thoughts, rather thrown together in the shape of memoranda or commonplaces than digested after any definite and certain method, although there was some appearance of order.[23]

The first draft bears a preface dedicated to a certain friend (unidentified) who stands ". . . firm in prudence and moderation . . ." ". . . amid those tumults of vain opinions with which giddy spirits disturb the peace of the church." In the preface Calvin anticipates the charge that his writing will disturb the unity and charity of the church, to which he responds: "We acknowledge no unity except in Christ, no charity of which he is not the bond; and therefore, the chief point in preserving charity is to maintain faith sacred and entire."[24] This in 1534 at Orléans, perhaps in the late summer. Calvin sent a copy of the first draft to the Reformer Wolfgang Capito at Strasbourg for his advice on publishing it. Capito's response which Herminjard dates toward the end of 1534 dissuaded Calvin from this and sent him "back to the drawing board" so to speak. Here are Capito's words:

> . . . As to publishing it, if you pay attention to us, you will by all means make plans for it at a more appropriate time. Now sects are raising an uproar everywhere, and the Germans in the great religious calamity have found that fighting errors makes them better known; that the surest way to take care of the afflicted churches is to depict Christ most carefully.

23. OC X, 51-2.
24. Op. cit. in note 8 above, p. 416.

> . . . I would prefer that you begin your literary endeavors in a more praiseworthy matter. . . . To sum up: the tortured state of the French churches demands that you rather withdraw from all contentions.[25]

Capito suggests that constructive scriptural exegesis would be more appropriate, pointing to his own work on Hosea. But this advice came during the negotiations of the German princes and reformers with the French authorities looking toward a religious peace and a reforming council. October 1534 was to see the affair of the Placards at Paris, the bloody persecutions of the French Evangelicals in the months that followed, then the cataclysm of Münster and the official justification of internal religious oppression by the French crown, that the offenders were all, indiscriminately, subversives. Calvin took Capito's advice concerning the *Psychopannychia* (which he however revised in 1535 during his Basel sojourn after completing the *Institutes*). But remain silent he could not to the charge that he and his compatriots were trying to destroy political order in France. And so in his preface to the French King, having alluded to his original catechetical intent—which we have already quoted—he immediately and passionately launched on why he decided to give his work a second purpose:

> But I perceived that the fury of certain wicked persons has prevailed so far in your realm that there is no place in it for sound doctrine. Consequently, it seemed to me that I should be doing something worthwhile if I both gave instruction to those I had undertaken to instruct and made confession before you with the same work. From this you may learn the nature of the doctrine against which those madmen burn with rage, who today disturb your realm with fire and sword. And indeed I shall not fear to confess that I have here embraced almost the sum of that very doctrine which they shout must be punished by prison, exile, proscription, and fire and be exterminated on land and sea. Indeed, I know with what horrible reports they have filled your ears and minds, to render our cause as hateful as possible to you. But, as fits your clemency you ought to weigh the fact that if it is enough merely to make accusations, then no innocence will remain either in words or deeds. [*Inst.* p. 1]

Essentially the same story is told by Calvin in his Preface to the *Commentary on the Psalms*, but perhaps even more pointedly:

> But it happened that while I was dwelling at Basel,
> Hidden there as it were, and known only to few people,
> Many faithful, holy men were burned in France,
> And reports of this having spread to foreign countries,
> A great part of the Germans
> Reacted with grave disapproval
> So as to conceive a hatred
> Toward the authors of that tyranny.
> In order to quiet things down,

25. Herminjard, III, No. 490

It was arranged to circulate
Certain shameful pamphlets
Full of lies, to the effect
That only Anabaptists and seditious person
Were being treated so cruelly,
Who by their dreams and false opinions
Were overturning not only religion
But the whole political order.
It appeared to me that these tools of the court[26]
Were by their disguises trying
Not only to keep this shameful shedding
Of innocent blood
Buried under false charges and calumnies
Brought against the holy martyrs after their death,
But also that thereafter they might have a means
Of proceeding to the ultimate extremity
Of murdering the poor faithful
Without anyone having compassion for them.
Unless, then, I strongly opposed them
To the best of my ability,
I could not justify my silence
Without being found lax and disloyal.
This was the reason that roused me
To publish my *Institutes of the Christian Religion*:
First, to answer certain wicked charges
Sowed by the other,
And to clear the memory of my brethren
Whose death was precious
In the presence of the Lord; [Ps. 116:15]
Secondly, as the same cruelties
Could very soon thereafter
Be exercised against many poor people,
That foreign nations might at least
Be touched with some compassion
And concern for them.
For at that time I did not publish
The book as it now is,
Full and laborious,
But it was only a little booklet
Containing in summary form
The principal matters.
I had no other purpose
Than to acquaint others
With the sort of faith
Held by those
Whom I saw

26. ab aulicis artificibus . . . See Bohatec, op. cit., p. 128.

These wicked and faithless flatterers
Villainously defaming.[27]

We see, then, that two things led Calvin to write his first edition of the famous *Institutes*: the catechetical needs of his religious brethren; and the need to plead their case before the King, that persecution might cease. And the latter purpose called forth a double theological response from Calvin, the rejection of institutionalized Roman Catholicism and at the same time of its extreme opposite, the revolutionary, disruptive spiritualism of what at that time he lumped under the name "Catabaptists." Hence, Calvin's future theological course was determined: to hold a middle direction between the right and left. This was not a prudent compromise, but a judgment securely grounded on Calvin's own independent study of Scripture. The later development of his theological system is an extending and perfecting of this initial polarity.

B. The Dedicatory Letter to the French King

1. An Apology among Christian Apologies. A study of the classic apologies of the Christian religion, particularly those early writings of the Church Fathers prompted by pagan Roman persecutions of the infant Christian Church, will demonstrate the creative impulse apologetic gave to Christian theology. The church found itself caught between Jew and Gentile, and more intimately between tendencies within its ranks which sought on the one hand to perpetuate its Jewish heritage and on the other to repudiate that heritage. Already in the experience of Paul himself these forces are at work; by the Second Century the future of the faith lay in holding to the unity of the testaments against the Jews who would deny the New and the Gnostics who would reshape the New shorn of its historic roots in the Old. The Apologists also had to convince the authorities that the Christian movement did not wish to destroy the Roman state and that its refusal to go along with official paganism and the emperor cult was not an act of political sedition but a religious preference which in no way weakened the Christian's support of the state. Even in Paul, and especially in the Pastoral Epistles of the New Testament this assurance of peaceful, nonrevolutionary coexistence is sounded.

In trying to bridge the gulf which these conflicts seemed to open, the Apologists, Justin Martyr notably, began the long process of the domestication of Greek philosophy in the Christian tradition, following Philo Judaeus, in the First Century of our era.

It may seem an unwarranted digression to speak of these early writers here but for the fact that a significant parallel in literary tone and even in argument may be pointed out between their writing and Calvin's. To mention but one striking item: the early Apologists were faced with the pagans' question: what

27. *The Piety of John Calvin*, Ford Lewis Battles, trans. & ed. (Grand Rapids: 1978), pp. 31-32.

authority does this new cult born a little over a hundred years ago have in comparison with other faiths such as the Egyptian that goes back thousands of years? To this the Apologists, insisting on Christian continuity with the Jewish Scriptures, said: "Our faith is as old as creation itself." To the charge that they were plotting to overthrow established religion and in fact the whole political establishment, they pointed to the purity of their life, the exemplary character of their worship and their loyalty to the emperor. To the charge that their faith was a thing of patches hastily sewn together from bits filched from ancient philosophy, they asserted that on the contrary their faith was the original from which these later pagan aberrations derived.

No wonder that Calvin eagerly scanned the whole history of the church and especially its earliest centuries! Like his fellow apologists of the early church, Calvin was by his apologetic effort really constructing a new synthesis of the faith. To the charge of novelty leveled by the Sorbonnists, Calvin asserted his faith was the authentic apostolic message, theirs the late medieval aberration. To the charge that the French Evangelicals were plotting to topple the monarchy, Calvin pledged the political loyalty of the Evangelical party. No man ever put to better use the force of history in the service of the faith.

The letter to Francis I is, therefore, to be set beside the apologies of Justin Martyr and his mid-second Century contemporaries, also beside the apologies of Tertullian, Origen and Eusebius.

2. *The Content of the Dedicatory Letter.* Let us look at the structure of the Letter. Calvin does not break it up into sections as he did the chapters of the latest editions of the *Institutes*. The printers set it in solid type. But one may discern eight parts, already noted in our translation of the 1559 edition, and here reproduced.

(1) We have already quoted from and discussed the first section, which we may entitle: "Circumstances in which the book was first written." Here, after outlining his double purpose, Calvin asks Francis I, a truly Christian King (as his title claims) for a full and fair inquiry into the Evangelicals' case.

(2) Next Calvin pleads for the persecuted Evangelicals, casting in stark relief their Scriptural faith and heroic martyrdom over against the Romanists' neglect of that Scriptural faith and insistence upon the Mass, purgatory, pilgrimages and like trifles.

(3) Thereupon Calvin takes up four basic charges of the Catholics against the Reformed faith: that it is new, unknown, uncertain and unsupported by miracles. The antithetical approach once again had come to Calvin's aid: God's word is hardly new! Unknown the Reformed faith may be, but the reason is that true doctrine has long lain buried and forgotten through man's impiety. How can you call our faith "uncertain" seeing our assurance over against their doubt? As for supporting miracles, you should sift the difference between true and false miracles.

(4) In the next section, Calvin disposed of the oft-repeated argument that the Evangelicals have thrown out the Church Fathers because they fail to support

their teaching. Calvin has read his fathers and the standard historians of the church. From them he produces an impressive series of sharp antitheses. We summarize them here:

(a) God doesn't need gold or silver / Look at their lavish rites
(b) Christians may either eat meat or abstain from it / Lenten fasts
(c) Monks must work / idle, licentious monks of our day
(d) no images of Christ or saints / churches crawling with images
(e) after burial of the dead let them rest / perpetual solicitude for the dead
(f) bread and wine remain in the eucharist / transubstantiation
(g) all present must partake of the Lord's Supper / public and private masses put grace and merit of Christ up for sale
(h) rash verdicts without basis in Scripture disallowed / jungle of constitutions, canons, etc., unbased on God's Word
(i) marriage affirmed for clergy / celibacy enjoined
(j) God's Word to be kept clear of sophistries / look at their speculative theological brawls!

(5) After this heavy cannonade of the Roman Catholic position, Calvin turns to the next circle of defense of the papal stronghold, the appeal to custom. Most Roman Catholic polemicists had stood firm in the assertion that these Protestant Johnny-come-latelies were sacrilegiously mangling the established and hallowed customs of Mother Church. Here, Calvin's humanist training shows its clearest strength. Most custom, he asserts, is the result of the private vices of the majority which become public error and wrongly take on the force of law. Over against such public error stands the eternal justice of God's Kingdom which we are called upon fearlessly to follow. In ringing terms Calvin asserts that, though the whole world may fall into the same wickedness, strength of numbers does not sanction or excuse it.

(6) Where then is the true church to be found? The Romanists have asserted that the form of the church is always observable; that this form of the church rests in the Roman church and its hierarchy. To this Calvin makes rejoinder with the Pauline marks of pure preaching and lawful sacraments, the same marks Luther had earlier asserted in the ecclesiological debate with Rome. Historically, both in the Old Testament and in subsequent Christian history, this true church often went underground and was without visible form. Yet though it seemed to disappear, a thin line of true witnesses to it was marvelously preserved by God even through the darkest times. When Elijah asked where the true worshipers were, God told him seven thousand there were who had not bowed the knee to Baal. The remnant still lived when mankind as a whole lay in spiritual slumber.

(7) Now, one of the most telling criticisms of the Romanists against the Reformed preachers, an argument to which harassed monarchs were especially sensitive, was that the renewed preaching of the Gospel was destroying peace and bringing in its train tumult and revolution. Calvin's reply to this rather strong

argument is to postulate a two-fold Satanic strategy. For centuries Satan kept the church asleep in worldly luxury. When, however, it started to wake up, in this new Apostolic age so to speak, he countered with a new strategy. He raised up contentions of all sorts, prompted religious strife, especially centering his ingenious new strategy on those Calvin calls the "Catabaptists." In this time of strife, we are in the same boat as the Apostles, but like them we have assurance of our faith.

(8) In the last section Calvin realistically sizes up the likelihood that his appeal will actually reach the King, and if it does, sway him in the least. Whether their earthly King listens or not to their plea, really recognizes them as loyal Frenchmen, the Evangelicals will ultimately put their faith in the King of kings, whose rule is perfect justice and who will hear their plea. So ends the letter to Francis I.

If we now turn from this impassioned appeal, to the very end of the *Institutes*, whether the third portion of the sixth chapter of the 1536 edition, or Book 4, chapter 20 in the edition of 1559, we will see a final plea of obedience to the earthly monarch, but at the very last the ringing assertion that obedience to man must not become disobedience to God. "We must obey God rather than men." This is the "political frame" of the *Institutes*.

At the heart of this letter, then, is the acute sense of contrast, not only between the evangelical faith and the doctrine and practice of the Roman Church, but also a contrast, not elaborated here, but to be worked out more fully later on, between the Evangelicals and the loose congeries of extremists (from Calvin's point of view) which he here conveniently if inaccurately labels "Catabaptists," the very term Zwingli had made current in his famous *Elenchus*, and which Bucer used in his commentaries to denominate that group. We may conclude that the *Institutes* took shape between these two opposing religious tendencies. We shall now turn to the six chapters that comprise the 1536 *Institutes*.

C. Analysis of the "Catechetical" Chapters (1-5).

The catechetical literature of the later middle ages, both in Latin and in the vernacular, took the form of simple expositions of the Law, Apostles' Creed, Lord's Prayer, etc. Luther found this form ready at hand when he compiled his *Small Catechism* of 1522 and the *Large Catechism* of 1529. It was natural, then, that Calvin would construct his first edition of the *Institutes* from the successive expositions of the Ten Commandments (ch. 1), the Apostles' Creed (ch. 2), the Lord's Prayer (ch. 3), the Sacraments (ch. 4). To this he appends first a refutation of the papal mass (end of ch. 4) and a long chapter rejecting on Scriptural and historical grounds the so-called five "false sacraments" (ch. 5). The concluding chapter contains three related essays, on Christian Freedom, Ecclesiastical Power, and Political Power, which we propose to treat separately as really a part of the apologetic aspect of the book, more perhaps than the catechetical.

In dealing with these basic documents of the faith, Calvin quite often seems to follow, but always in his own independent way, Martin Luther. This is especially true in his treatment of the Decalogue. (Later editions of the *Institutes* will show a greater independence of treatment of the separate commandments.) Yet we must candidly remark that the well-known difference between Luther and Calvin on the Law is already apparent. Our analysis of these chapters will not be exhaustive but will concentrate on the polarities they present.

1. Chapter 1: On the Law. After the theological restatement of Calvin's faith which serves as a preface and which we have already discussed, Calvin launches into an exposition of the Decalogue. Most of the commandments are paraphrased in the briefest terms, but four of them call for fuller discussion: the Third evokes an essay on images and idolatry with application to the Roman Catholic cultus; the Fourth offers an opportunity to reject the Anabaptist teaching on oaths; the Fifth on Sabbath observance, since it stands between the moral and ceremonial law, calls for something other than a literal exegesis; the Tenth or "Deuteronomic" Commandment is more extensively discussed because of its practical consequences: if the family is extended to include the larger political groupings (one is reminded here of Aristotle's *Politics*) one may subsume under it the honoring of the king, prince, magistrates, etc. Here is a scriptural restatement of the classical notes on the *Pater Patriae* as set forth in the *Seneca Commentary.*[28]

The concluding discussion of the chapter moves on to the uses of the law and to justification: this logically brings in the contrast between faith-righteousness and works-righteousness, and such subsidiary Roman Catholic notions as works of supererogation. The influence of Luther (and of Paul) is obvious here. In later editions fuller support will be drawn from Augustine as this material is broken up, expanded and distributed to new chapters.

2. Chapter 2: On Faith. This chapter, containing an exposition of the Apostles' Creed, was the chief casualty of the later editions, being fragmented to provide substance for a radically altered structure. The centrality, existentially speaking, of faith to Calvin's whole religious view, demanded more than a mere reliance on an ancient and post-Scriptural epitome of evangelical teaching, such as the Apostles' Creed.

Basically, in 1536, the chapter consists of a theological essay on the nature of faith and the Trinity, an exposition of the Creed, and a concluding section on the relation of faith, hope and love. Strong antitheses, some against the Roman Catholics and others against the Anabaptists and anti-trinitarians mark the chapter.

Let us look at the chapter in more detail. True vs. false notions of faith mark the opening pages, largely against the Roman Catholics. The section on the Trinity seems to be directed against unnamed contemporary antitrinitarians, who are credited with "mocking us for confessing one God in three persons," the indiscriminate use of "Spirit" by some, the criticisms of others leveled against the use of technical non-Biblical theological terms are refuted by Calvin

28. See *Calvin's Commentary on Seneca's De Clementia* (cited in Note 6 above), pp. 105, 121, 171, 237, 107.

with the help of ancient church history parallels. Some authorities think that the proposed meeting of Calvin with Servetus in Paris in 1534 (?) which never occurred may be hinted at here; at any event, these kernels of refutation were later reused and expanded in the Servetus quarrel as reflected in the latest edition of the *Institutes* (1559). Our endnotes mark points of contact with Servetus' two earliest treatises.

In discussing the Creed, Calvin utilizes the first article to assert God's omnipotence and providence against any vestigial Pelagianism of the Sorbonne.

The second article carries a strong critique by Calvin of an unidentified position which had asserted Christ was God's Son only according to his humanity (by the virgin birth) and charged Calvin and his party with a "two-Christ" doctrine.

Calvin in dealing with the descent into hell reiterates the nonliteral interpretation of the *Psychopannychia*, thus setting a further antithesis with the Anabaptists; but this position of Calvin is also taken implicitly over against the Roman Catholics. The session at God's right hand is simply stated in a way that presages the remarks on Christ's risen body in Chapter 4 (On the Sacraments): "Therefore, although lifted up to heaven, he has removed the presence of his body from our sight, yet he does not refuse to be present with his believers in help and might, to show the manifest power of his presence." Here we see his distinction not only from the Roman Catholics but from Luther and from Zwingli as well. This affords the clue to Calvin's Christological difference from the Lutherans.

The fourth article is chiefly a brief positive statement of Calvin's view of the church, based on a thorough-going theology of grace, marked by election and predestination, but the most corporate and least developed statement of his doctrine in all of Calvin's voluminous writings on this hotly contested doctrine.[29] It is very much here a churchly doctrine, cast as it is in the midst of the discussion of the ecclesiastical article of the Apostles' Creed. Not all of Calvin's ecclesiology is confined to this chapter, however; aspects are dealt with in Chapters 3-6 as well.

The concluding essay of Chapter 2, on faith, hope and love, argues the primacy of faith, rejects the Roman Catholic notion of *fides informis* and also the Roman Catholic teaching that we are justified by love rather than faith.

It is interesting to note that the antitheses sketched here against the "left wing" of the Reformation are utilized in much expanded form later on against Servetus, other Antitrinitarians, and also against certain Anabaptists (as Menno Simons on Christology).

3. Chapter 3: On Prayer. This chapter owes a great deal to Martin Bucer's *Commentary on the Gospels* (1530), as Alexandre Ganoczy has shown, and as

29. Smits' previously cited (Note 15 above) careful study of Calvin's use of Augustine reveals that Calvin does not quote *On the Predestination of the Saints* until the edition of 1539.

is documented in our endnotes. Here let us be content with summing up the antitheses it contains. The most obvious antithesis is between Christ as sole Mediator and the many human mediators in the invocation of the saints. Implied throughout the chapter is the general antithesis between the false aspects of Roman Catholic worship and the purity of Evangelical worship, a subject to be more polemically treated in the following chapters. This included the localization of the holy, the superstitious use of set times (cf. Calvin's earlier exegesis of the Fifth Commandment, and his later adiaphoric treatment of rites in the second essay of Chapter 6), the use of Latin rather than the vernacular, and passivity vs. action of the congregation (implied in his remarks on singing). These points were later to be greatly expanded by Calvin.

4. *Chapter 4: On the Sacraments*. This chapter is divided into four sections, the first three corresponding roughly to the order of the sacramental chapters of the 1559 *Institutes* (4.14-18): the initial essay deals with the sacraments in general: it is followed by essays on baptism and the Lord's Supper, and the short concluding piece discusses the administration of the two dominical sacraments. In the marriage of physical with spiritual which is a sacrament, Calvin uses the exegetical principle of accommodation.

Parenthetically, we would like to note that many years later, in 1556, when Calvin was writing his Second Defense against Westphal, his chief Lutheran opponent on the Lord's Supper, he referred to his early reading on this topic:

> Beginning gradually to leave the darkness of the Papacy and having taken a little taste of healthy doctrine, when I read in Luther that Oecolampadius and Zwingli left nothing in the sacraments but bare figures and representations without truth, I confess that I turned from their books, with the result that I abstained from reading them for a long time. But before I began to write they had conferred together [1529] at Marburg.[30]

That Calvin had read Zwingli, or through some other source knew his position when he wrote this chapter, will be apparent from the position our reformer took. In defining a sacrament, Calvin rejects on the one hand "those who weaken the force of the sacraments and completely overthrow their use," and on the other hand "those who attach to the sacraments some sort of secret power with which one nowhere reads that God had endowed them." This latter tendency embraces two groups: those who teach that the sacraments of the new Law justify and confer grace, "provided we do not set up a barrier of mortal sin" (obviously referring to the Roman Catholics); and those who believe a hidden power is "joined and fastened to the sacraments to distribute in them the graces of the Holy Spirit, but only if the Holy Spirit accompanies them." Calvin does not identify this last group. So we may see that Calvin's *general* sacramental position lies between Zwinglianism and Roman Catholicism, emphasizing as it

30. "Second Defense . . . to the Calumnies of Joachim Westphal," *Tracts and Treatises*, II, 252-3.

does the sacraments as "seals" upon the document of faith, as God's accommodation to our weak capacity to understand.

Calvin's chief opponent in his discussion of baptism would seem to be the Anabaptists whose demand for believer baptism and Donatistical insistence on rebaptism he rejects; but Calvin also refutes the Roman Catholic view, resting upon a defective grasp of original sin, that baptism releases us from original sin and restores us to the righteousness and purity of Adam before the fall. Briefly alluded to is the Zwinglian minimal view of baptism as "but a token and mark by which we confess our religion before men." That Calvin senses his mediating position may be seen in his refutation of the Anabaptist demand for rebaptism by identifying them with the ancient Donatists: "Such today are our Catabaptists who deny that we have been duly baptized because we were baptized by impious and idolatrous men under the papal government."

Calvin's essay on the Lord's Supper sets forth in a briefer fashion the essential points made at greater length in his mature theological expression. There are several striking features of this earliest eucharistic discussion of his: first, it shows remarkably wide reading and independent reflection upon the infinitely varied views previously expressed on the Lord's Supper. While deeper study of Augustine and Chrysostom was to be evidenced in the 1539 edition, Calvin had in the edition of 1536 canvassed historically the development of the Lord's Supper, had examined the pertinent Scriptural passages deeply, and had reviewed the various positions on the Supper expressed in his own time. Two testimonies to this preparation for his task come from later writings. We have the text of two speeches he gave at the Colloquy of Lausanne in early October 1536, a discussion organized by the Bernese authorities between the Roman Catholics and the Reformed spokesmen on the Lord's Supper.[31] In this, Calvin quoted extensively from the Church Fathers. In 1556 in writing his *Second Defense* against the Lutheran Westphal he made the statement previously quoted about his early reading on the sacraments. Taken literally as some scholars do, this statement in the Westphal essay would push Calvin's theological awakening back to his days at Bourges and associate this interest with the influence of his teacher Melchior Wolmar. But it probably refers rather to Calvin's post-conversion religious studies in 1534-35.

A second feature of Calvin's earliest eucharistic statement is that it enters the debate not as a new voice just beginning its labors, but as if Calvin had long been debating the points at issue, either as spokesman for a party he does not identify or possibly as the self-appointed continuator of true Christian orthodoxy as he, fresh from his initial studies, understands it.

A third feature is that Calvin's grasp of the various tendencies, combinations and alignments of parties is so deep that he in brief anticipates later full-blown developments of theological controversy; in fact, much of his material

31. OC IX, 877-886

here possessing a general application is later adapted and augmented to apply to specific controversies in which he is subsequently engaged.

Without entering into all the subtleties and details of Calvin's eucharistic teaching, one may ask the question, where does his position lie with regard to the major alignments of parties? He sees two opposing faulty views on the Lord's Supper, expressed perhaps more succinctly in his exposition of the *Consensus Tigurinus* (1551): if the dignity of the sacraments is too highly extolled, superstition easily creeps in; on the other hand a cold and less elevated discussion of their virtue and fruit leads to profane contempt of them. The main cause of controversy over the Supper, he asserts in the *Institutes* of 1536, is that men have asked the wrong question: "How do we eat Christ's body?" They should have asked: "How does Christ's body become ours?" He rejects the idolatry of the Mass. He rejects a discipline that allows only the perfect (Anabaptists) or the perfectly shriven (Roman Catholics), to communicate. He rejects the rationalistic reductionism of Zwingli but sides with him on the limits of the glorified body against the real presence (differently advanced by the Roman Catholics on the one hand and by the Lutherans on the other); he accepts an "as if" physical presence, a sort of ubiquity of God's power which marvelously bridges the otherwise unbridgeable spiritual gulf between heaven and earth. These are subtle distinctions taken in conscious differentiation from the manifold positions taken by other theologians both of the past and of his own time, but dictated primarily by a living faith proclaimed to men in the Scriptures but fortified, "sealed," by the sacraments for the sake of man's weakness and incapacity. Faith does not make the sacraments mere signs, nor do the sacraments by themselves do the work of faith: they work together—faith and sacraments. At bottom, these differences in eucharistic theology mark corresponding differences in theology and Christology.

The strong *pastoral* intent of Calvin is seen in his rejection of any theological position or liturgical practice that denies the benefits of the sacraments to the faithful.[32] He therefore concludes his chapter with a discussion on the administration of the sacraments. Briefly but succinctly he sets forth the evidence from the New Testament for sacramental practice, then discusses details which can be varied according to time and place without harm to sacrament or receiver. The touchstone of *true* vs. *false* sacramental theology and practice is Scriptural authority: all else is of human invention.

5. *Chapter 5: On the Five False Sacraments*. This chapter was perhaps to be in later editions the least altered in basic content and structure of all the chapters of the 1536 *Institutes*. From the copious side-notes of the original text at this point it is clear that Calvin has both the Scriptures and Gratian's *Decretum* and Peter Lombard's *Sentences* beside him as he writes this chapter. It is of course directed against the false sacramental teachings and practices of the Ro-

32. One of the worst features of the Roman Mass, in Calvin's view, is that it makes the laity into "second-class citizens" of the kingdom.

man Church, and draws at least some of its initial inspiration from Luther's *Babylonian Captivity of the Church* (1520). Each "sacrament" is examined in terms of the claims made for it, its actual history and the true teaching that should replace it. While Calvin lives up to his promise of brevity in discussing Confirmation, Extreme Unction and Marriage, he deals with Penance and Orders at length. Under Penance he treats such related topics as repentance, confession, absolution (the power of the keys), indulgences, the treasury of merits, satisfaction for sins, and purgatory. In later editions these will be detached to separate chapters, leaving only the original nucleus. Over against this false ecclesiastical structure Calvin lays the Scriptural view of repentance and forgiveness. In like manner, he deals at length with the "Sacrament" of Orders and its various divisions, setting over against it the Scriptural doctrine of ministry, a topic to be much more fully dealt with in the edition of 1543, after Calvin's pastoral experience at Strasbourg.

We have in this chapter, in a sense, the nucleus of Calvin's detailed refutation of the foundations of the medieval church order, if we add to it some details from the middle essay of Chapter 6, On Ecclesiastical Power. These two portions, taken together and skillfully patched, were to become the first half of Book IV in the final edition of 1559. In reaction to the ecclesiastical abuses of his time he reaches back through history for a better way. Much of what he says here is an expansion of the lean antitheses already set forth in the Letter to Francis I.

D. Chapter Six: Conclusion of the Letter to Francis I?

1. General Considerations. A comparison of the Dedicatory Letter to Francis I and the final chapter of the 1536 *Institutes* suggests that this, and not the end of the letter itself, is the real conclusion of the apology to the king. Chapter 1-5 are primarily the catechism Calvin initially had set out to write, although Chapter 5, as we have seen, is a careful examination of the unscriptural sacramental structure and related features of the Roman Catholic Church as well as a catechetical chapter. The three-fold structure of Chapter 6, however, particularly relates to the appeal to Francis I. The first essay, on Christian Freedom, claims on a Scriptural basis freedom for Christians in the spiritual (ecclesiastical) as opposed to the political (temporal) sphere. The second essay, On Ecclesiastical Power, both rejects humanly devised ecclesiastical laws and customs as violations of this freedom, and also tries to demonstrate to the monarch the fact that the Roman Catholic ecclesiastical establishment has usurped some portion of the secular power. There ought to be two kings: Christ over His church, and the earthly monarch over his domain. This latter topic is the subject of the third essay, On Civil Government, designed both to assure Francis of the Evangelicals' political loyalty, and to apprise him of their utter rejection of the false political views of the Anabaptists, and warn him that the ultimate spiritual stakes are in the hands of God the King of kings. While many details summarily covered in the Dedicatory Letter are dealt with in other chapters in passing, the chief arguments of the letter are formally rehearsed in Chapter 6 and rounded out.

In Chapter 6 Calvin specifically alludes to arguments of the Sorbonne theologians in support of the current Roman Catholic ecclesiastical structures and practices. By skillful Scriptural and historical arguments set antithetically against their views, Calvin seeks both to refute them, justify his own religious party in the king's eyes, and also (by implication) to detach Francis from his malign ecclesiastical advisers.

2. *Specific Content.* It will be useful, perhaps, to look in more detail at the three essays that comprise the final chapter.

A. Christian Freedom. In a sense the problem of freedom is the central theme of Chapter 6. Later editions, in fragmenting this chapter and distributing its elements to widely separated contexts, have sacrificed the pointed message. But, as the immediate apologetic task of the first edition receded into the past, new and more multifarious questions arose that called for the expansion of, and regrouping of the thought of this chapter.

Calvin throughout Chapter 6 is steering a middle course between the piling up of laws and the rejection of all laws; he is pleading for a spiritual freedom even in the midst of civil tyranny, unburdened by the yoke of illicit church regulations and at the same time unplagued by wild unbridled license.

Christian freedom means three things: (1) freedom from the law, (2) freedom of conscience willingly obeying without compulsion of the law, (3) freedom in "things indifferent." Such freedom must never be exercised to the harm of the poor or the weak. We should avoid offensive opulence in living, and sometimes should show our freedom by abstaining from exercising it, especially when by so doing we may endanger weak consciences. But the final determination is not offense against neighbor but offense against God. In pressing the freedom of the Christian conscience from human traditions and laws, Calvin postulates the distinction between spiritual and political government, more or less paralleling his distinction between soul and body.

This first essay on Christian freedom which with little alteration is ultimately moved to a new context (between justification and prayer) in the 1559 edition, serves in the 1536 edition as the introduction to the discussion of the two kingdoms, a concept already familiar in Luther. The constitutions of the Roman Church enslave consciences, and thus deprive the Christian man of his God-given spiritual freedom.

B. Ecclesiastical Power. Calvin lays down his views of church order between the radical rejection of all church laws (currently evidenced in the revolutionary kingdom of Münster) and the senseless heaping up of all sorts of doctrinal, disciplinary, and ritual requirements which (however recently originated) are claimed by the Romanists to have an apostolic or even dominical origin. The radical or Anabaptist notions are but mentioned in passing here; the main butt of Calvin's argument in his second essay is the Roman Church. Against claims that the faith rests solely upon the church's decision, that the clergy and councils of the church are inerrant, Calvin brings both scriptural and historical counter-evidence. In an interesting digression he displays the patrimony of the church—its usurpation of temporal power and perquisites—as due to the misguided but pious generosity of princes. Was this an oblique appeal to Francis I?

The church needs laws to govern itself, to achieve concord in the diversity of human customs; but such are not necessary for salvation: consciences are not to be bound by them. Here Calvin's view of Christian freedom, already enunciated in the prior essay is reiterated. And so Calvin distinguishes between impious ecclesiastical constitutions and legitimate church ordinances made either for public decency or based on the common usage of men—hours of worship and the like. The details are not important; that definite procedures are set is important. We see here how his adiaphoric principle, elucidated in the previous essay on Christian freedom, is put to use.

C. Civil Government. In the final essay, on civil government, the Anabaptists figure much more prominently. As we read these final pages of the book we clearly see Calvin lecturing the French King both on what loyal Evangelical Frenchmen believe, and how he as monarch of the French ought to conduct himself in his office. Calvin first discusses the necessity of civil government.

Earlier, we mentioned in passing that the defective teaching of the Anabaptists on soul and body, already criticized in the *Psychopannychia*, has political implications as well.

> Certain men, when they hear that the Gospel promises a freedom that acknowledges no king and no magistrate among men, but looks to Christ alone, think that they cannot benefit by their freedom so long as they see any power set over them. They therefore think that nothing will be safe unless the world is shaped to a new form where there are neither courts, nor laws, nor magistrates, nor anything similar which in their opinion restricts their freedom. But whoever knows how to distinguish between body and soul, between this present fleeting life and that future eternal life, will without difficulty know that Christ's spiritual kingdom and the civil jurisdiction are things completely distinct.[33]

The distinction between body and soul, infant baptism, and the distinction between the spiritual and political realms, are all of one piece. Also, the contrast between perfectionism held by at least some Anabaptist groups and by Calvin attributed to them all, and the Calvinian notion of gradual spiritual growth during the present life, is to be associated with this general antithesis.

Calvin's picture of the function of the establishment and protection of true religion by the civil authority is consciously constructed against Anabaptist repudiation of all government but also against Romanist usurpation of temporal functions to the ecclesiastical sphere. Yet we must admit that in his delicate balancing of church and state, Calvin laid himself and the city of Geneva open to frequent conflict between council and consistory.

33. See text below: p. 207.

> Let no man be disturbed that I now commit to civil government the duty of rightly establishing religion, which I seem above to have put outside of human decision. For, when I approve of a civil administration that aims to prevent the true religion which is contained in God's law from being openly and with public sacrilege violated and defiled with impunity, I do not here, any more than before, allow men to make laws according to their own decision concerning religion and the worship of God.[34]

Calvin's second topic, a discussion of civil government, is divided into three parts: magistrates, laws, and people.

What, then, does Calvin have to say on the office of *magistrate*? In what sense may the word "god" be applied to man? In their perfectionism the Anabaptists fancied themselves "gods," or so Calvin inferred; in their ecclesiastical usurpations, the Romanists took unto themselves, their saints, and their images and eucharistic hosts the name of "god." To Calvin, like Luther, following especially Psalm 82 and Romans chapter 13, the only human beings who could scripturally bear the name of "gods" were the magistrates. And so explicitly against the Anabaptist rejection of kings and civil authorities, and implicitly against Romanist incursions into the civil sphere, Calvin ringingly asserts the "godship" of the ruler. We are shocked by this sort of teaching until we read the high demands Calvin laid upon his civil magistrate. For him "civil authority is the most sacred calling before God, and the most honorable of all callings in the life of mortal men." As if reminding Francis I of his superlative title "Most Christian," Calvin pictures the high office:

> This consideration ought continually to occupy the magistrates themselves, since it can greatly spur them to exercise their office and bring them remarkable comfort to mitigate the difficulties of their task, which are indeed many and burdensome. For what great zeal for uprightness, for prudence, gentleness, self-control and for innocence ought to be required of themselves by those who know that they have been ordained ministers of divine justice? How will they have the brazenness to admit injustice to their judgment seat, which they are told is the throne of the living God? How will they have the boldness to pronounce an unjust sentence by that mouth which they know has been appointed an instrument of divine truth? With what conscience will they sign wicked decrees by that hand which they know has been appointed an instrument of divine truth? With what conscience will they sign wicked decrees by that hand which they know has been appointed to prescribe the acts of God? To sum up, if they remember that they are vicars of God, they should watch with all care, earnestness, and diligence, to represent in themselves to men some image of divine providence, protection, goodness, benevolence, and justice. And they should perpetually set before themselves the thought that 'all are cursed who do in deceit the work of God' [Jer. 48:10].[35]

34. Ibid., pp. 208-9.
35. Ibid., p. 210.

Revolutionaries who rail against this holy ministry as abhorrent to Christian religion and piety are reviling God himself. It is quite apparent that the conflict between Calvin and the Anabaptists is one concerning the use of Scripture. The Anabaptists rest their case primarily in Jesus' sayings viewed apart from their Jewish roots; for Calvin the teachings of Jesus must be seen in the light of the Old Testament as well as the New; and the Pastoral Epistles, at the other end of the Scriptures, also buttress his case. You confuse the office of Apostle and King, Calvin warns the Anabaptists. Applying to Scripture the ancient classical distinction between the private and public man (on which Calvin had laid so much emphasis in his *Seneca Commentary*), he uses this in the remaining pages of the chapter as the foundation principle in discerning the interworking of magistrate, laws, and people.

The sole endeavor of the magistrate should be to provide for the common safety and peace of all. In fulfilling his function the magistrate has the power of judicial murder, for in sentencing to death he is but carrying out God's judgments. This would be an unpopular stand to take in modern penology! Here again, an exegetical principle is at stake. The pacifist Anabaptists took a simple Biblical prohibition against killing both as a Christian repudiation of the judicial process and especially of capital punishment and the right to wage war. Other radicals were not pacifists, but still repudiated worldly government. It is not improbable that Calvin had in mind the chaos of Münster when he wrote:

> Now if their [the magistrates'] true righteousness is to pursue the guilty and the impious with drawn sword, should they sheath their sword and keep their hands clean of blood, while abandoned men wickedly range about with slaughter and massacre, they will become guilty of the greatest impiety, far indeed from winning praise for their goodness and righteousness thereby![36]

Throughout this essay on the civil government, there are strong echoes of the *Seneca Commentary.* Earlier, we tentatively spoke of the former as the "first draft" of Calvin's apology to Francis I; unquestionably Calvin is here reworking from this new evangelical Christian vantage point the whole classical teaching on the monarch. This connection between the two writings is especially close as he turns to clemency, clue to the best king, and *epiekeia*, the well-spring of law-giving and its application.

True leadership in the state lies between excessive cruelty and exaggerated gentleness. Thus, the use of war must be only as a last resort. Kings must restrain their wrath; they must also restrain their greed and their passion for magnificence; for ultimately the public chest, raised through the right to tax his subjects, is "almost the very blood of the people."

Calvin now turns to the *laws*, the second aspect of civil government, reworking again materials already familiar to readers of the *Seneca Commentary.* As he often does, Calvin begins with the repudiation of an exaggerated position.

36. Ibid., p. 213.

Jacob Strauss, Andreas Carlstadt, and others had proposed literally substituting the entire Mosaic code of the Old Testament for the civil laws of the European nations. In response to this Calvin sets forth his famous distinction (shared with Melanchthon) of law into three layers: moral, ceremonial, and judicial or civil. Moral law, which has already been discussed in Chapter I (but without benefit of this tripartite distinction) is nothing else than a testimony of natural law and of that conscience which God has engraved in the minds of men. In his discussion of the Fourth Commandment in Chapter 1 and of rites and ceremonies in Chapter 5 and Chapter 6, part 2, Calvin has already dealt with the ceremonial law. He now concentrates on judicial law. *Epiekeia* (equity) and adiaphora are two principles that inform his discussion of the topic. Equity is the goal and limit of all laws, determining their right framing and their right application in later generations. Among the nations of the world there is and has always been an incredible variety of laws and punishments to be meted out; these varying details are adiaphoric. Fundamental to all laws, however, is their identical end: to punish those crimes which God's eternal law has condemned, but according to the specific needs of particular times and places.

The final topic is the *people*, for whom magistrates and laws exist, and who are to respond in obedience to him. Again, Calvin sets the stage for his discussion by sketching exaggerated views: in I Corinthians Paul had referred to the passionate litigiousness of certain Corinthian Christians. These constitute one extreme—the persons who use the law courts to excess. At the other end are the Anabaptists who hold the courts of law to be superfluous among Christians. Calvin's exposition of the Christian people's course is a mean between these two extremes. Use the law courts? Yes, with Christian love toward one's legal opponent. To repudiate the courts is for Christians to repudiate God's holy ordinance. Do not lust for revenge, but with equity and moderation of mind use the God-given office of magistrate and court to seek justice.

Calvin reserves to the very end of the *Institutes* the vexed question of what sort of obedience the subjects owe their sovereign. Here he is speaking both to Francis I and to his own countrymen. To the magistrate (under whatever political system one lives) is owed obedience because he is the vicegerent of God. Amassing evidence especially from the Old Testament history (e.g., Daniel, Jeremiah) Calvin argues for obedience not only to the just ruler, but even to the unjust, for the latter is a judgment of God upon the people. Private men have no right to take the law into their own hands.

However, God does provide some relief from oppression, in his own good time. He raises up, history teaches us, two kinds of avengers against unjust rulers: his public servants, lesser magistrates whose task it is to defend the people (ephors in Sparta, tribunes in Rome, and the three estates in France are given as examples); secondly, others who in their rage unwittingly do God's will.

Lastly, Calvin reminds Francis I and his persecuted Evangelical Frenchmen that there is but one King of kings. When obedience to the ruler leads away from obedience to God then: "We must obey God rather than men." The last lines of the Book then re-echo and amplify the closing words of the Dedicatory Letter.

Acknowledgments

Hughes, P.E. "Jacques Lefèvre d'Etaples (c. 1455–1536). Calvin's Forerunner in France." *Calvinus Reformator* (1982): 93–108. Reprinted with the permission of the Institute for Reformational Studies, Potchefstroom University for Christian Higher Education. Courtesy of the Institute for Reformational Studies.

Eells, Hastings. "Martin Bucer and the Conversion of John Calvin." *Princeton Theological Review* 22 (1924): 402–19. Courtesy of Yale University Divinity Library.

Pauck, Wilhelm. "Calvin and Butzer." *Journal of Religion* 9 (1929): 237–56. Courtesy of Yale University Divinity Library.

Hunter, A. Mitchell. "The Education of Calvin." *Evangelical Quarterly* 9 (1937): 20–33. Courtesy of Yale University Divinity Library.

Salley, Louise L. "A French Humanist's Chef-D'Oeuvre: *The Commentaries on Seneca's 'De Clementia'* by John Calvin." *Renaissance Papers* (1968): 41–53. Reprinted with the permission of the Southeastern Renaissance Conference, Duke University. Courtesy of the *Renaissance Papers*.

George, Timothy. "Calvin's *Psychopannychia*: Another Look." In E.J. Furcha, ed., *In Honor of John Calvin, 1509–64* (Montreal: Faculty of Religious Studies, McGill University, 1987): 297–329. Reprinted with the permission of the Faculty of Religious Studies, ARC, McGill University. Courtesy of the Faculty of Religious Studies.

Tylenda, Joseph N. "Calvin's First Reformed Sermon? Nicholas Cop's Discourse—1 November 1533." *Westminster Theological Journal* 38 (1975–76): 300–18. Reprinted with the permission of the Westminster Theological Seminary. Courtesy of Yale University Divinity Library.

Divita, James J. "The Italian Sojourn of John Calvin: 1536." *Italian Quarterly* 14 (1971): 85–111. Reprinted with the permission of the *Italian Quarterly*. Courtesy of Yale University Sterling Memorial Library.

Littell, Franklin H. "What Calvin Learned at Strassburg." In John H. Bratt, ed., *The Heritage of John Calvin* (Grand Rapids, MI: William B. Eerdmans Publishing Company, 1973): 74–86. Reprinted with the permission of the Calvin College & Seminary. Courtesy of the Calvin College & Seminary.

Patte, Edward. "John Calvin and Choral Music." *Choral & Organ Guide* 18 (1965): 6–17. Reprinted with the permission of Roy Anderson, Editor and Publisher. Courtesy of Yale University Seeley G. Mudd Library.

Strand, Kenneth A. "John Calvin and the Brethren of the Common Life: The Role of Strassburg." *Andrews University Seminary Studies* 15 (1977): 43–56. Reprinted with the permission of the *Andrews University Seminary Studies*, Andrews University Press. Courtesy of *Andrews University Seminary Studies*.

Payton, Jr., James R. "History as Rhetorical Weapon: Christian Humanism in Calvin's Reply to Sadoleto, 1539." In E.J. Furcha, ed., *In Honor of John Calvin, 1509–64* (Montreal: Faculty of Religious Studies, McGill University, 1987): 96–132. Reprinted with the permission of the Faculty of Religious Studies, ARC, McGill University. Courtesy of the Faculty of Religious Studies.

Battles, Ford Lewis. "Introduction." In Ford Lewis Battles, ed., *Institutes of the Christian Religion* (Grand Rapids, MI: William B. Eerdmans Publishing Company, 1986): xvii–lix. Reprinted with the permission of the William B. Eerdmans Publishing Company. Courtesy of Yale University Divinity Library.